THE E-BUSINESS FORMULA FOR SUCCESS

Other Titles of Interest From Maximum Press

THE E-BUSINESS FORMULA FOR SUCCESS

How to select the right e-Business model, Web site design, and online promotion strategy for your business

Susan Sweeney

MAXIMUM PRESS
605 Silverthorn Road
Gulf Breeze, FL 32561
(850) 934-0819
www.maxpress.com

Publisher: Jim Hoskins

Manager of Finance/Administration: Donna Tryon

Production Manager: ReNae Grant

Cover Designer: Lauren Smith Designs

Compositor: PageCrafters Inc.

Copyeditor: Andrew Potter

Proofreader: Kim Stefansson

Indexer: Susan Olason

Printer: P.A. Hutchison

Recognizing the importance of preserving what has been written, it is a policy of Maximum Press to have books of enduring value published in the United States printed on acid-free paper, and we exert our best efforts to that end.

Library of Congress Cataloging-in-Publication Data

Sweeney, Susan, 1956-
The e-business formula for success : how to select the right
e-business model, web site design, and online promotion strategy for
your business / By Susan Sweeney.
p. cm.
Includes index.
ISBN 1-885068-60-3 (alk. paper)
1. Electronic commerce. 2. Internet marketing. 3. Internet
advertising. I. Title.
HF5548.32 .S94 2001
658.8'4—dc21
2001000317

Acknowledgements

This book was very much a team effort and I would like to extend my thanks to Ed Dorey, Andy MacLellan, and Matt Bell—part of the dynamite team at Connex Network. It was an extremely busy year, but we did it! Thank you for your time and dedication on this project.

Special thanks to my mom and dad, Olga and Leonard Dooley.

As always, special thanks to my husband Miles, and our three wonderful children—Kaitlyn, Kara, and Andrew—for their love, encouragement and ongoing support. Love you more than the last number.

Thanks to Maximum Press. As always, it has been a pleasure to work with Jim Hoskins and Donna Tryon. Thanks to ReNae Grant of PageCrafters for all her support and patience. I look forward to working on future projects with you all.

I would like to end by thanking all those individuals and organizations that share their information so freely with everyone on the Net. Sites like WilsonWeb.com (*http://www.wilsonweb.com/*), E-commerce Times (*http://www.ecommercetimes.com/*), Portals like Internet.com (*http://www.internet.com/*), About.com's e-Business section (*http://ebusiness.about.com/industry/ebusiness/mbody.htm*) and great newsletters such as AudetteMedia's I-Sales and I-Search, as well as WebPromote Weekly (*http://www.webpromote.com/*), ICONOCAST (*http://www.iconocast.com/*) and iEntry's WebProNews are all truly invaluable resources.

Disclaimer

The purchase of computer software or hardware is an important and costly business decision. While the author and publisher of this book have made reasonable efforts to ensure the accuracy and timeliness of the information contained herein, the author and publisher assume no liability with respect to loss or damage caused or alleged to be caused by reliance on any information contained herein and disclaim any and all warranties, expressed or implied, as to the accuracy or reliability of said information.

This book is not intended to replace the manufacturer's product documentation or personnel in determining the specifications and capabilities of the products mentioned in this book. The manufacturer's product documentation should always be consulted, as the specifications and capabilities of computer hardware and software products are subject to frequent modification. The reader is solely responsible for the choice of computer hardware and software. All configurations and applications of computer hardware and software should be reviewed with the manufacturer's representatives prior to choosing or using any computer hardware and software.

Trademarks

The words contained in this text which are believed to be trademarked, service marked, or otherwise to hold proprietary rights have been designated as such by use of initial capitalization. No attempt has been made to designate as trademarked or service marked any personal computer words or terms in which proprietary rights might exist. Inclusion, exclusion, or definition of a word or term is not intended to affect, or to express judgment upon, the validity of legal status of any proprietary right which may be claimed for a specific word or term.

Your "Members Only" Web Site

The Internet world changes every day. That's why there is a companion Web site associated with this book. On this site you will find updates to the book and other Web site promotion resources. However, you have to be a member of the "e-Business Formula Insider's Club" to gain access to this site.

When you purchased this book, you automatically became a member (in fact, that's the only way to join), so you now have full privileges. To get into the "Members Only" section of the companion Web site, go to the Maximum Press Web site located at *www.maxpress.com* and follow the links to the companion Web site for "e-Business Formula for Success." When you try to enter, you will be asked for a user ID and password. Type in the following:

- For your user ID enter: formula
- For you password enter: cold

You will then be granted full access to the "Members Only" area. Visit the site often and enjoy the updates and resources with our compliments—and thanks again for buying the book. We ask that you not share the user ID and password for this site with anyone else.

Table of Contents

Part 1: Understanding e-Business

Chapter 4: Laying the Foundation 18

Part 2: The Right e-Business Model

Part 4: The Right Traffic

Part 1

Understanding e-Business

1

e-Business Overview

"We are crossing a technology threshold that will forever change the way we learn, work, socialize and shop. It will affect all of us, and businesses of every type, in ways far more pervasive than most people realize."

Bill Gates, Comdex 1994

Bill Gates was very prophetic when he made this statement in 1994, eons ago in terms of the Internet. Communicating with customers and other businesses has changed drastically over the past century. It started with print, then radio, television, phone, fax, and now the fastest medium yet—the Internet. The future is bright for businesses that utilize the Net as a primary medium of communication and sales.

The opportunity is there for anyone to create a dynamite business online if it is done right. Unfortunately, it's not a matter of just developing a Web site, putting it online, and having the world beat a path to your door. To achieve success online, you have to choose the right business, choose the right e-Business model, develop the right Web site directed toward your target market, and then generate substantial traffic to your Web site. The online customer who visits your site is much more demanding than a typical offline buyer in many ways. The online buyer knows what he wants, how he wants it, when he wants it, and at what price. The product and service must be exactly what was ordered and must be delivered immediately to the correct place and for the lowest price he can find. Competition is fierce on the Internet, and you must do a number of things to succeed online. First, you have to create a professional and secure e-Business presence. Second, you have to target the demographic of Internet users who will use your product or service. Finally, you have to work diligently to attract traffic. Serious marketing research is required to successfully target and attract the appropriate customers.

What Is e-Business?

The term "e-Business" is used commonly, but e-Business means different things to different people. To some people, e-Business is simply having a Web site with a toll-free number visitors can call to place an order. Other people think e-Business is having a Web site that enables customers to submit their credit card information online, even though their orders may then be processed manually just like a fax or telephone order. Still others believe that e-Business means being able to place a secure online order, having immediate credit card verification, and having a fully integrated backend database that automatically updates and informs the customer of the latest prices and whether or not an item is in stock. The point is, how you define e-Business and how you implement e-Business on your site will depend upon your business and the type of products or services you are marketing on the Web.

For instance, a software development company that sells a downloadable software application (i.e., has no physical boxed version) has no inventory. Therefore, they would not require a backend inventory database to be integrated with their e-Business system. All they might need is an e-Business system that automatically verifies credit card information and takes payment. On the other hand, if you have an online business that intends to sell books, and you want to become the next Amazon.com, you will require a full-blown, full-featured, fully integrated e-Business system to compete with the Amazon.coms of the world. Otherwise, potential customers will shop at Amazon.com because their e-Business system is more convenient and easy to use.

Industry Overview

The size and demographics of the online population that makes up the Internet universe is an important component of the industry as every business must have an in-depth understanding of their target audience in order to be successful. In general, the number of Internet users is growing at a staggering rate. The Computer Industry Almanac has reported that by the year 2002, 490 million people around the world will have Internet access; that is 79.4 per 1,000 people worldwide, and 118 people per 1,000 by year-end 2005. There are currently 374.9 million Internet users worldwide. From a demographics standpoint, Internet users are typically well educated, technically inclined, and financially well off. Popular uses of the Internet are for research purposes, entertainment, e-mail, chat, and for shopping. As the Internet expands so to does the number of opportunities for businesses.

The Internet has been known as a marketplace consisting of predominantly young, professional males. Over the span of 2000 we saw the demographics that make up the online universe expand and diversify. Shifts in Internet demographics are expected to continue in the foreseeable future as the use of the Internet continues to become an accepted part of every day life. The first quarter of 2000 marked the first time the number of women online in the United States surpassed that of men, according to a report by Media Metrix and Jupiter Communications. The number of seniors online is one of the most rapidly growing segments of the Internet. The number of seniors online at the beginning of was estimated at more than 23 million according to several sources. IDC, a leading industry analyst, expects the number of seniors online to grow to 34.1 million by 2004—an estimated 20% of all new Internet users. With the growth in the number of seniors taking to the online world, you will see an increase in the number of opportunities available to businesses who target this segment. Recent surveys by Harris Interactive found that "young people" in the U.S. between the ages of 18 and 24 have a significant amount of buying power, and are spending an estimated of $164 billion per year. This represents an attractive segment for businesses, because a respectable portion of the $164 billion spent is spent online and e-Business spending among this age group is more than four times the rate of e-Business spending among all adults.

e-Business brings forth a number of beneficial opportunities for existing businesses and new start-ups alike. Not only does it open the doors to new markets, but also it can open the door to new market opportunities. Consider the travel industry. Traditionally consumers would consult with their personal travel agent for vacation packages and flight information. The advent of the Internet and e-Business changed the rules for the travel industry, and new companies such as Travelocity.com and Expedia.com were able to enter into the already highly competitive market by offering rock bottom pricing and empowering the consumer with the ability to quickly and easily plan their own trips without interacting with a travel agent. These new companies were able to provide their services to an enormous market and at a much lower cost than could traditional travel agents at the time As a result, they have been quite successful. This is only one example of how businesses can be successful through e-Business.

The Internet expansion into all business and personal communications is inevitable. What was considered a "trend" is becoming the "norm." As people are becoming more familiar and trusting of online transactions, the consumer relationship is being improved each month due to new security-based technologies that are being developed. New media support groups are also speeding up the learning curve of the average Internet users.

The future is bright for e-Businesses. Not everything is available on the Internet... yet. Hot items for sale online have always been and continue to be apparel, computer hardware/software, music, books, electronics, toys, and travel, but more and more people are coming up with new business ideas every day to meet consumers needs and changes in the online demographics. A recent survey conducted by Roper Starch found that Internet users are becoming much more open to using the Internet to conduct personal business, such as banking, and to shopping online. According to the study, in 1998 31% of people surveyed shopped online, 16% conducted personal banking online, and 11% traded stocks. In 2000, each of these numbers increased to 56%, 25%, and 16% respectively. Several studies indicate these numbers are going to continue to increase over the next few years, presenting many opportunities to businesses looking to extend their operations online. With respect to the B2B (Business to Business) marketplace, the Yankee Group estimates that 90% of all small to medium sized businesses will make at least one purchase online this year.

Online revenue is expected to increase to $3.2 trillion by 2004, according to Forrester Research. These are encouraging numbers, but for dot com businesses the year 2000 was filled with many difficult challenges. No longer can an e-Business succeed based on a good idea alone—you need the right e-Business model, the right Web site, and the right volume of targeted traffic. This year you will see e-Business move from being an option to a common aspect of many businesses daily operations—it has already begun. Whether you are a dot com or a bricks and mortar, an established business or your business is just a dream, this book will assist you in taking your business online and serve as your guide on the path to e-Business Success.

2

Demystifying e-Business Myths

There are many myths and misconceptions relative to Web development, Internet marketing, e-Business, your online presence, and who's responsible for what online. It is important to dispel these myths at the outset and have a reality check. This chapter covers some of the more popular misconceptions.

Myth #1 "Anyone Can Build a Web Site."

Many people believe that literally anyone can build a Web site. There are many software programs, wizards, and templates to make it easy. There's nothing to it. Web design is often viewed just like word processing or creating a flyer using a basic graphics and text software program. We get our brothers, uncles, and kids to design our professional Web sites. We hear it all the time: "His nephew is getting paid $50 per page and he does it in the evenings… there can't be that much to it."

REALITY: "NOT MANY DO IT RIGHT."

It may be easy to build a Web site, but it's a little more difficult to do it right. Our teenage kids may be quick with typing and be able to use graphics programs, but we wouldn't consider having them develop our corporate brochure or marketing materials. Why, then, do so many people assume that these kids are capable of developing their corporate Web presence just because they can type and use a Web development software program?

When developing your Web site, you ideally start with the clear identification of your Web site objectives, your target market, and your products and services. Without identifying your primary and secondary objectives and articulating them to your Web developer, it is impossible for the developer to design and develop a site that is going to achieve your objectives. The site should be designed for your target market. If you don't identify your target market to the Web developer, it will be tough for her to develop graphics that appeal to your target demographic.

In an ideal world, your site will be developed with input from several different disciplines. For instance, you will have input from a graphic designer. Your site needs dynamite graphics that "speak" to your target market. You will also have input from an individual with a public relations or advertising background. Your site needs succinct text that grabs the reader's attention, gets the intended message across, and encourages the reader to take action, all in a screen or less. People in advertising are experts at this. You will have input from an individual who is great at programming. Your Web site should be robust and browser friendly. Most sites today include some Java, and possibly Macromedia Flash. If you have databases, it is very important that they be designed and built by someone who has expertise in this area. You will have input from an individual with expertise in Internet marketing. Your Web site must be search engine friendly. An Internet marketer knows what it takes to optimize each page of your site to achieve high ranking in search results. The Internet marketer also knows which repeat traffic generators, permission marketing techniques, and other elements are appropriate for your target market to help you achieve your online objectives.

So in light of all this, although our kids may be able to use a Web development program, I think we should leave this job to the experts. Your Internet presence provides you with an enormous opportunity. Do it right! You don't get a second chance to make a first impression.

Myth #2 "If You Build It, They Will Come."

Since the Internet emerged as a part of our lives and conversations, the belief has been that once you create a Web site, the world will automatically know it exists and will beat a path to your door to do business with you. The idea is that once you have taken the time and effort to publish a Web site, the job is done and all you have to do is make sure the site is live and wait for the e-mails to come in.

REALITY: "BUILDING A WEB SITE IS JUST THE FIRST STEP."

Getting business from your Web site is a lot like getting business from a great brochure. You can have the best brochure in the world, but it isn't going to bring you any business if it sits in the bottom drawer of your salesperson's desk. The same is true with your Web site. You can have the greatest Web site in the world, but it will not bring you any business if you do nothing to let your target market know the site exists and encourage them to visit.

You need a strategy to reach your target market online and offline that encourages them to visit your site. Search engine registration is one element, and there are many more. Your strategy could include the following marketing techniques:

- Mail list marketing
- Newsgroup or forum participation
- Electronic press release distribution
- E-zine article submissions
- Cybermall participation
- Listings in meta indexes and industry-specific directories
- Banner advertising
- Links from sites frequented by your target market

It is critically important that you spend as much time planning and implementing the marketing of your site as you did in the planning and development of the site, if not more.

Myth #3 "My Online Store Will Offer the Same Products and Services as My Offline Store."

Business owners who have a bricks-and-mortar location sometimes assume that their online storefront is an extension of their offline storefront and that they will provide exactly the same products and services online as offline.

REALITY: "CONSUMERS HAVE HIGHER EXPECTATIONS ONLINE THAN OFFLINE, AND THE CONSUMER RULES!"

In some cases fewer products are offered online than in the physical store. This is often the case where you are test-marketing, but also where some of the products you sell in your physical location are not appropriate for online sales due to competitive pricing or shipping logistics.

In other cases your online store will offer more products or services than the bricks-and-mortar location. For example, your offline bookstore may not offer shipping or gift-wrapping. If your online bookstore does not offer these services, you will lose a lot of business to your online competition. When a site's product offerings include items that are appropriate for gift giving, it is essential to also offer wrapping, customized cards, shipping to multiple addresses, and shipping options. The consumer is king and is very demanding. You have to meet and beat your consumers' expectations online to garner market share. People shopping for gifts online are looking for convenience, and the site that provides the greatest convenience and the greatest products at the greatest price will be the winner.

Myth #4 "My Web Developer Takes Care of That."

It is amazing how people assume that just because a person or company develops a Web site, that company will take care of everything related to the site and its marketing online. Not only do they expect the Web developers to build the site without much direction, but they also expect the Web development company to:

- Get it placed high in the search engines
- Monitor the positioning and resubmit when needed
- Let the world know the site exists

- Attract a lot of traffic to the site
- Update the site's content and graphics when it is needed

And here is the real kicker—the average client expects ALL this for the price of the initial Web development.

REALITY: "MANY ASSUME THAT THEIR WEB DEVELOPER IS RESPONSIBLE FOR GETTING THEIR SITE PLACED IN THE SEARCH ENGINES AND GENERATING TRAFFIC TO THEIR SITE."

When you hire a print advertising company to develop your corporate brochure, you don't expect them to research your target market and then distribute the brochure and then follow up with the potential clients. For some reason, people expect Web development companies to "do it all."

In some instances a full-service Internet marketing and Web development company may be able to provide additional services other than site development. Tasks such as search engine submission and generating links to your site can be provided, but generally it is your responsibility to handle these tasks. It is important that your company have an Internet marketing strategy in place to generate significant traffic to your site. You should also have a site maintenance strategy and implementation schedule. You may choose to outsource some of the elements in your Internet marketing strategy, but it is your responsibility to make sure that you have control over what is being done and who is doing it.

Myth #5 "My Web Site is the Same As My Corporate Brochure."

Many assume that a Web site is basically the corporate brochure in electronic format. They provide the company brochures and marketing collateral to the Web development company and expect, from that material, that the Web development company can build their site.

REALITY: "YOUR WEB SITE IS YOUR CORPORATE BROCHURE, ONLINE AD, ONLINE STORE, AND ONLINE PRESENCE. IT'S YOUR BUSINESS IN VIRTUAL FORM, AND IT'S THE MOST EFFECTIVE RECEPTACLE OF TARGETED MARKETING INFORMATION WE'VE EVER HAD ACCESS TO."

A Web site can be an online brochure or advertisement for your business, but it has the potential to be so much more. It is the most cost-effective way to promote and communicate with your niche market customers, so using it simply as an ad is a huge missed opportunity. Keep in mind that for the most part people do not return to an ad they saw or tell friends about an ad they liked or found useful.

Your Web site is the virtual window to your business because you can keep it constantly updated with the latest information. Your online store may mirror the products and services of your physical location; a business Web site is more like a branch office—a place of doing business. It's like opening a second office, except this office is open 24 hours, 7 days a week, holidays included.

Your Web site is also a perfect way to provide customer instructions, support information, and a section for frequently asked questions specific to your business.

Myth #6 "E-business is e-Business is e-Business."

It's a package I can buy. It's an option my Web developer provides. It's all point and click, simple as pie! There is a standard way of conducting e-business that all online businesses follow.

REALITY: "THE IDEAL E-BUSINESS MODEL THAT IS APPROPRIATE FOR YOUR BUSINESS DEPENDS ON YOUR PRODUCTS OR SERVICES, PAYMENT PRACTICES, TARGET MARKET, OBJECTIVES, BACK END SYSTEMS, BUDGET, AND SO FORTH."

There is no one e-Business model that is universally acceptable to all businesses. The e-Business model that is appropriate for your business will depend on a number of things. The products and services you provide will impact the e-Business model that is appropriate for your business. Your target market will impact the appropriate e-Business model for your company. Your business practices of how and when you take payment as well as how and when you deliver the goods will dictate the payment taking and processing elements of your e-Business model. Many other things like your budget, your back end systems, and the number and variety of products you offer all have an impact on the model you implement.

The following chapters on the e-business models will help to dispel this myth and to help you choose the appropriate e-Business model for your business.

3

The e-Business Formula

What is e-Business success? The answer starts with the e-Business formula introduced in this chapter.

Understanding the Formula

How do you achieve it? There are three essential components that make up e-Business success—the right e-Business model, the right Web site, and the right volume of targeted traffic to your site. If you think of e-Business success as a formula, this is how it would work:

the right e-Business model
+
the right Web site
+
the right Web site traffic, and lots of it
=
e-Business success

All pieces of the formula are co-dependent on one another. If you omit any one of these components from the equation, you cannot achieve e-Business success. You can have a great Web site using the right e-Business model, but with no traffic, you are not going to achieve online success. Likewise, you can have a great Web site and lots of traffic, but if your e-Business model doesn't fit the requirements of your business and the needs of your consumer, you're not going to make many sales.

Everyone is Different

When developing your e-Business strategy, you have to take into account:

- Your online goals and objectives
- Your company's budget and financial position
- The size and type of operation you run
- The products and services you sell
- The needs and wants of your target market

The scope of your e-Business strategy is a factor of all these things. A Bed and Breakfast that wants to be able to take online reservations has different needs from an online business selling tools and hardware. As the Bed and Breakfast, you may need a simple, attractive, easy-to-use Web site with a form that contains a customer's name, address, phone number, and details about his reservation request in order to hold a room for him.

An online hardware store would need to consider a wide variety of options. The hardware store needs to be able to present the products for sale to customers in a visually appealing manner that is easy to follow and use. The hardware store also needs some kind of a shopping cart so that customers can add and remove items they wish to purchase at will. In addition, the hardware store will need to know information about the consumer who is purchasing the merchandise.

What about payment? Would you sell hardware to a consumer and tell him or her, "Oh, don't worry about it, you can pay me later"? Not if you want to stay in business for any extended period of time. The hardware store needs to be able to accept payment for the merchandise sold online. What if the items to be purchased are going to a different location from the purchaser's home? Maybe the items are a gift for someone. The hardware store should provide the customer with the option to ship the merchandise to different locations. If you were the customer, would you want to pay to have the merchandise shipped to your home only to turn around and spend additional money to have the items reshipped to the recipient of the gift? I doubt it. And in keeping with the theme of gift giving, thought should be given to a gift-wrapping service as well.

Different types of businesses are going to require different e-Business strategies, and it is important for you to understand what strategies work best for your type of business. Recognize as well that the e-Business needs of your business will likely change over time as a result of your own success or due to external influences such as competition, changes in technology, or the mindset of your target market.

Applying the Formula

There are a lot of steps to the e-Business process and many decisions to be made, but you can achieve e-Business success if you take the time to do it right. Remember:

the right e-Business model

+

the right Web site

+

the right Web site traffic, and lots of it

=

e-Business success

Each component of the e-Business success formula works with the others as a cohesive unit, so it is important that you do not discount any single part of the equation.

In the following chapters you will read about what options are open to you and learn how to select the right e-Business model. You will also learn what you need to do to build a dynamic Web site that is search engine friendly, meets your objectives, and meets the needs of your target market. Once you have selected your e-Business model and have constructed your Web site, you need targeted traffic. The last section of the book discusses many proven tips, tools, and techniques for driving targeted traffic to your Web site. By the time you have finished reading this book, you should have a firm understanding of what it takes to achieve e-Business success and how you can do it.

4

Laying the Foundation

There's an enormous amount of opportunity on the Web for existing businesses and startups alike. A number of research firms are projecting e-commerce revenues of $100 billion by 2003. Before you can build your online empire, however, you need to understand the e-commerce options available to your business. Selecting e-commerce products and services that cannot meet your needs can result in lost sales, while implementing systems well beyond your needs can result in unnecessary expenses that impact negatively on your bottom line. In this chapter you will learn about a number of common mistakes made when moving a business online as well as the background information you need to know to be able to take payments online. You will also learn about the various types of storefronts available to you and the features you should consider when selecting which storefront option to go for.

Some Things to Consider

Don't go overboard during the planning process of your e-Business. Many companies never make the jump to e-commerce or never get started because they in effect scare themselves away from it. Often, companies select the best of the best because they think they need it—they don't understand the technology at their disposal. They gain a perception that e-Business is too expensive, when all they really need to build their e-Business is completely within their means.

Are your products and services appropriate for sale online? What sells in "traditional" storefronts will not necessarily sell in the "online" world. Some companies fail because they do not do the appropriate research to determine whether or not the product(s) they want to sell can be done so effectively online. From a business standpoint, would it make sense to develop a site exclusively to sell ice pops online? Probably not.

Do not underestimate your competition. Many companies tend to undervalue the threat or ignore their online competitors, which can result in failure. Take the time to research your online competition so that you are aware of their capabilities and can plan appropriate strategies to remain competitive in the future. There are sites available to the Internet consumer that will scan the web for pricing information on a particular product and return results based on price or some other predetermined criteria. AltaVista Shopping (*http://shopping.altavista.com/*), as shown in Figure 4.1, allows you to compare products and prices from over 600

Figure 4.1. Comparison shopping sites allow consumers to compare prices from around the Web.

stores across the Internet. Another product comparison site is mySimon (*http://www.mysimon.com/*).

Do not assume you can sit down and learn everything there is to know about doing business online overnight. It's impossible to learn everything there is to know about e-commerce, storefront solutions, payment options, hosting, site design, and so forth, in one sitting. If you're just testing the e-Business waters, it may be in your best interest to allow companies that specialize in the technical aspects of the business to take care of these things for you. Most high-quality storefront/hosting services, such as Yahoo! Store, will take care of the behind-the-scenes details such as maintaining the hardware and software needed to run your online store.

In a similar fashion, do not try to do everything yourself. It's great to have a dream and to want to pursue it on your own, but that dream may be easier to realize with the help of others. Many online businesses fail due to a lack of general business, strategy, accounting and marketing knowledge. It may be in your best interest to consult with a friend or colleague with professional experience. Like with all businesses, to survive and thrive, online businesses must be run efficiently.

Taking Payment

One of the key components of doing on business online is the ability to take payment for goods and services online. Essentially, taking payment online involves the ability to successfully transfer payment from the buyer to your bank account. There are a number of factors you need to be aware of before venturing out and developing your online business. The main form of payment online is the credit card, which is the focus of this section. Currently 95 percent of all purchases online are made using credit cards.

The Advantages of Taking Online Payments

The ability to take payment for goods and services online presents several significant advantages to you as a business owner. Many Internet users expect speed and convenience. They want what they want, when they want it. By offering Internet shoppers the ability to make a purchase and pay for it online, you're helping to facilitate their needs and desires. You're enabling them to make their purchase at any time of day or night. Basically, your online storefront is open for business 24 hours a day, 7 days a week, 365 days a year. By allowing users to purchase goods and services online, you're allowing them to pay for items on their own terms as well. Independence and freedom play a role. The user is able to make the purchase on his own, without relying on another individual. He does not need to wait for the assistance of a sales associate to make his purchase, he does not need to wait an extensive period of time for approval of that purchase because everything is automated, and he does not need to write down a phone number or other contact information to contact someone to make the purchase. It's on his terms and he likes that.

Automated online payment processing can benefit your business in the form of reduced costs. You do not need to pay someone to process your transactions, and you do not need to pay to produce paper invoices and statements. Think of the additional time automated online payment processing can save you as well. You and your employees will not have to spend time processing payments yourselves. Your time will be free to be better used on more important business matters.

Having your site set up to take online payments portrays a professional image and boosts the credibility of your operation in the eyes of the consumer. It shows that you have taken the time and invested the money to develop a well-run operation.

You may experience increased sales. Why? Many of the purchases made online are impulse buys. Living up to consumer expectations is key to your e-Business's success!

Acquire an Internet Merchant Account

What do you need to do to begin taking payments online? Before you can accept credit card payments online, you need to acquire an appropriate Internet merchant account. Your other option is to utilize that of third party, which we discuss later. An Internet merchant account allows you to accept credit card payments for goods and services. You may be saying to yourself, "I already have a merchant account" if you currently operate a business; however, you will need a merchant account that allows you to take payment over the Internet and you will need a merchant account for each type of credit card you plan to accept. To get an

Internet merchant account or to change your merchant account to the correct type, you must contact your financial institution or bank.

When you approach your financial institution for an Internet merchant account, you will have to prove to them that you deserve it and that you are a safe investment. They will want to know a significant amount of detail about your online business, but the most important issue is your credit history. Your type of business (products and services you offer), the length of time you have been in business, and your existing relationship with the financial institution will influence their decision on whether or not to issue you an Internet merchant account. They will likely also want to know how you plan to process transactions, what your payment processing company of choice is, and so on. They may ask you to provide details of how an actual transaction on your Web site will work.

The Internet is significantly different from doing business at a traditional bricks-and-mortar storefront location because the credit card and the cardholder are not present at the point of sale. Some banks have no problems issuing an Internet merchant account because as far as they are concerned it's just like any other sale where the transaction does not take place at the point of sale (e.g., a mail order catalogue). On the other hand, some banks are a little uneasy when it comes to doing business online and may be hesitant to issue you a merchant account for such transactions. In fact, they may not be willing to work with you at all, in which case you will have to approach another financial institution for assistance.

Because there is a higher perceived risk with doing business over the Internet, the issuing financial institution may present you with a higher discount rate. A discount rate is simply a percentage fee of each transaction charged to the merchant, based on the perceived risk. The higher the risk, the higher the discount rate. Feel free to talk to other banks and find out their feelings on online business—you may be able to get a lower discount rate. Those banks that are accepting of home and mail-order businesses generally tend to be more accepting of online business and will likely offer a better discount rate.

In addition to the discount rate, you will be responsible for various other fees. There may be an account application or setup fee, a per-transaction fee, a monthly fee, a statement fee, support fees, and possibly other related fees. Make sure you cover these details with your financial institution! One financial institution may require a security deposit of up to 20 percent of annual sales before they are willing to issue you an Internet merchant account; another may have you set up and operational in 24 hours with no security deposit at all.

You can opt to use a third-party alternative, also known as an Internet payment service. One such company is InternetSecure (*http://www.internetsecure.com/*). The main advantage of using another company's Internet merchant account is that you avoid a lot of the hassle with setting up your own Internet merchant account. The third party will let you use theirs for a fee. Like the bank, there will be various fees such as setup fees and transaction fees. These fees are often more than those of having your own merchant account because you're paying for the privilege of using someone else's account. The choice is yours as to whether you use a third-party company or acquire your own Internet merchant account, but base your decision on your needs and objectives.

Protecting Your Customers

Security has been a major issue with e-commerce ever since the day e-commerce began to propagate across the Internet. Thanks to recent innovative technologies, consumers are feeling better about the security measures many e-commerce sites now employ. Although the general consumer fear of conducting online transactions has dissipated to some extent, there are still a lot of folks who need convincing and others who will not purchase an item online unless they are assured the site is secure. You should protect your users by ensuring your site's security. This protects the consumers and it protects the future of your business. Most, if not all, of today's online payment service solutions use secure technologies. Whenever security on the Internet is discussed, two common terms always come up—SSL and SET.

SSL, which means Secure Socket Layers, was developed by Netscape and is supported by all leading Web browsers. SSL currently is the implied standard encryption protocol in the industry for managing the security of file transmissions around the Internet.

SET is short for Secure Electronic Transaction. SET is implemented to protect the security of electronic financial transactions on the Internet. Whatis.com (*http://www.whatis.com/*) provides an excellent overview of how SET is implemented, as described next:

Assume that a customer has a SET-enabled browser such as Netscape or Microsoft's Internet Explorer and that the transaction provider (bank, store, etc.) has a SET-enabled server.

1. The customer opens a Mastercard or Visa bank account. (Any issuer of a credit card is some kind of bank.)

2. The customer receives a digital certificate. This electronic file functions as a credit card for online purchases or other transactions. It includes a public key with an expiration date. It has been digitally switched by the bank to ensure its validity.

3. Third-party merchants also receive certificates from the bank. These certificates include the merchant's public key and the bank's public key.

4. The customer places an order over a web page, by phone, or some other means.

5. The customer's browser receives and confirms from the merchant's certificate that the merchant is valid.

6. The browser sends the order information. This message is encrypted with the merchant's public key, the payment information (which is encrypted with the bank's public key and can't be read by the merchant), and information that ensures that payment can only be used with this particular order.

7. The merchant verifies the customer by checking the digital signature on the customer's certificate. This may be done by referring the certificate to the bank or to a third-party verifier.

8. The merchant sends the order message along to the bank. This includes the bank's public key, the customer's payment information (which the merchant can't decode), and the merchant's certificate.

9. The bank verifies the merchant and the message. The bank uses the digital signature on the certificate with the message and verifies the payment part of the message.

10. The bank digitally signs and sends authorization to the merchant, who can then fill the order.

If you are going to accept payment online, then you should take the necessary steps to ensure the security of your customers' personal information and payment information. Implementing measures to make your site secure also encourages sales as consumers will feel more comfortable handing over their payment information. Be sure to post your security policy on your site in a clear location using plain English. Keep this in mind when reading the following section on selecting a payment processing company.

Locate a Payment Processing Company

Your merchant account, your online storefront, and your payment processing company must work together effectively for you to be able to integrate your online business and operate successfully. A payment processing company links everything together and provides real-time payment authorization. Some real-time payment processing companies are:

- Authorize.net, *http://www.authorize.net/*
- CyberCash Inc., *http://www.cybercash.com/*
- MSBill.com™, *http://www.msbill.com/*
- Nobil IT, *http://www.nobil.com/*
- VeriSign Payment Services, *http://www.verisign.com/payment/*

One of the biggest considerations to make when selecting your payment processing company is whether or not it is compatible with your online storefront package. InterShop's (*http://www.intershop.com/*) storefront software has several payment processing companies preconfigured as default selections. Watch out for compatibility with your Internet merchant account as well. If you're a Canadian company and you select an American payment processing company, you should make sure that they are able to use Canadian Internet merchant accounts.

Find out what methods of payment the payment processing company can handle. Be sure to look at the accepted currencies if you plan to do business outside of your own borders as well. Is there a limit on the number of transactions you can process per month? Are there any hidden costs you should be aware of? How does the payment processing company protect its clients against fraud? These are all relevant issues to consider before you move ahead with selecting a particular payment processing company to handle your business transactions.

The ability to track your transactions is an important feature to watch for. You should find out whether the payment processing company provides regular statements of transactions made on your site or if there is some other way you can monitor your transactions. A record of your transactions is useful for your own knowledge, strategic planning, accounting, and budgetary planning, as well as in the event of a dispute with a customer.

Most payment processing companies can process a transaction and approve or reject a payment within 5 to 20 seconds. When looking for a payment processing company, be sure to find out how long, on average, it takes to process a transaction. Some companies will tell you it can take a minute or more. The faster the transaction can be processed, the better. In general, Internet users are not known for their patience, and you do not want them trying to back out of a transaction because they're tired of waiting or that they think that something went wrong.

VeriSign's Payment Services offers clients a number of benefits, such as an unlimited number of credit card and Internet check transactions at a fixed monthly fee, acceptance of multiple payment types (credit cards, purchase cards, debit cards, ACH, and Internet checks), and real-time credit card and check authorization in approximately three seconds. VeriSign also offers customizable back office reporting tools and 24-hour customer service to its clients.

Find out how the payment processing company handles chargebacks. Doing business online increases the risk of chargebacks because there is no real way to verify the actual cardholder online. They are rare, but they do occur, so you should be aware of them. A chargeback occurs when a cardholder disputes a transaction and the bank charges a sale back to the original merchant. The specifics are beyond the scope of this book, but a dispute may occur if, in the event of credit card fraud, the cardholder is unhappy with a product purchased, or if the purchaser does not receive the item within a reasonable timeframe. Be prepared to deal with such situations. Be sure that you ask the user for appropriate contact information, including an e-mail address. You or your transaction processing company should be able to grab each customer's IP address for verification purposes. Discourage fraud on your site by posting messages in appropriate locations that state that fraudulent activities will be processed to the full extent of the law. Make sure your return and exchange policies are clearly laid out. Finally, send an e-mail notification to the client stating that her transaction has been approved. This can be done by you or automatically by your storefront software, or sometimes the payment processing company will take care of this.

Sending an e-mail notification to the customer allows you to reiterate how a sale will appear on the consumer's monthly statement so that the charge does not take her offguard. A consumer may become confused and dispute a charge if she does not recognize your company name or the name of the payment processing company. She may only be familiar with your URL, so it helps to clarify how the purchase will appear on the credit card statement. Sending an e-mail notification is also a good opportunity to insert marketing information relative to future promotions or to encourage the customer to come back to your site.

Storefront Solutions

Depending on your online objectives, your products and services, and your budget, you might have to develop an electronic storefront for your business. An electronic storefront is the interface that a customer sees when purchasing goods on a Web site. The need for an electronic storefront varies with the level of e-Business that your company chooses to implement. The various levels of e-Business are discussed in more detail later in this chapter.

When developing a storefront for your business, you have a number of options available. You can:

- Use a storefront template service
- Use the ASP model
- Purchase storefront development software
- Program and develop your own storefront

- Use a hybrid storefront system

Each option has its strengths and weaknesses, and some are more appropriate than others depending on your products and services, your budget, your online marketing objectives, and the features you want in your storefront. Prior to making the decision about which storefront solution to use, you should review and evaluate the following optional storefront features and select the ones that are most appropriate for your business. After you have determined which features you want to have, you will be in a better position to determine which storefront solution will best meet your needs. We discuss the storefront solution options in greater detail later in the chapter.

Select Storefront Features That Meet Your Objectives

There are many different features available with different electronic storefronts. Features vary depending on how advanced the storefront option that you have selected is. Typically, higher-end software has more advanced features from that of a template service; however, some of these features may not be essential or even appropriate to run your particular online business. Before moving on to the storefront solutions, it is important for you to review the following list of features. Note which ones are essential, which ones would be nice to have, and which ones can be discarded, and keep this information in mind when looking for and implementing a storefront solution. We provide you with a convenient checklist for this purpose in Appendix C.

Shopping Cart

An electronic shopping cart is an excellent feature for sites that sell multiple products or services. The online shopping cart system operates much like an actual shopping cart. You can add items to your carts as you please, and you can remove items just as easily. As the customers add and subtract items from their shopping cart, a running total of their purchase choices is dynamically updated.

If you have a wide variety or a large number of product offerings, then this feature is extremely valuable, both to you and to your customers. The shopping cart manages each item the user selects to purchase and displays it to him in an organized manner. A common shopping cart displays a number of things to the online consumer:

- Items in the cart
- The quantities of each item in the cart
- A description of the products in the cart
- The price of each item or group of items
- A subtotal of all items in the cart

Backend Integration

Does the software enable you to integrate the storefront with your backend systems? Backend systems refer to the company's internal accounting, inventory, contact management, order management, and customer and other supporting software systems. Do you want to integrate all backend systems or do you just want to integrate one or two of them? The option to integrate certain backend operations is a fantastic feature for companies that sell multiple products online, that want to build better relationships with their customers, or that simply want everything to run independently of manual processes.

Take storefront integration with the backend inventory system as an example. By integrating the backend with your storefront, you can track inventory levels to (1) ensure you don't run out of a certain product or (2) notify customers that you are out of stock before they make a purchase. The use of inventory management integration may also give you the option of accepting pre-orders for specific items, depending on which storefront solution you implement. Amazon.com allows people to place books on order prior to their release date.

Want to build a better relationship with your customers and increase sales? Consider implementing CRM (customer relationship management) techniques by integrating your storefront with your customer database. This is a feature found more in high-end solutions such as full-featured e-commerce software packages and customized storefront design. Amazon.com is a good example. When you log in to their site using your username and password, they present you with purchase suggestions based on your personal information and purchase history. Amazon.com also greets users by name when they visit the site.

If you plan to use some form of integration, then make sure the solution you select is compatible with your existing backend systems. If your inventory is hosted in an Oracle database, what good is it to you if you select a storefront solution that supports Sybase, MSSQL, Informix, and MYSQL but not Oracle? Although all databases are founded on SQL (structured query language), each has its own subtle differences and unique operational commands.

Integration requires a serious investment of time and money. If you do not have an existing product database and want to use this option, know that it can take months of planning, design, and testing before your database is operational and ready to be integrated. For integration to be useful, your databases must be able to be updated in real time. If someone purchases 100 widgets, then your storefront solution will have to be able to communicate with the database to tell it that you now have 100 fewer widgets on hand. It will also have to be able to associate the sale with the consumer's account, with any order management systems in place, and with your accounting systems. A small business with small product assortment may find that investing the time in constructing one or more databases and integrating them with the Web site is not feasible from a business standpoint, whereas for big businesses it is basically essential.

Thumbnail Image Capability

Your storefront software should enable you to place small thumbnail images of the products next to their listing. The user can then click on the image to enlarge it and see a better view of the product. This enhances the overall listing for each of your products in your storefront. Thumbnails also assist in optimizing your site's download time. It takes much less time to download several thumbnailed 2K images as opposed to several full-sized 50K images.

Searchable Product Database

Practically a necessity for companies selling hundreds of products online, this feature enables a consumer to visit your site and search through your database of product listings. Often consumers will know what they want when they visit your site; thus, offering this feature will enable them to go directly to the product SKU (also known as a stock keeping unit) that they want, rather than searching through multiple pages trying to find the product. A SKU is similar to the ISBN number you find on the back of books—it is a numerical value that identifies an individual product.

Some storefront solutions will allow the consumer to search for a particular string such as a product category, brand name, keyword, SKU, ISBN number, and so on. If having a searchable product database is important for your business, take the time to define the search capabilities required on your online storefront.

Tax Calculations

Depending on the laws in your local area or country, different tax rules will apply, or there may even be no taxes at all. There are over 30,000 tax jurisdictions across the United States alone. If you require the ability to perform appropriate tax calculations, then this is a feature you should look for when selecting your storefront solution. MerchandiZer, pictured in Figure 4.2, allows the user to easily update sales tax rates.

If you are doing business internationally, you may need to be able to calculate value added tax (VAT). Some storefront solutions come with specific international tax settings in place and others do not, but they allow you to add them in yourself. You might want to arrange international tax according to specific zones, such as all European Union countries are charged *X* amount on their purchases. When doing sales internationally, be sure to consider how the particular storefront solution you're considering handles international taxes. Does it include predefined tax settings? Do they update themselves in real time? Does the solution allow you to configure your own tax settings? Determine what will be important to you.

Shipping and Delivery Options

Another way to provide excellent customer service is by offering different shipping options to your clients. This feature enables your customers to select a shipping option that best suits their needs during the checkout period when they are finalizing their order on your web site. Some people like to receive their purchases immediately and are

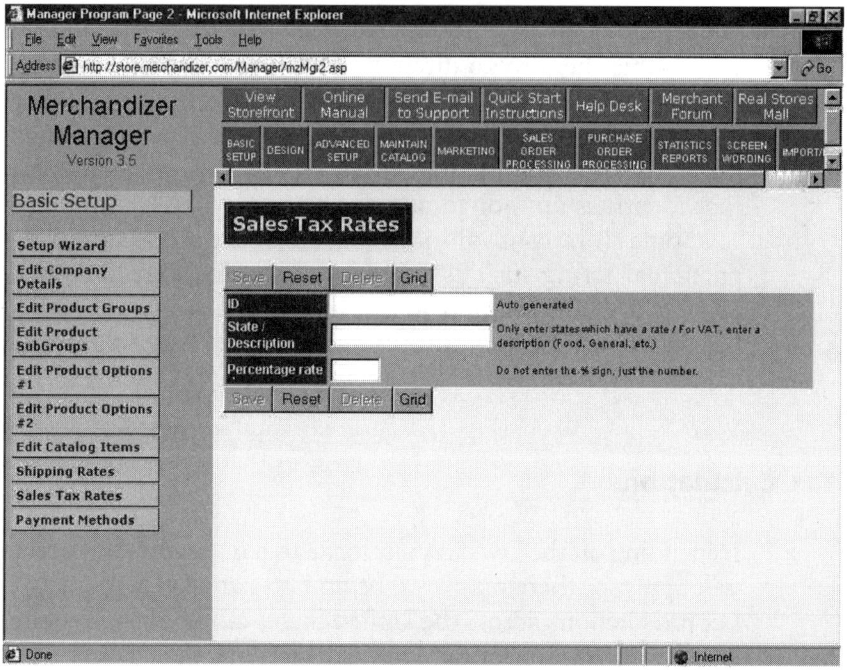

Figure 4.2. Merchandizer customers can quickly and easily insert or update tax settings.

willing to pay a premium for overnight delivery, while others prefer to save a little money and are willing to wait a few days.

By offering a variety of shipping and delivery options, you have an opportunity to upsell (that is, add to your sale) by utilizing different price points for different delivery periods. You could set a specific price point for each of your delivery options, which may include "next day," "2–3 days," "surface, 1–2 weeks," and so on.

The key is, when implementing different shipping options, be sure to do so in a logical manner. Consider for a moment that you're selling jewelry and someone purchases a ring valued at $600. Assume that customer is only a couple hundred miles (or kilometers) away in a neighboring state (province). What are you going to charge for shipping? Some companies base their shipping rates on a percentage of the overall sale, such as 10 percent. Would you be willing to pay $60 in shipping fees for a box no bigger than a package of sticky notes? Probably not, and neither will your customers. The fees you charge for shipping could be based on a number of things:

- The ZIP or postal code of the end destination for the package. The farther the item is traveling, the more it will typically cost. People know this; it's a common fact.

- The size of the package. The bigger it is, the more you can expect to pay to have it shipped.

- The weight of the package. The heavier it is, the more costly it will be to ship it.

- The dimensions of the package. The dimensions of a package can have an effect on how much it will cost or even if the package can be shipped at all. In Canada, Canada Post will not send letter envelopes that are in the shape of a triangle.

- The time frame in which the package is to be delivered. If you want to send a package across the country overnight as opposed to regular mail, you can expect to pay a premium for the rush service.

Calculating shipping fees can become complicated. Many businesses choose to simplify the process by defining set procedures for calculating shipping charges. This makes it easier for the company to track and it makes it easier for the customer to understand. Newline Cinemas' online store bases its shipping charges on location (U.S.A., Canada, or internationally) and on the price of total order. (See Figure 4.3.)

A number of options to consider when defining your shipping policy are:

- To charge a standard fee per item.

- To offer free shipping over a certain specified amount. For example, "all orders over $100 are shipped for free."

- To charge a specific fee based on the value of the total order.

These are just a few of the many combinations available. What you choose to do is up to you, but just make sure it makes logical sense! Different storefront solutions will usually contain preconfigured shipping options as well as allow you to define your own. Select the storefront solution that best fits your needs.

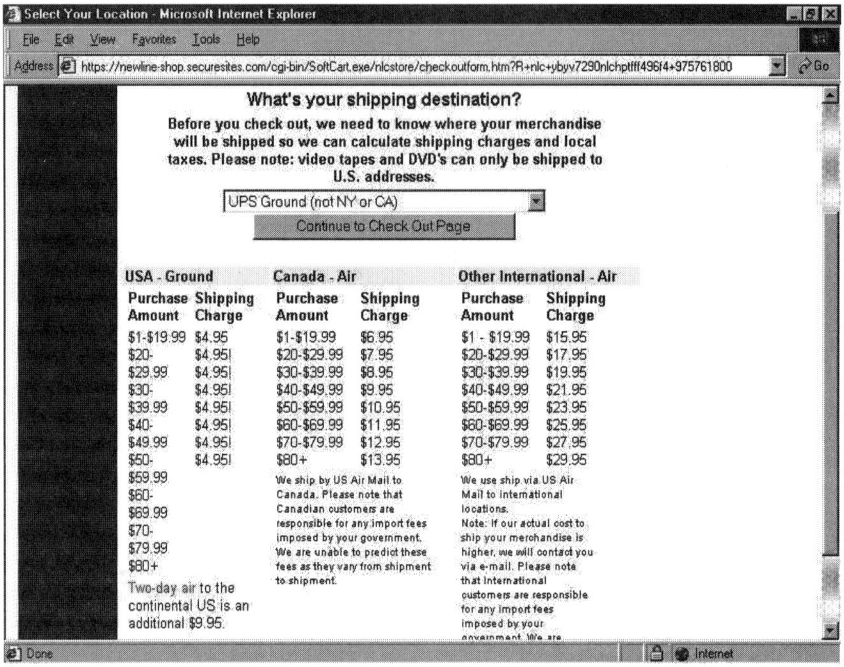

Figure 4.3. Simplifying shipping procedures makes it easier for you and your customers.

Automatic Purchase Notification

This feature enables the merchant to be notified via e-mail whenever a purchase is made on its Web site. The e-mail typically states the product purchased, the amount of the purchase, the purchaser's contact information, and any other relevant information pertaining to the purchase. This feature is terrific if you use offline methods to authorize credit card purchases (i.e., the telephone). You can simply pull up the e-mail message on your screen and call in to receive an authorization number.

Customer Email Notification

This feature enables you to automatically send your clients an e-mail directly after they purchase an item on your Web site. The message will confirm that you have received their order, and you can also take the time to thank them for doing business with your company. This is a great way to provide quality customer service to your clients.

Order Tracking

Order tracking encourages both new customers and repeat customers. People like to know what the status of their purchase is. Some storefront solutions will allow you to empower users to log on using a username and password to check the status of their orders. Knowing that an order has already been shipped or what the status of your backorder is increases consumer confidence as they are not wondering whether or not their package has been shipped or if it ever will be. This is an extremely important feature for online businesses selling big-ticket items. Clients want to know exactly where their purchase is at a given time.

Customer Information

Allowing users to create an account on your online storefront with a unique username and password can be a valuable asset to your online business. It allows them to store their personal information, such as their name, phone number, credit card information, and place of residence, on your site. Every time the customer visits your site, she logs in using her username and password. When the user goes to make a purchase, she will not have to enter her personal information each time because it is already on file. This saves her time and facilitates her needs—a great way to encourage repeat sales and build consumer loyalty.

If you're selling a product or service that is likely to be purchased only once by the consumer, then this option is not a necessity for you. On the other hand, if you're operating a B2B (business-to-business) and are a supplier to a whole network of other businesses on a regular basis, then this option becomes quite a necessity. If a customer is visiting your site each week to make a purchase, he's not going to want to have to enter his personal information each time he visits.

Some solutions allow customer payment information to be stored on hand. This works in the same way as storing personal information in that the user will not have to enter the payment information each time she makes a purchase. If storing payment information is an important option for you, be sure that the storefront solution you select is capable of effectively encrypting the data to protect your business and your customers from fraudulent activities.

If you expect to have a large customer database, then giving users the option to change their personal information without having to contact your company is a great asset. It saves you time and it saves the consumer time. You do not want to answer the phone or your e-mail box 50 times a day to change a customer's phone number, and they probably don't want to have to contact you either—it's a hassle.

Ship-to Addresses

Some customers may prefer to send their purchases to a location other than their place of residence. A customer may order something and want it shipped to his place of work, or he may order something and want it shipped to another city as a gift. Giving the user the option to send each item to a different location is a great feature to include if it is likely that your clients are not always going to send their purchases to the same address time and time again.

Some storefront solutions will remember the ship-to information that is entered when the user returns to the web site again. This is a valuable feature if your customers are going to consistently send items to different locations. For example, you may have a buyer for an entire company with ten subsidiaries located in a head office in New York. This buyer may be responsible for sending product to each of the ten subsidiaries. Unless the company has a central distribution warehouse through which all product must pass, the buyer will probably not want you to ship all product to her location so that she then has to turn around and send all of the product out again to each individual subsidiary. This results in unnecessary time delays and costs.

Technical Support

Above all, whether you purchase storefront development software or choose to use a template service, you should always ensure that the service provider has excellent customer support. If you have any problems with your storefront, you should be able to call your service provider and receive immediate assistance to remedy your problem. Downtime or malfunctions in your storefront can hinder your business's professionalism, so you should have the best technical support available to help you solve any problem you may encounter.

Tracking and Report Generation

Planning for the present and the future is an important part of being a successful business. How do you do that? Understanding your business is a big part. Different storefront solutions offer different options for tracking sales and trends.

This feature is important for all businesses! You're going to want to know what was sold, when it was sold, how much was sold, who bought it, sales trends, and so forth. This information helps you plan what products and services you should emphasize and which ones you should drop.

If you have a large selection of products, you will want to be able to check whether or not the description, pricing, SKU, graphic, and so on, are correct for each of your products. This is where reports that detail discrepancies will come in handy. If you have to physically go through each product on your site, a lot of time will be wasted.

Yahoo! gives users a number of options for monitoring their site and transactions. (See Figures 4.4 and 4.5.)

Payment Platforms

If you want to be able to accept forms of payment other than credit cards, then this feature is a necessity. Some storefront solutions are able to accept checks, digital cash, coupons, Air Miles, gift certificates, and so on. Some storefront solutions are able to communicate with the customer's e-wallet. An e-wallet resides on the consumer's computer and stores all of her payment information such as credit card information.

If you are going to accept coupons as payment, then your storefront must be able to handle coupons as a form of payment services. Likewise, if you are a member of the Air Miles program, your storefront will have to be able to communicate with the Air Miles program to accept points as an exchange of monies.

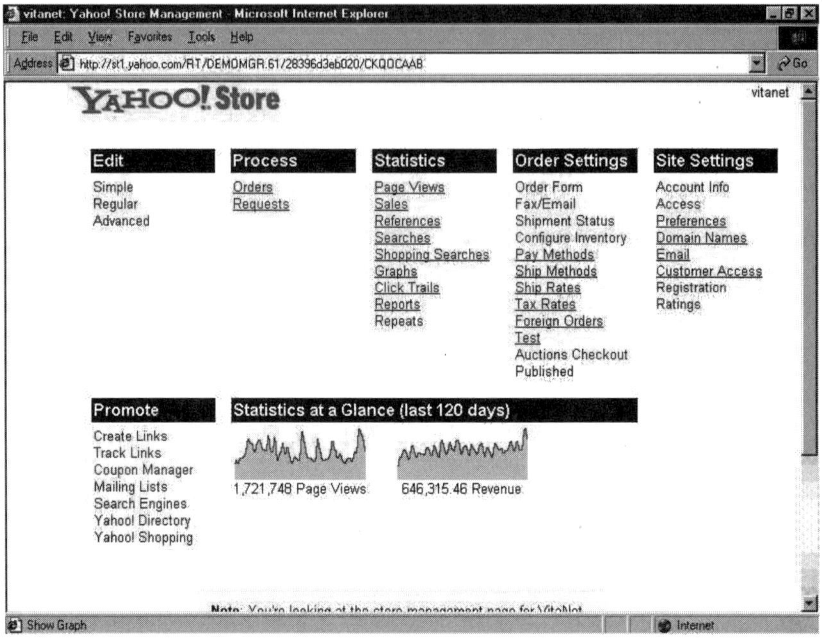

Figure 4.4. Yahoo! Store enables store owners to analyze a series of pertinent statistics.

Promotions and Discounts

Many companies use online promotions and discounts to build traffic to their sites and to increase online sales. Most storefront solutions offer some support for promotional activities because it is common occurrence in business practices.

This feature ties in closely with payment platforms, just discussed. For example, if you want to offer a two-for-one special on your site, then your storefront needs to be able to account for this.

Do you need to be able to offer discounts on your online store? Are discounts going to be determined as a percentage, quantity, weight, a fixed rate, and so on? Are discounts permanent or are they going to run for a defined period of time? If discounts are an important part of your regular business, then the storefront solution you select must be able to manage this for you.

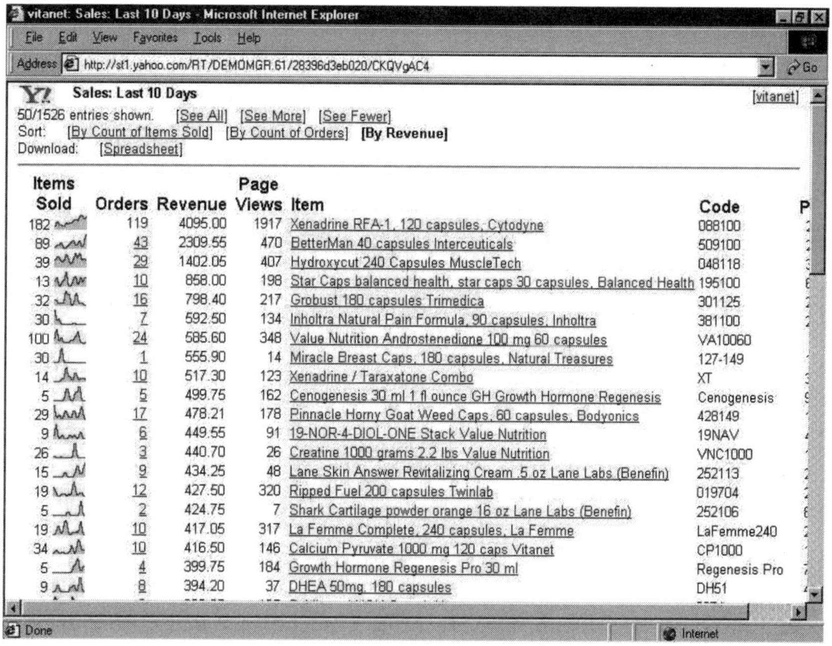

Figure 4.5. You can view sales per item over a specified period of time with Yahoo! Store.

Third-Party Support

Third-party support is extremely valuable if you want to automate certain processes on your site. If you're running an operation that requires the online storefront to be integrated with your inventory management system, what good is a storefront solution that cannot integrate the two? Sometimes your financial institution will require you to use a specific payment processing company if you want to be able to accept online orders and automate the payment process. What purpose does a storefront solution serve if it does not support the payment processing company you are required to use? These are examples of questions you should ask yourself when selecting your storefront solution.

Many storefront solutions support products and services of other companies with regard to accepting payment, tracking orders, shipping, backend integration, third-party payment support, and so on.

If you want to offer order tracking as a service to your customers, then you're going to need a storefront that can communicate with a shipping company such as UPS to provide the appropriate information. Select a storefront solution that meets your needs.

Domain Name Support and Storefront Hosting

Some storefront solutions require you to use their domain name, whereas others allow you to use your own domain name. Your storefront would then be a subdomain or a subdirectory of their domain. For example:

- *http://www.YOURSTORE.yourprovider.com*
- *http://www.yourprovider.com/YOURSTORE/*

Using the domain name of a solution provider is appropriate for companies with a limited budget or that are not committed to e-business. But if you are serious about your online presence, you will want a solution that supports the use of your own domain name.

Some storefront solution providers require you to host the entirety of your online store on their server. This is common of storefront solutions that require you to use their domain name. Other storefront solutions require only part of your online storefront (CGI processes) to be hosted on their servers, and still others enable you to host all aspects of your own storefront locally. In general, however, the more control you wish to have, the more you can expect to pay for the solution.

Maximum Product Limit

How many products are you going sell? One? Ten? A hundred? Ten thousand? The storefront solution you select will need to be able to support your requirements.

Digital Content Sales

Are you selling an intangible product such as downloadable software? If so, when evaluating your options you will need to look for a storefront solution that is capable of managing the sales of informational property and its distribution.

Template Customization

If you are managing your online presence yourself, then your level of HTML knowledge and experience comes into play here. Some storefront solutions offer limited customization and only one or two template layouts to choose from. This is more common of an online storefront service. In contrast, some solutions offer unlimited possibilities—especially if you're designing your own storefront from scratch. The solution you choose will be based on your requirements. The use of a template service or storefront software package will meet the needs of most online businesses.

Many storefront software packages come with multiple default templates you can use to construct your storefront with little or no HTML knowledge. Multiactive Software's (*http://www.multiactive.com/*) ecBuilder solution is packaged with 40 templates and over 700 graphical layout combinations. You do not need HTML knowledge to set up their storefront. Mercantec's SoftCart provides the user with many templates as well. In addition, you can build your own template, but you need the technical know-how to do so in order to design the layout and to be able to effectively link it to your Web site.

International Options

Although there is an enormous potential in doing business internationally, there are a number of factors you need to consider before selecting a storefront solution to do business across international borders. Tax, which was covered earlier, is one of them. The solution you select must also be able to process shipping to other countries and manage multicurrency transactions if you want to offer this option.

When selling overseas, you will probably not want to conduct business in every country. There will be certain countries where the risk is too high or your product is inappropriate for sale. Some storefront solutions allow you to restrict the countries in which you do business.

Flexibility and Value-Add Components

This section is intended to expand on the previous sections and has been included to provide you with some insight into some little extras that may be very important to your business. For example, many companies like the ability to have their latest products prominently displayed with an accompanying "New" message for a specified period of time. This draws attention to your latest products and services.

If the products you sell are appropriate for gift giving, then consider a gift-wrapping service. This is a great value-add, and it gives you the opportunity to upsell. You can charge a fee for gift wrapping. You might charge $1.95 per item for standard wrapping, $4.95 for wrapping and a bow, and maybe $7.95 for wrapping, a bow, and a personalized message.

Is the ability to view purchase history important to your customers? If so, then you will want to find out if the solution you're considering is capable of doing so. Many consumers and business customers will want to review their purchase history for a number of reasons—there might be a discrepancy on their credit card bill, the company may need it for account purposes, and so forth.

From time to time people forget their passwords. You may wish to implement a storefront solution that can provide the customer with a password auto reminder such as a skill testing question or a brief e-mail with the password enclosed. This is a convenient feature for a couple of reasons. It means that the consumer can figure out his password on his own without waiting for a response from you. If a user forgets his password he may just leave your site never to return or may create a new account and increase redundancies in your consumer database. You're saving yourself maintenance time and you're providing a valuable service to your customers.

What if the customer makes a purchase only to realize a couple of hours later she bought the wrong product? Empowering the user with the ability to make changes to her order is great customer service!

Some storefront solutions give consumers the ability to control how information is displayed to them on the Web site. There are certain people who may only be interested in seeing specific content or products on a site at a given time. For example, if you sell books, videos, and music, the storefront solution would enable the customer to customize the site so that every time she logs in she is given a listing of the latest video releases or whatever her preference happens to be.

From the perspective of the merchant, is the storefront solution user-friendly? Are you able to make product changes easily or does the solution require knowledge of HTML scripting? Can you change tax settings and shipping configurations through the use of a convenient graphical user interface or does the solution require editing the actual code?

These additional features can make doing business online easier for you from a maintenance standpoint, and they can help to increase your online profitability through value-add features that assist in encouraging sales and building relationships with your target market.

Once you have evaluated the storefront options in terms of what is (a) essential, (b) nice to have, and (c) unnecessary, review the storefront solutions available to you and compare them with the criteria you have determined as being important to your business's objectives.

Use a Storefront Template Service

Typically, this storefront option is appealing to businesses with smaller budgets and weaker technical skills. There are hundreds of businesses online that provide storefront template services. Storefront templates are very easy to use. You simply register to use the service, and once you have been approved you key in the appropriate information for your product listings. This service is usually provided through a Web browser interface, which enables you to quickly and easily update your product listings online. Some of the more popular storefront Web-based template services include:

- Yahoo! Store (*http://store.yahoo.com*)
- ShopBuilder (*http://www.shopbuilder.com*)
- MerchandiZer (*http://www.merchandiZer.com*)

Quite often template service providers can also assist you in taking online payments or can refer you to an associate company that can help you. For first-time online business operators this can help the process run more smoothly as the support of the service provider can help you to gain a clearer understanding of what is involved in running an online business. Yahoo! Store can be seen in Figure 4.6. An example of a business using Yahoo! Store's service can be viewed in Figure 4.7.

To use a template service you typically have to pay a monthly service fee. Fees can range from US $10 to US $250 depending on which features the template service provides. These fees cover the setup and daily maintenance of your virtual storefront. Some template services provide you with relevant statistical information such as page views for a period of time and a comparison of your sales history. More advanced features such as real-time credit card processing usually cost more. Many storefront template services charge a base fee for allowing you to set up shop and host your site and charge additional fees for value-add options. For example, Yahoo! Store requests $100 per month for a storefront with the ability to list 50 items. To list 1,000 items the monthly fee becomes $300, and so on.

When using a storefront template service, your storefront is hosted by the template service on its server. What does this mean? If you were using Yahoo!'s storefront template service, then all of the information and data pertaining to your online business would be hosted by Yahoo!.

Although storefront templates make it very easy for you to set up your online business, they may not be appropriate for some forms of business. When you're using a template service, you have to understand that your storefront will look similar to other businesses' store-

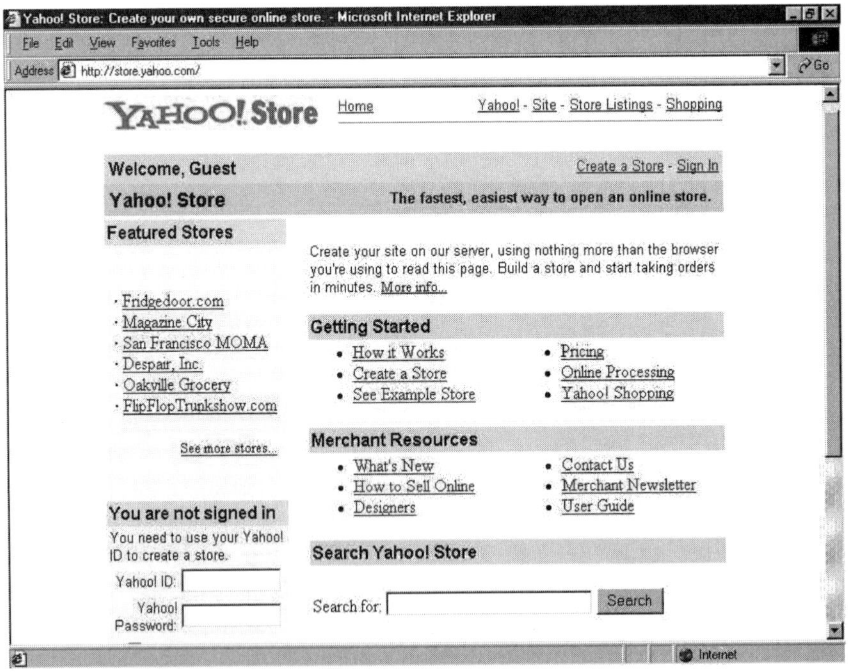

Figure 4.6. Yahoo! Store allows individuals to build their own online storefront.

Figure 4.7. Gardener's Supply Company is an example of a storefront using Yahoo!'s template service.

fronts that are using the same service. To smaller businesses with smaller market share this is tolerable, but to others this makes their site less distinguishable on the Internet.

Storefront template services often restrict the amount of customization that you can do to the templates. They usually have a standard layout, which limits your ability to customize the template and means that all storefronts using the same solution have a similar look and feel. If you host the main body of your site on an ISP of your choice, then when a visitor chooses to browse through your selection of products he is taken to a page that may not be consistent with the overall appearance of your site. For many businesses this is not an issue, but if you are looking to maintain a unique look and feel, then this option may not be a viable one for you. Not all act in this manner, however. In fact, some offer a number of different template options or even allow you to customize the appearance of your storefront as you see fit.

Using an ASP

ASP stands for Application Service Provider. The ASP owns the storefront software and operates its own e-commerce server. As an ASP, it licenses out the use of its software and e-commerce hosting services to clients that desire to sell products and services online. The software is hosted on the ASP's server, and as the client you pay the ASP to use its software and server. This option is often much cheaper than purchasing your own storefront software package.

When researching ASP solutions, understand what features you want the storefront to include and compare the different solutions based on this. You do not want to pay for features you do not need, and you do not want to pay for an ASP's solution when it doesn't meet all of your objectives.

The ASP's storefront solution can be integrated with your existing web site. The portion of the storefront that is hosted on the ASP's server can be customized to duplicate the appearance of your site and use the same navigation system. This adds to the level of professionalism and maintains a sense of consistency across all pages of your site and the purchase process.

Each client is given a unique username and password to allow for easy management of her account. The information hosted on the ASP's server can be modified at any time—you can add or remove products at your convenience, alter the layout, change prices, and so on.

This solution is ideal for businesses that are looking to maintain their own site, but that do not want to be responsible for configuring and maintaining the technical aspects of the e-commerce system. The ASP model is usually easy to configure for individuals with limited HTML knowledge and can be set up and running in a very short time frame. One provider of such a solution is W3 Internet Services (*http://www.w3internet.com/*). (See Figure 4.8.)

Purchase Storefront Development Software

There are a variety of storefront software development packages available that you can purchase to enable you to develop your online storefront for your business. This is generally a more expensive approach compared to using a template service; however, there is a lot more flexibility as to what you can do with your storefront. If you choose to use this approach, a more technical knowledge of computers will be required and you will have to find an Internet service provider to host your electronic storefront.

The advantage of using a software package to develop your storefront is that you have more control over the layout and design of your storefront. Unlike some template services, software packages enable you to develop the storefront to be consistent with the rest of your Web site. Consistency in appearance across all pages of your site is important. The only downside is that you need some degree of technical knowledge to design a complex storefront for your business.

Software packages also offer more advanced features that can help you to provide better internal and external control over your business. These features were covered earlier in the chapter and include things like multiple currencies, tax calculations, shipping calculations, and so on. In general, larger online businesses use these software packages when developing their online businesses because of these features. Make sure you know which features you are look-

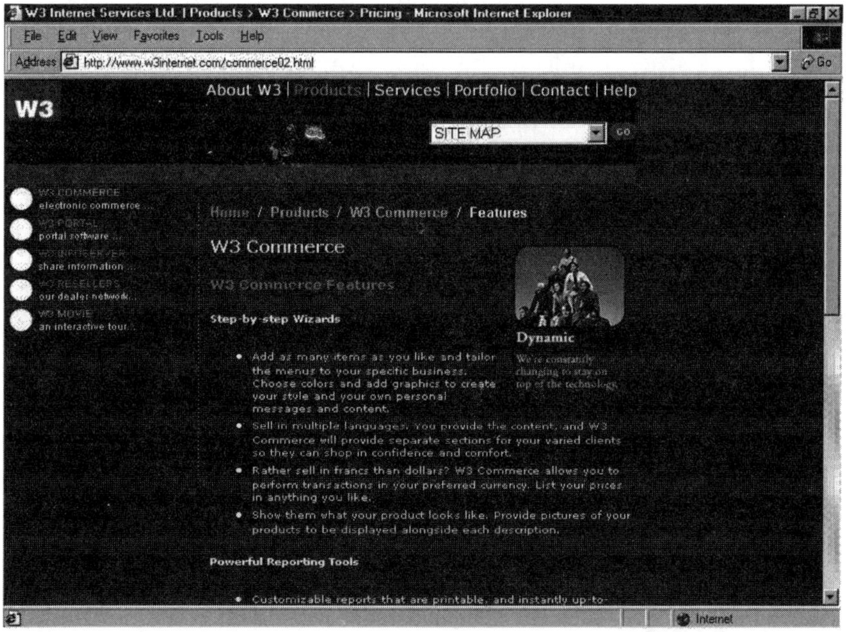

Figure 4.8. W3 is an up-and-coming ASP.

ing for prior to your software selection. If you plan to sell only 10 to 20 products, there is no need to pay a premium for a software package than can handle 5,000 SKUs. Similarly, if you do not plan to sell outside your country's borders, the ability to accept multiple currencies is probably not a necessity for you.

Review the list of storefront features to determine those that are essential to your business, ones that would be nice to have, and the ones you can omit because they have little value to your operation. A large business that sells internationally will have different needs from a small business doing business locally. In general, larger businesses handle higher volumes of sales and carry a broader line of products. The large business may require a searchable product database to assist its customers as well as the ability to accept currencies from around the globe. These features are appealing to such businesses because the software gives them the flexibility they need to control sales activities and enables them to provide better customer service to their clients.

Storefront software is commonly installed on the same server as your web site. This can be a more involved process, and in some cases it may be necessary to hire a person with the appropriate technical knowledge to set up and maintain your storefront. Many medium- to large-sized businesses have their own in-house team to manage their e-Business operations. Do some research before you select the storefront option that best fits your business requirements. The resource section at the end of this chapter suggests some valuable sites for obtaining more information. One popular solution is InterShop's (*http://www.intershop.com/*) Enfinity, as pictured in Figure 4.9.

Another popular storefront software is Mercantec's (*http://www.mercantec.com/*) SoftCart series. They have four versions of their product: Start-Up, Lite, Pro, and Suite. You can select the package that best suits your needs now and, should you need more capabilities in the future, simply upgrade.

Program and Develop Your Own Storefront

If you have a broad product line or a complex array of products and services, you may want to consider developing your own storefront. This requires in-depth technical knowledge and programming capabilities. If you don't have the technical capability in-house, you can outsource this activity to a firm capable of developing such a program for your business, or hire an employee or team to handle the storefront development. Keep in mind that developing your own storefront from scratch can take a long time, and it will require a significant monetary investment.

There are many software packages available that have an enormous range of capabilities. The option of building your own storefront from scratch is best for companies that are in a unique situation where a software package or an alternative solution cannot meet their needs.

If you decide to develop your own storefront software, you should ensure that everything is running smoothly before you launch the storefront into cyberspace. Every aspect of the storefront selection and purchasing procedure should be tested and retested to ensure that there are no bugs, miscalculations, or errors in the process. Once you are sure that everything is working correctly and smoothly, you then have to find a place to host the storefront, whether it be on your own server or on an ISP's server. From that point on, your only recur-

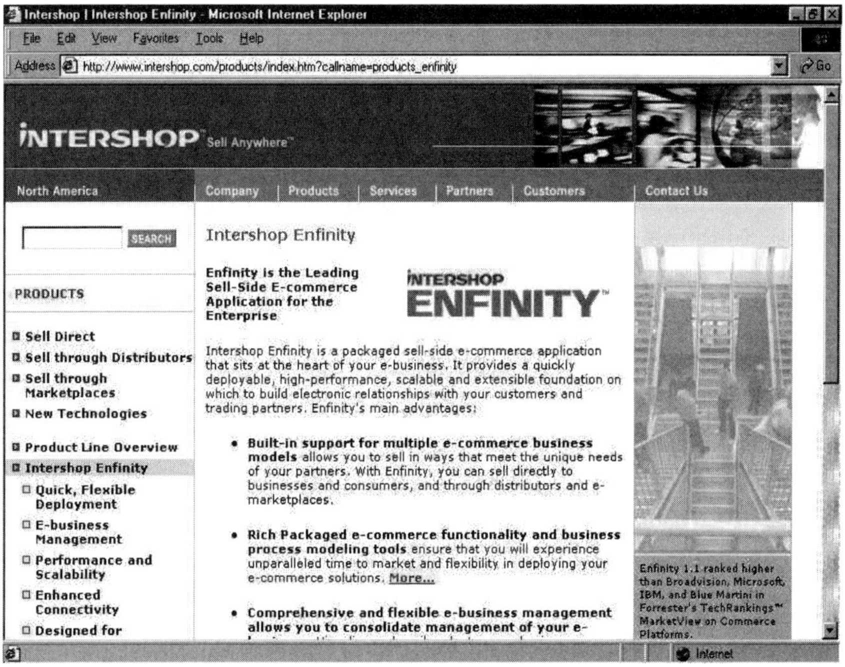

Figure 4.9. InterShop is one of the most recognized names in the business.

ring expense is that of hosting your storefront, and payment processing and authorization charges from a payment processing company.

Use a Hybrid Storefront System

A hybrid system is a combination of more than one storefront solution. What happens here is that you may use part of one solution and part of another to achieve your desired outcome. For example, you could purchase a storefront software solution and hire a Web developer to integrate the software with your web site. This may be a cost-effective solution for a company that wants its storefront set up professionally but that does not have the necessary capital to have a solution developed completely from scratch or the knowledge to integrate the software solution in-house.

Customer Service

Customer service is possibly the key component to closing sales and building your base of repeat customers. In addition to making the experience pleasant for the user from the Web site design and storefront points of view, you need to make their experience pleasant behind the scenes as well.

Good customer service can have a major impact on the performance of your business online. Some people will not make a purchase without some kind of human interaction; this is especially true for big-ticket or customized products. Ensure that you prominently display your company's phone number and e-mail address for customer service. Be sure that you have the staff to maintain superior customer support. People will not sit by the phone waiting on hold for 30 minutes, nor do they want to wait a week for an e-mail response. Another option is to offer real-time customer service via Web chat. This allows the customer to communicate with you and get an immediate response without disconnecting from the Web to make a call. The knowledge of a customer service representative can often close the sale. Likewise, the customer representative can cross-sell and promote your products when talking to the customer. Overall, great customer service makes customers feel more secure and comfortable in doing business with you.

Part of providing good customer service comes from living up to your promises. If you tell a user you're going to send her order out, do it—don't wait a week so that you can send a group of orders out together just because it's more convenient for you.

Respect the privacy of your customers. When users sign up to be a member of your site or your newsletter if you have one, they expect you to keep their personal information to yourself, and why shouldn't they? Do not sell or distribute your members' personal information. This will keep your customers happy and help to keep your online business moving along. Providing a detailed privacy policy that Web site visitors can view helps in building your relationship with your customers because it tells them that you respect their privacy.

Internet Resources for This Chapter

MerchantWorks
http://www.merchantworkz.com/
This is a good site that provides objective information for small businesses on the Web. This site contains rate comparisons for merchant service providers, E-Commerce Solutions, and so forth.

MerchantSeek
http://www.merchantseek.com/
This site assists companies in finding a merchant account provider. The site also contains articles, a glossary, and books as well as additional information on credit card acceptance.

The Electronic Commerce Guide
http://ecommerce.internet.com/
This guide is packed with the latest e-commerce news, trends, and tips. You will also find information on many storefront options and payment processing solutions, including costs—a great place to start!

E-Commerce Research Room
http://www.wilsonweb.com/research/
An excellent collection of articles, resources, and links compiled by Dr. Ralph F. Wilson, E-Commerce Consultant.

E-Commerce Times
http://www.ecommercetimes.com/
This site presents daily e-commerce news about trends in e-Business, new technologies, new products, and anything else that's going on in the industry. In addition, there is a Small Business Advisor section that looks at e-Business strategies for entrepreneurs.

Part 2

The Right e-Business Model

5

e-Business Model 1—Electronic Order Taking

E-Business Model 1 is the most basic form of conducting e-Business online. It consists of the ability to take orders or reservations through e-mail or an online form on your Web site. It does not include exchange of money on a Web site.

Is Model 1 for You?

The answer to this question depends on a number of things. What products or services do you offer? What is the scope of your product or service line? What kind of budget do you have laid out for your online endeavors? What are your online goals and objectives? These are just some of the questions you need to ask yourself.

The primary function of this level of e-Business is to enable your business to accept electronic orders. This level of e-Business is very simple in comparison to the other e-Business models in that it does not involve transaction processing of any kind, the organization of a storefront, or integration with your supporting business systems such as inventory.

You will find this level of e-Business used by newcomers to the online business realm who have a restricted budget or are exploring their options online. The dynamics of the business itself also influences the model chosen. If you are a business that has little to worry about with respect to inventory or you are a business that cannot put a specific price on a product or service, then this model may fit your objectives.

An engineering or marketing firm often cannot put a price on their services as this is decided on a case-by-case situation depending on the size of the project being negotiated. The purpose of their e-Business presence is to generate awareness of their services and to encourage potential customers to request a proposal or to contact the respective firm for more information. These businesses must communicate extensively with their target market about their needs and objectives in order to determine the extent of work required before agreeing to do a project for a certain value.

Exploring e-Business Model 1

The primary advantage of this level of e-Business is that the company is able to conduct business online with minimal effort. The business does not need to worry about selecting and setting up an e-commerce software package, finding and paying to use a payment processing company, or ensuring that all of their online and offline systems are integrated and working properly.

A Bed and Breakfast operation may opt to provide a reservation form on their Web site to encourage bookings. An online form certainly makes booking a room simple and convenient for the customer. It allows the customer to take care of the reservation then and there—she does not need to worry about having to write down information in order to phone and make a reservation at a later date. White Point Beach Resort, as pictured in Figures 5.1–5.3, is one such resort that facilitates the needs of its target market by allowing them to make bookings directly on its Web site.

The ability to accept orders on your Web site gives you a significant advantage over your competitors that do not offer this option. You can make the sale then and there; they can't.

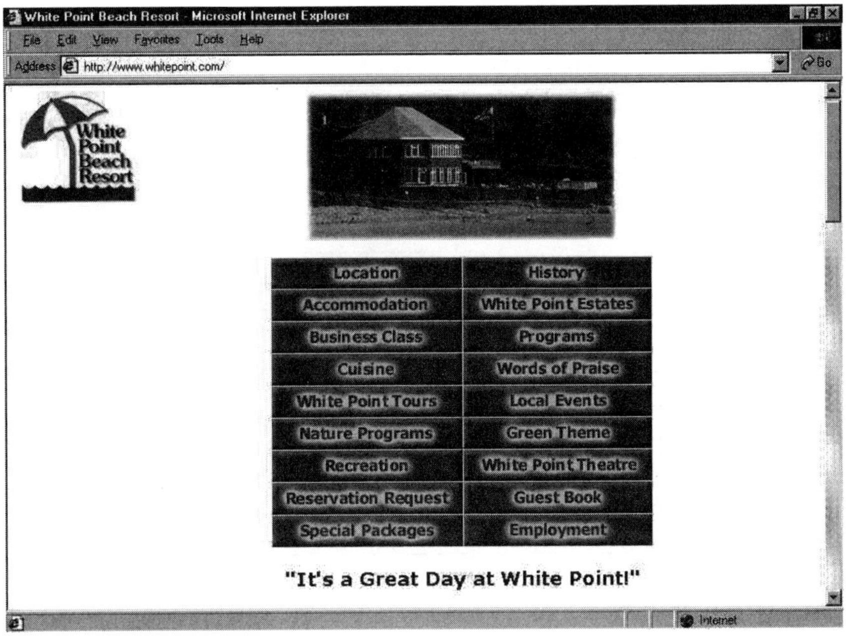

Figure 5.1. White Point Beach Lodge's home page.

If you are a business looking to sell a variety of products with set prices online, this level of e-Business will not be adequate for you. One of the other levels described in the upcoming chapters will better fit your e-Business strategy.

Ordering Alternatives

As discussed in the early chapters of this book, Internet consumers typically have extremely high expectations—you want to cater to their needs and expectations. Some of your potential customers may not feel comfortable with placing an order directly on your Web site even though no payment information is required.

To increase your chances of making the sale, you should provide the consumer with additional methods of placing his order. If you do

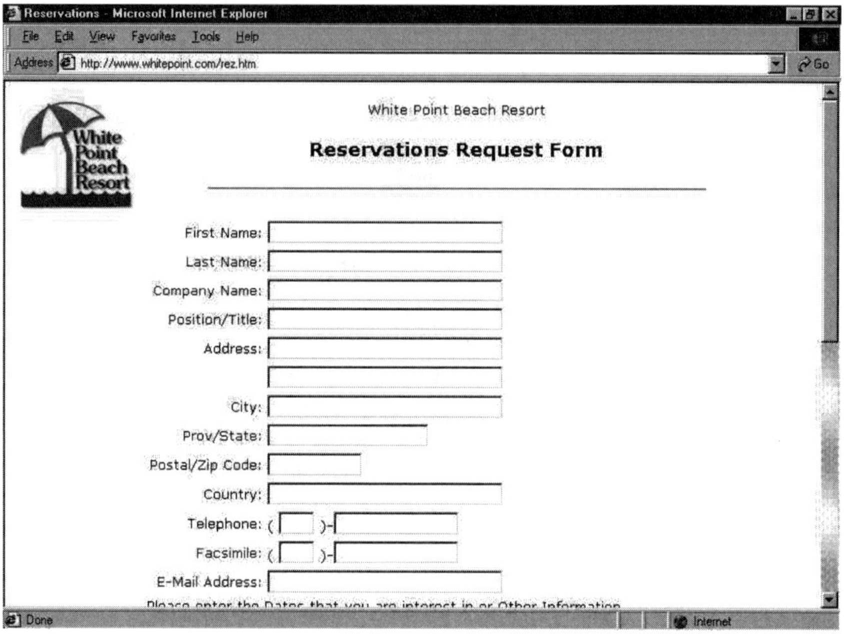

Figure 5.2. Customers can easily fill out the online form to make a room reservation.

not already have a toll-free number (1-800, 1-888, etc), consider getting one. Remember, many people who visit your site are likely from another state or out of the country, and you increase your chances of capturing the sale if you provide them with a method of placing an order at no additional cost to the consumer.

Make use of your fax machine by providing your target market with your fax number. You can allow your customers to print off the order form on your site and fax it in to complete their order. Another option to consider is to provide your target market your mailing address so that they can mail in their order. It may take longer, but if that's what they're comfortable with doing, then they should be allowed to do it.

Be sure to design your site with future upgrades in mind. If you want to add payment processing options in the future, you do not want to have to redesign your entire site from the ground up.

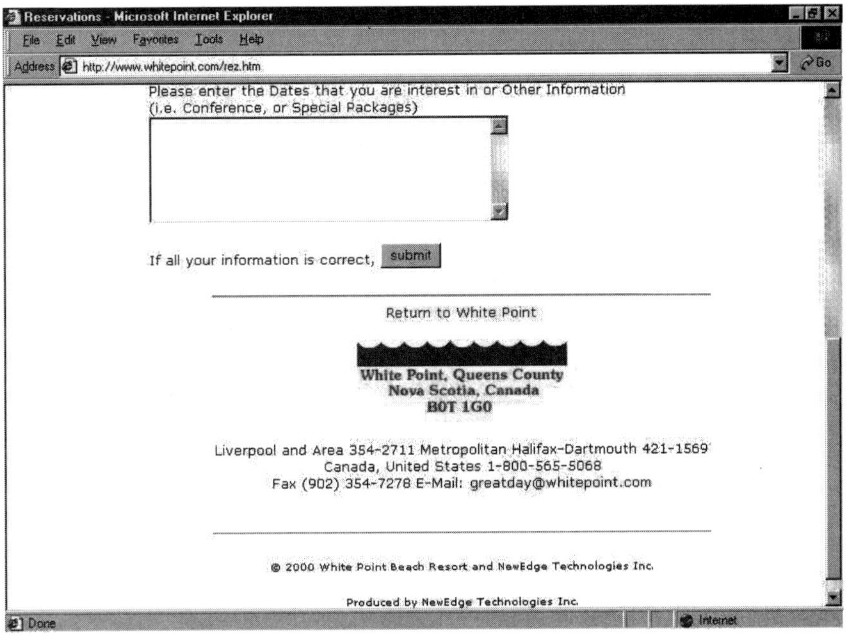

Figure 5.3. White Point provides its 1-800 number, its fax number, its e-mail address, and the physical address to customers.

Behind the Scenes

What happens behind the Web site will play a major role in the success of your online endeavor. Ensure that you have the capability to accept, process, and confirm customer orders. You do not want your customers waiting three weeks for a confirmation on their room reservation. If someone orders a particular product or service through the form on your Web site, you do not want to wait a week or two before calling them to confirm the receipt of their order and request their payment information. It's too late. They probably aren't interested anymore or have forgotten they even placed the order.

Have appropriate systems in place to manage day-to-day business. If you accept an order, call to confirm it within 24 hours and to collect payment. Poor customer service is a common reason that Internet users do not buy online and why many businesses fail online. Do not be a statistic. With the right planning and effort, you can achieve e-Business success.

6

e-Business Model 2—Accepting Electronic Payment

E-Business Model 2 moves a step beyond Model 1; however, it is important to begin by reviewing e-Business Model 1. It is the most basic e-Business model that enables the use of the Internet to conduct business electronically. This may be through the use of your company Web site to accept orders/reservations, or it may be the use of e-mail to communicate digital documents between yourself and a client, and so forth. The fundamental principle behind e-Business Model 1 is that e-Business is conducted without the transfer of payment. E-Business Model 2 extends the first model by incorporating the ability to accept electronic payments. Read on to find out if this model is appropriate for you.

Is Model 2 for You?

The answer to this question involves asking yourself the same questions you did when reviewing the first e-Business model, such as:

- What products or services do you offer?

- What is the scope of your product or service line?
- What kind of budget do you have laid out for your online endeavors?
- What are your online goals and objectives?

And so on.

When you are deciding on an e-Business model, everything always comes back to the basics—your goals, your objectives, your products and services, your target market, your commitment to the Internet as a sales vehicle, your budget, and so forth. Is the ability to accept payment over the Internet important to your business? E-Business Model 2 is appropriate when the price of your product or service is set, when payment is required on delivery of the final product or on promise of delivery, and when inventory is not a significant issue. Examples of business types that would follow this strategy include organizations that sell:

- Downloadable software
- Accommodations for which a deposit is required
- Seminar/course registration
- Theme park admittance
- Memberships
- Ski lift tickets
- Magazine subscriptions
- Gift certificates
- Products for which supply is not a big issue

Before moving on, you need to keep in mind that your online business consists of two core functional areas—the front end and the back end. The front end of your online business is essentially everything that your target market interacts with. It is your Web site, your online storefront. The back end refers to all supporting operations that take place behind the scenes, such as inventory management, accounting systems, and processing of special offers or discounts. This level of e-Business does not involve integrating the front end of your business with back-end operations. Each operates as a separate entity, but in such a way that the business runs efficiently.

A Bed and Breakfast does not need a complex storefront or systems integration to be able to accept room reservations with a deposit. All they need is a simple, secure Web site form that the customer fills out and inputs payment information. By requiring the customer to place a deposit online, the Bed and Breakfast is cutting down the number of "no-shows" and is increasing short-term cash flow. When people place a deposit on something, regardless of what it is, they are more likely to complete the transaction or contact you for a return on the deposit because you are in possession of their money. Some businesses request a deposit or full prepayment to even out seasonal fluctuations in cash flow.

Exploring e-Business Model 2

How do you accept payment for your products and services over the Internet? The first thing you need is an Internet merchant account. You can acquire your own or use that of a third party. This is discussed in depth in Chapter 4.

You can tackle the actual processing of online payments for goods and services in two ways. Many businesses implementing this level of e-Business will choose to process payment information manually. Quite often you will notice that sites using this type of payment strategy will require the customer to fill out some kind of online form that requests their personal information (name, address, etc.), purchase information (details about the purchase, color, quantity, etc.), and credit card information (type of card, number, expiration date). When the customer submits his information through the form, it then goes to a specific location where you, as the business owner, can access it. You would then manually verify the user's credit card information and process the sale. Once the sale is authorized, you or whoever takes care of ensuring that sales are processed should notify the customer that his transaction was approved and his item(s) is on the way.

Automatic payment processing is the second option available to you for accepting payment over the Internet. This enables you to have all payments processed without human interaction and deposited automatically into your bank account. Using the services of a payment processing company is required here. Consult with Chapter 4 on selecting and implementing the services of a payment processing company.

You must select the most appropriate method for your business. Processing payment manually may be more time-consuming than having your transactions processed automatically in real time by a payment processing company, but it may be more cost-effective for smaller businesses. Also, if your company does not sell large quantities of product, then the additional time required to process transactions may cause no interference in daily operations—they would be processed in exactly the same way regular business transactions are conducted.

This level of e-Business is very simple to implement and quite affordable. A good example of a company that would use this level of e-Business would be an online teleclass or teleseminar company. Since an unlimited number of people can dial into a bridged phone line, the company does not have to worry about inventory issues. The number of people participating in each class would likely not pose a problem for the Web server hosting the presentation slides as well. The teleclass company can simply design a generic payment form that takes all contact and payment information. The form may have a couple of additional fields asking users which presentation they're signing up for and on which date, but other than that the form would be straightforward. This e-Business strategy has low costs and low overhead, and is easy to implement. Figures 6.1 to 6.5 demonstrate an example of a tour operator's use of e-Business Model 2 to accept online bookings.

Figure 6.1. Prince of Fundy Cruises gives their customers the option to book online.

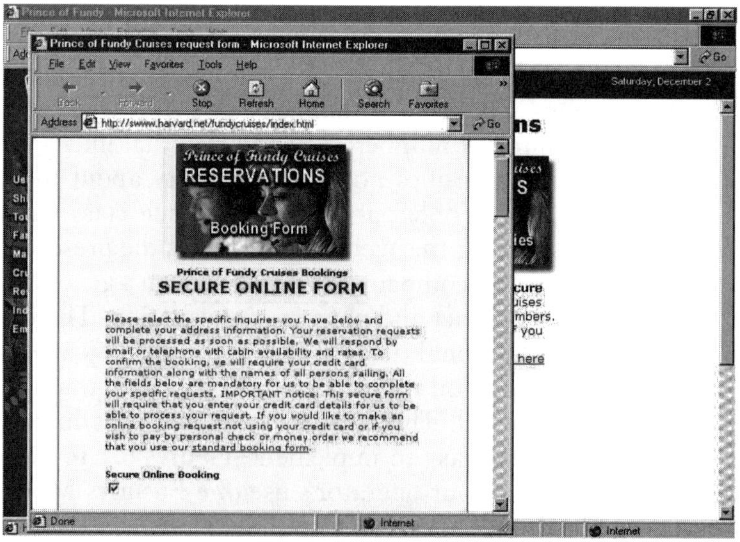

Figure 6.2. Simply select Reservations from the main navigation bar and the secure online form appears.

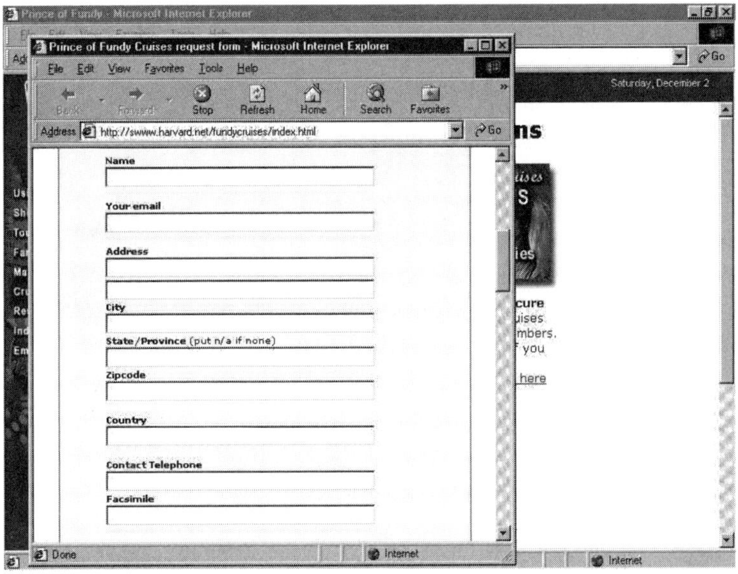

Figure 6.3. Enter the required details in the available fields.

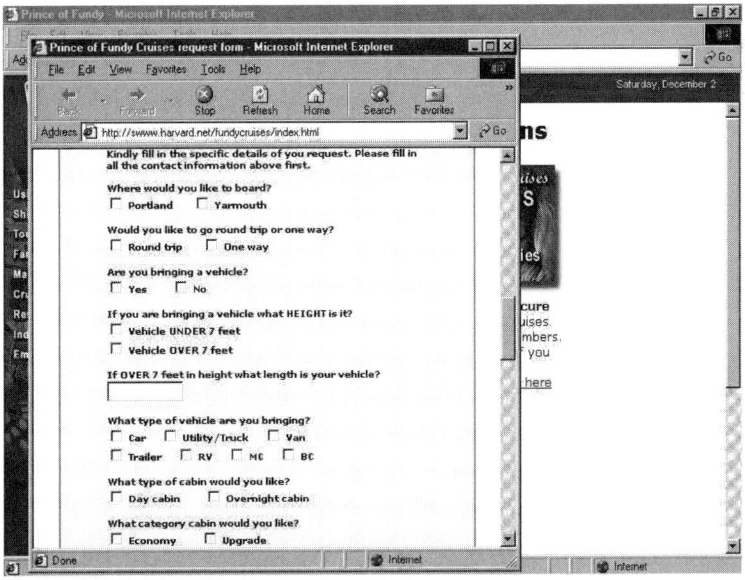

Figure 6.4. Select the options for your trip.

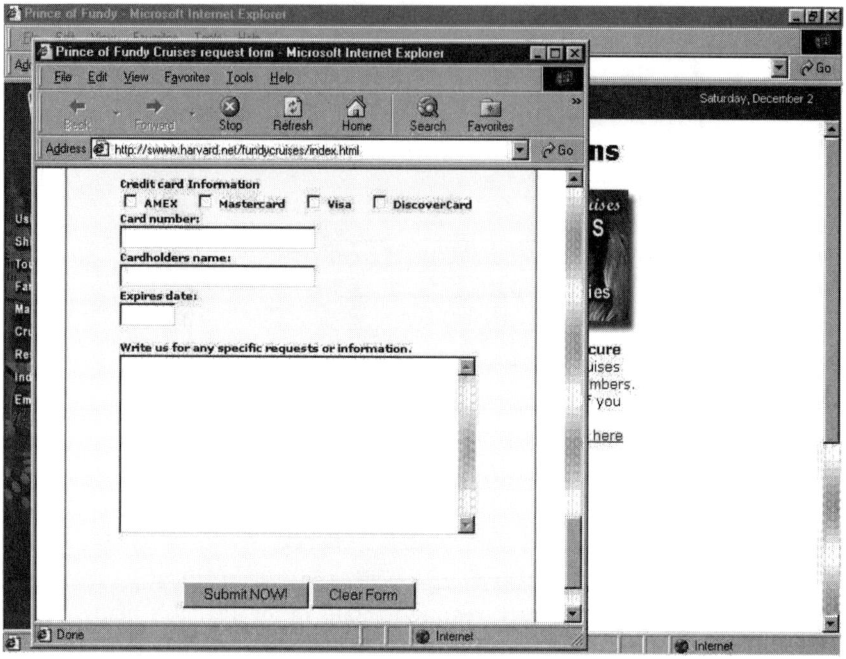

Figure 6.5. Complete the form by filling in your payment information and any specific requests you may have.

7

e-Business Model 3—Storefront Selection and Payment Automation

The first e-Business model represents the most basic level of conducting business online. The second model extended e-Business capabilities with the inclusion of allowing for paying online. With the third e-Business model, you're maintaining the implementation of online payment taking, but you're extending the use of your Web site by utilizing an online storefront. E-Business Model 3 is covered in greater depth in the upcoming section.

Exploring e-Business Model 3

E-Business Model 3 is similar to operating a catalogue sales business, but doing so online. If you are going to be selling a variety of products or services on your Web site, then this is an option you should consider. Model 3 uses an online standalone storefront and electronic payment processing. The company's inventory and other backend or internal systems are not integrated with the Web site. A company could have a number of reasons for not integrating supporting systems. For example, current business systems may not support backend integration; it may not be necessary for the business to integrate the backend; the company may operate only online; or the company may not have the available funds at its disposal to make integration worthwhile.

Because company systems are not integrated, businesses that choose to use this e-Business approach constantly have to monitor inventory levels and ensure there is adequate supply, remove the out-of-stock items from the site, or make sure that an appropriate "item temporarily out of stock" message is displayed to the consumer.

There are many storefront solutions available to users. They can choose to use one of the many template storefront solutions, an ASP or application service provider solution, a packaged storefront software solution, a custom software solution, or a hybrid of these solutions. Details on each of these solutions are provided in Chapter 4. Within each of these solutions there are many products and services available.

Similar to Model 2, with this model you are responsible for setting up your payment processing system and acquiring a merchant account. Once this has been established, you will be able to take payment for your products and services on your Web site. At this level of e-Business, the ability to process transactions over a secure connection and in real time is extremely important.

Who Uses e-Business Model 3?

This is a relevant question to consider as it can help guide you in selecting in the e-Business model most fitting for your business. Many types of businesses use this model.

You will find this model employed by businesses where availability of inventory is not an issue—for example, a software developer that has a number of titles available for sale and offers them to consumers via an online storefront. The customer would select the title of interest, pay for it, and then download it to his system. The software can be downloaded by as many consumers as are interested in the product. Inventory is never an issue, so there is no need to have a more complex system.

This model is popular with businesses where there is an online presence only—no bricks and mortar. In businesses where there is only an online presence, there is no need to integrate inventory. There are no physical store locations selling the same products at the same time and from the same pool of inventory.

Businesses that have a number of products and services and wish to make them available online also find this model appealing. The use of an organized storefront solution and shopping cart allows businesses to offer their products or services to their target market in a visually appealing, structured, and easy-to-use manner.

Backend systems may influence the decision as to which model is appropriate as well. If a particular company is using an old legacy inventory system that is not Web-enabled and is incompatible with current storefront solutions and the company has no plans for upgrading its existing legacy system in the near future, then e-Business Model 3 will suit its current needs. Also, if a company does not update its inventory in real time, but rather polls the inventory or updates it once a week or once a month, then there is no need to integrate the online storefront with inventory.

In addition, businesses often will employ this e-Business model when testing the Internet as a sales vehicle. Developing and implementing an online storefront can be done at a reasonable cost, whereas stepping up to full integration requires a large financial and managerial commitment to the online endeavor. This makes this model very attractive for businesses looking to evaluate the user of their Web site as a point of sale.

Before You Get Started

Understand your needs. It is impossible to make an informed decision regarding the development of your online storefront if you do not have a clear understanding of what you want your storefront to do and be. The process of selecting relevant storefront features and determining the appropriate storefront solution is best done through the process of elimination. You begin by considering all of the storefront features and solutions that are at your disposal. You then review your business requirements and determine which online storefront features are required as well as the storefront features you feel complement your business. Then you compare your needs and wants against several storefront solutions and make your selection based on your budget, your objectives, and the fit with your business.

Before you select the storefront solution for your online business, it is important that you first develop a list of all of the features that you are going to need for your site broken down into three categories: (1) features that are essential to run your business effectively, (2) features that would be nice to have, and (3) features that are not necessary. Some common features include the use of a shopping cart, different ship-to addresses, order tracking, and customer e-mail notification. Automatically sending the customer an e-mail to inform her that her purchase was successful is important to ensuring customer satisfaction. You do not want your customers wondering whether or not their order has gone through—this can lead to frustration and a loss of customers. This information is detailed in Chapter 4 and in Appendix C, which lays out each storefront option in a tabular format for you to use when deciding on online storefront features for your business.

The next step in this process is to select the preferred storefront solution. There are many solutions available. You might decide to use a template service storefront solution, an ASP (application service provider) solution, a packaged storefront software solution, a custom-built storefront solution, or a combination of these solutions. A closer look at each is provided later in this chapter. After you understand the different options that are available, you should then compare each of the options against your "feature sheet" that you developed in step 1 of this process. The storefront solution that you select in the end must meet the requirements of your business and meet the needs of your target audience.

When deciding on your storefront solution, you need to consider other factors as well, such as the Internet merchant account and your payment processing solution. How do these factors influence the decision-making process? Consider this example: Assume you selected and paid for a specific storefront solution and that it has a number of payment processing companies configured as selections. Based on this, you pick a payment processing company because it is one of the ones supported as a default selection, but you do not have your Internet merchant account as of yet. You then approach your financial institution to get your merchant account, only to find out this institution does not recognize the payment processing company you selected as a valid choice. This causes a ripple effect in that neither the payment processing nor the storefront solution you selected is valid—at least with your preferred financial institution. You have two choices at this point. You can either pursue an Internet merchant account from another financial institution or go back to square one based on the requirements of the financial institution. Regardless, the result is that unnecessary expenses are incurred and valuable time is wasted.

Storefront Solutions Recap

Let's take a closer look at each of the storefront solutions. Consider the examples before selecting your storefront solution; they may help you choose the solution with the best fit to your business. For specific details on each solution, refer back to Chapter 4.

Storefront Template Service

Many storefront template services can be established with little or no programming knowledge. To recap the details covered in Chapter 4, template services, in general, are the most basic of all the storefront development solutions, but they offer a number of significant benefits. They are cost effective and are also quick and easy to set up.

A great example of a storefront template service is 5click.com (*http://www.5click.com*). This solution is easy to use, there are no setup fees, and a free 15-day trial period is offered. The cost of this service is $75 American or $100 Canadian per month. An example of an online store that uses this service can be seen in Figure 7.1.

You can sign up to try 5click.com's trial version directly on the Web site. Figures 7.2 to 7.7 show a walkthrough of the five-step setup process in the trial version. The first step involves entering your personal and contact information so that the company has a record of you and so that you can login to update your site at a later date. The second step defines your site; you are asked to provide a name for your site, select a URL, and so on. In the third step you select the layout of your site. This encompasses the color scheme and the presentation of your site's content. The fourth step requests you to enter inventory information. The fifth and final step of the wizard asks you to confirm the information you filled out in the previous steps. After

Figure 7.1. Terrabridge Wireless Gear uses 5click.com's services.

you have completed the five steps, 5click.com sends you an e-mail with the location of your storefront and the access information you will need to maintain it.

Let's take a look at maintaining your online storefront. Figures 7.8 through 7.12 show the maintenance section of the online storefront where you can change your site's configuration, update inventory, gather your orders, and so on.

One of the benefits of using a template service is that you can login anywhere through your browser and manage your storefront. There are also no downloads, installs, long-term obligations, or programming knowledge needed to get your store up and running. If you're a small business looking to test the e-Business waters, then this may be the solution you're looking for.

It is possible to set up a good online store without having to invest money for the actual development. FreeMerchant.com (*http://www.freemerchant.com/*) (shown in Figure 7.13) is an excellent service that is offered essentially for free. What's the catch, you ask? There really isn't one. FreeMerchant.com generates revenue from partners who pay to advertise on merchant sites; however, you as the

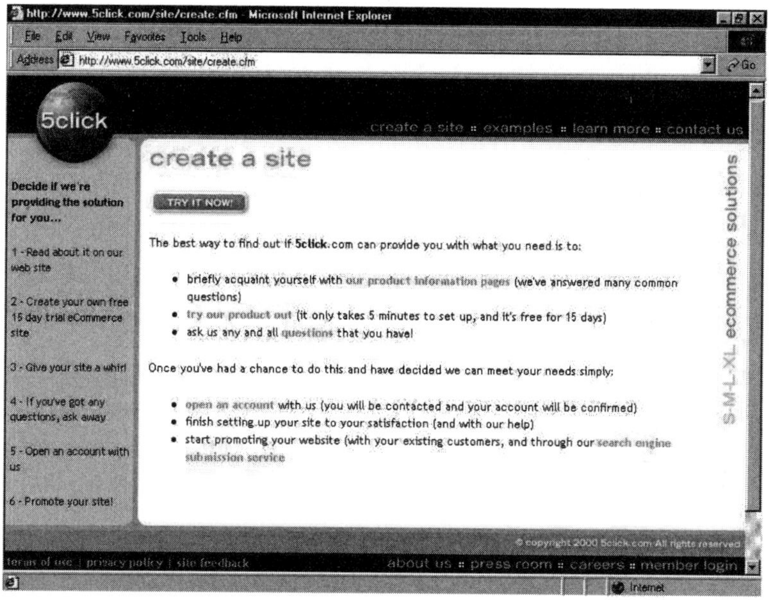

Figure 7.2. You can try out 5click.com's service free for 15 days.

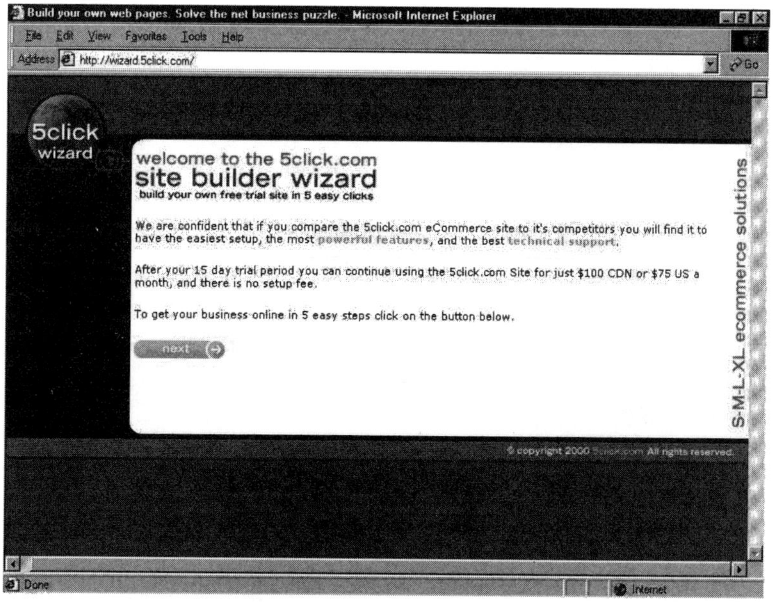

Figure 7.3. A wizard guides you through the process of setting up your trial online storefront.

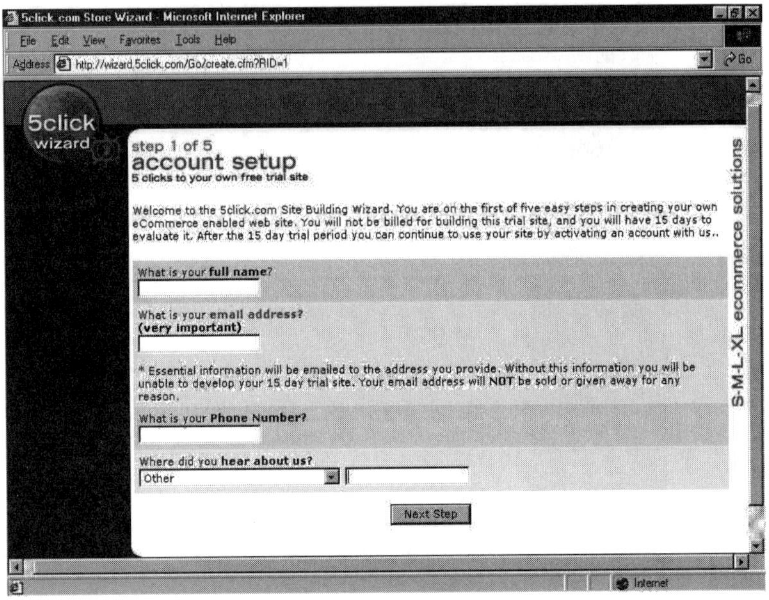

Figure 7.4. Step 1 covers the account setup.

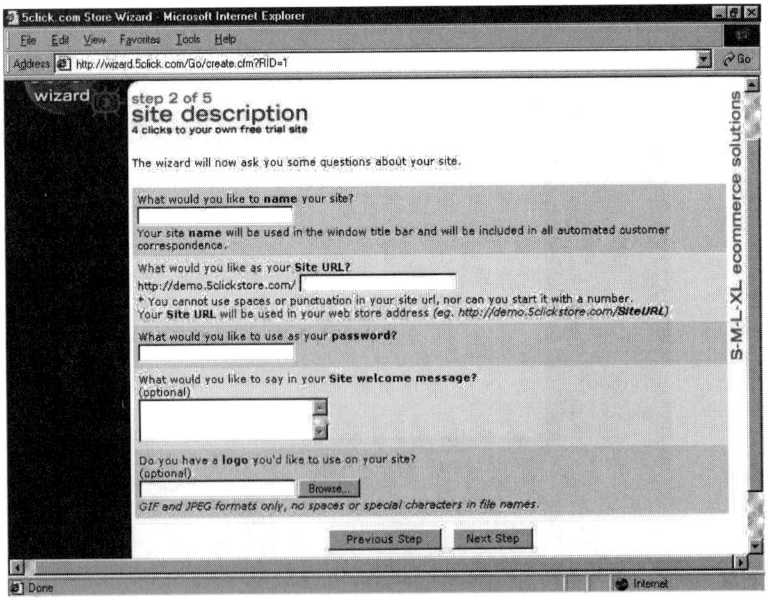

Figure 7.5. Step 2 covers the site description.

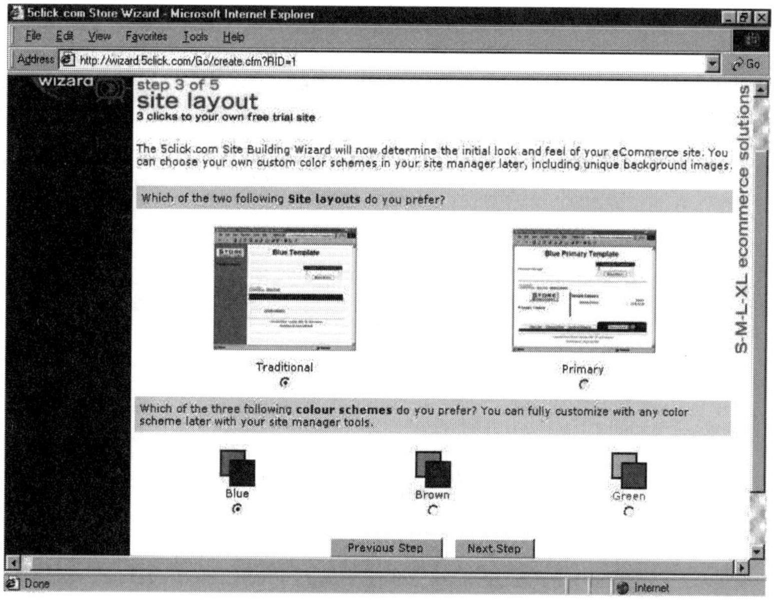

Figure 7.6. Step 3 covers the site layout.

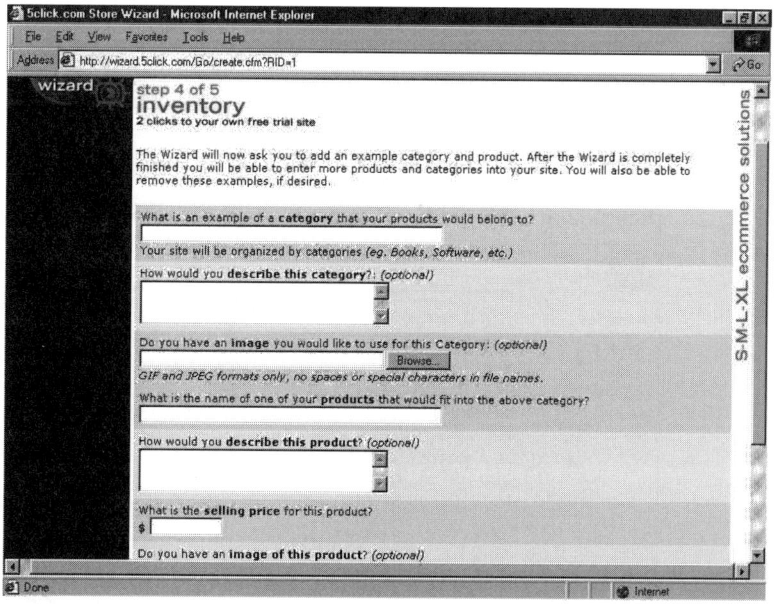

Figure 7.7. Step 4 covers inventory.

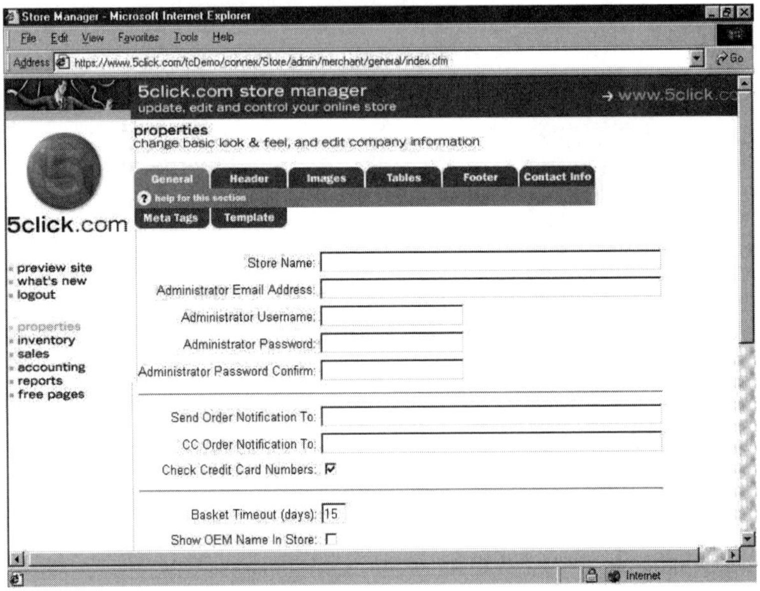

Figure 7.8. You can edit your storefront using the store manager.

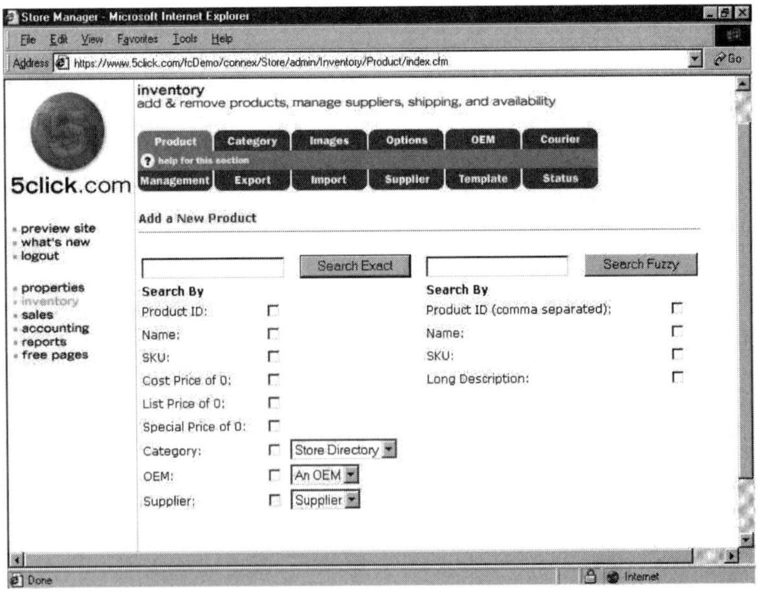

Figure 7.9. Manage your inventory through the easy-to-use interface.

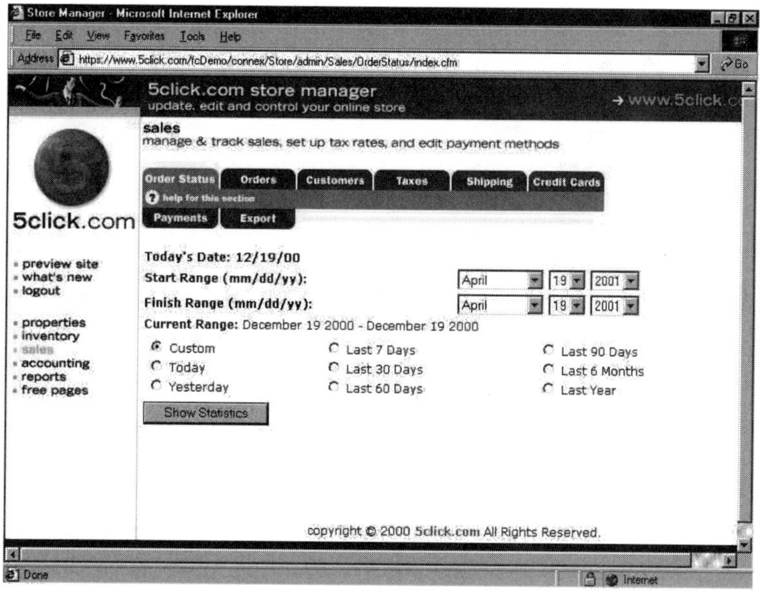

Figure 7.10. Check orders, edit taxes, set up shipping options, and edit payment methods.

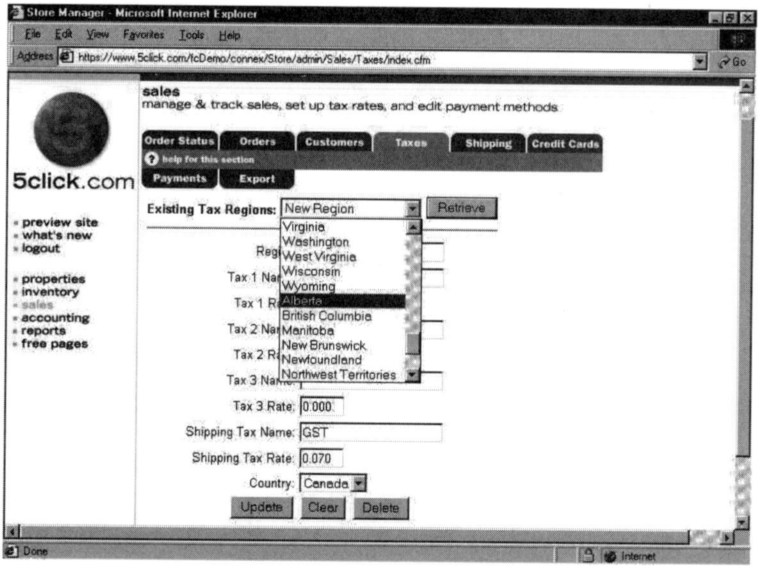

Figure 7.11. 5click.com has preconfigured tax rates for all the states and provinces.

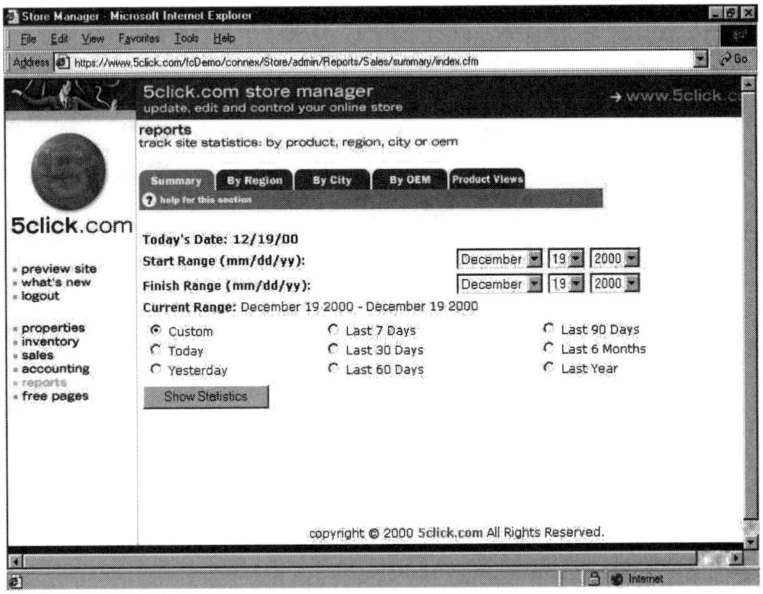

Figure 7.12. You can monitor your site statistics through the store manager.

Figure 7.13. FreeMerchant.com enables merchants to set up an online storefront for free.

merchant have the option of allowing or not allowing advertising on your site.

FreeMerchant.com gives merchants the option of using an extension of its safeshopper.com domain (such as yoursite.safeshopper.com), or they can use their own. Merchants can choose from a large number of templates when developing their site, as well as a broad range of features such as the ability to upload an existing inventory list in Microsoft Excel, dbase, Lotus 1-2-3, and so forth. A nice feature offered by FreeMerchant.com is its inventory tracking capability. It will automatically update your storefront to inform customers of whether or not a particular item is in stock. An example of a site using FreeMerchant.com's service can be seen in Figure 7.14.

Using ASP Services

When using an application service provider (ASP), you license the use of the provider's software and e-commerce hosting services. ASPs are usually more customizable than template services in that you can

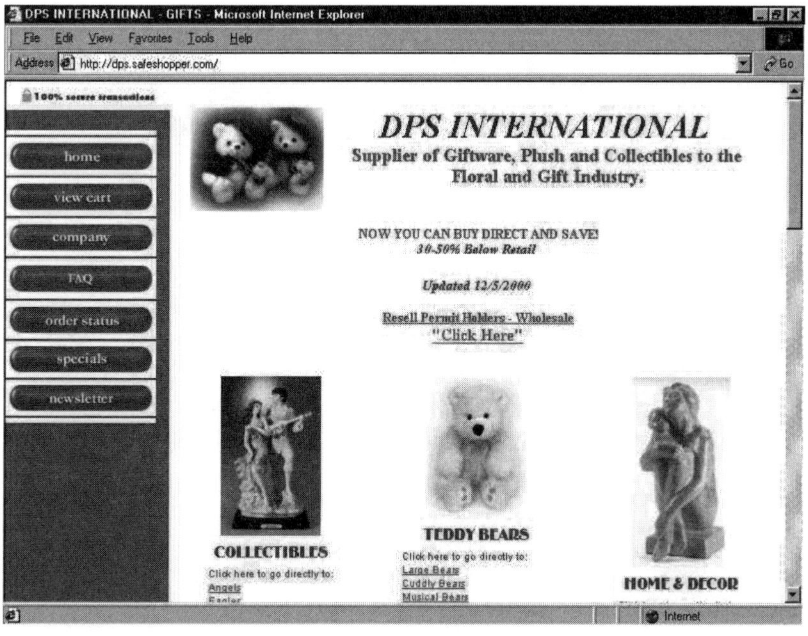

Figure 7.14. DPS International uses FreeMerchant.com's service.

configure your storefront to look like your existing site. Also, because the e-commerce aspect of your site is hosted on the ASP's server, you do not need to worry about the technical issues of maintaining your storefront software. This is handled by the ASP.

I operate an Internet marketing company called Connex Network. Over the past couple of years, I have written a number of books including *101 Ways to Promote Your Web Site*, *Internet Marketing for Your Tourism Business*, *101 Internet Businesses You Can Start from Home,* and now this book. I wanted to be able to sell these books directly from my Web site. My area of expertise lies in marketing, not coding HTML, and I was looking for an option that I could set up myself. I was also looking for an option that I could get up and running in a short period of time. I chose the W3 Internet Services (*http://www.w3internet.com/*) e-commerce solution because it was very affordable and it best fit my needs. My books were available for sale online in less than half a day. Figures 7.15 to 7.17 show my online storefront. My books are available for sale 24-7, 356 days a year, on my Web site. When a customer visits my site and clicks on

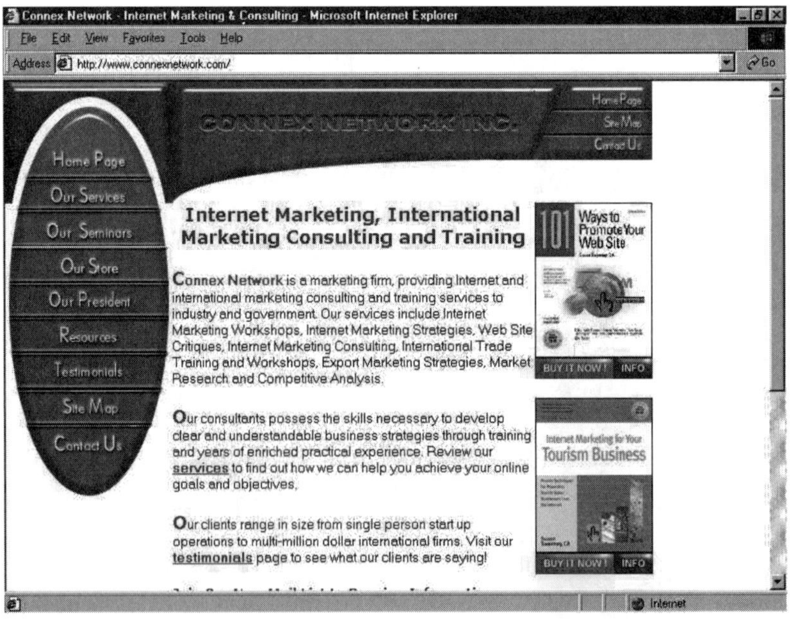

Figure 7.15. Connex Network's homepage.

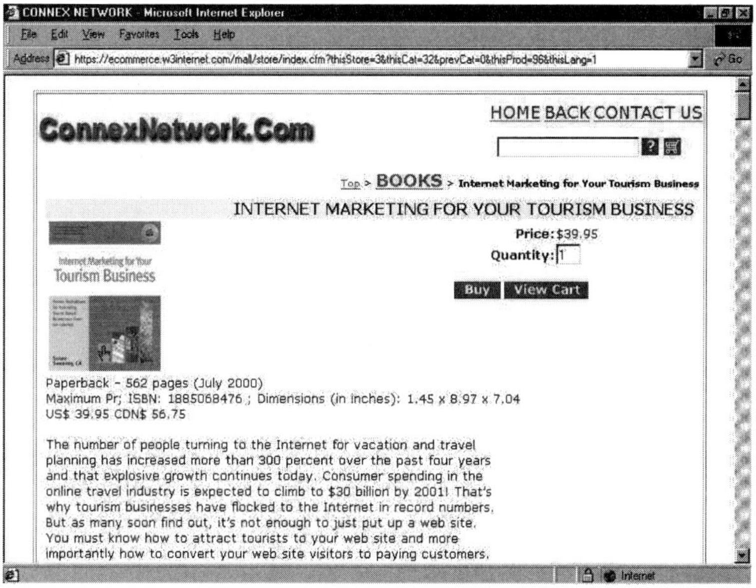

Figure 7.16. When the customer clicks on a product, he is taken to W3's e-commerce server.

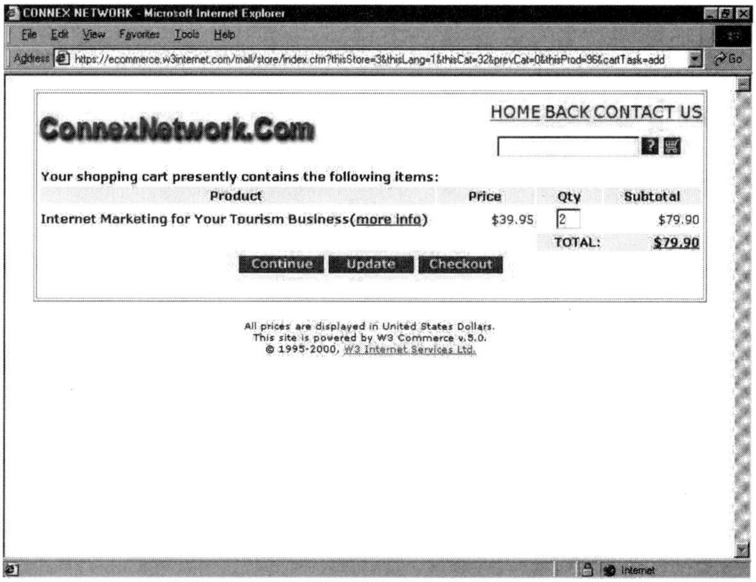

Figure 7.17. Connex Network's shopping cart.

one of the book titles, he is transported to W3's e-commerce server, which can be customized to look like your existing site.

Figures 7.18 to 7.20 show some of the "behind-the-scenes" maintenance activities such as retrieving purchase order summaries and adding new products to inventory using W3 as an example.

Storefront Development Software

Storefront development software packages are used by small, medium, and large businesses alike and are installed on the desktop or server, depending on the software. The features and capabilities of the software package often vary in price.

Actinic (*http://www.actinic.com/*) has a number of e-commerce products such as Actinic Catalog, Actinic PortalBuilder, and Actinic Business. Actinic Business is a great software package for businesses looking to move operations online with minimal difficulty. A free 30-day trial version is offered which you can download from the site or

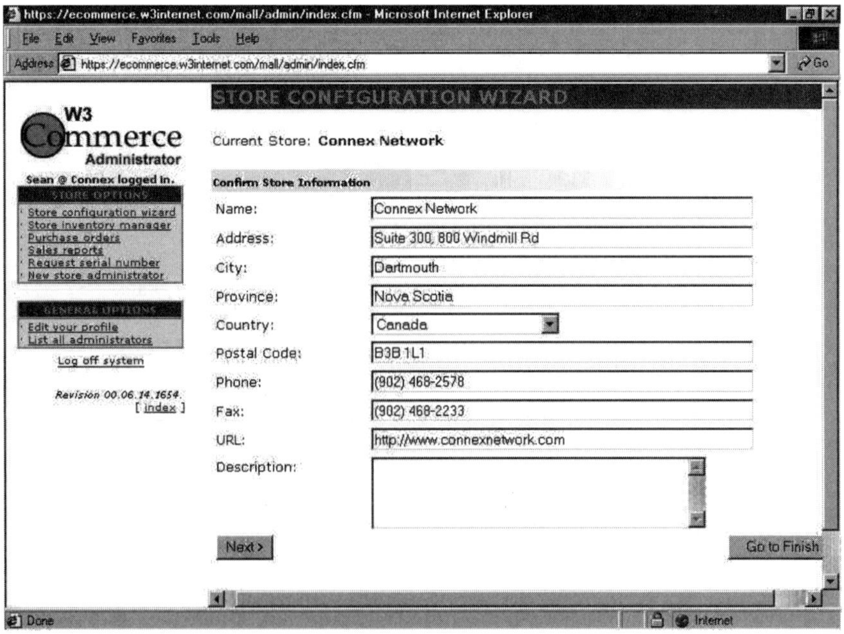

Figure 7.18. W3's Store Configuration Wizard.

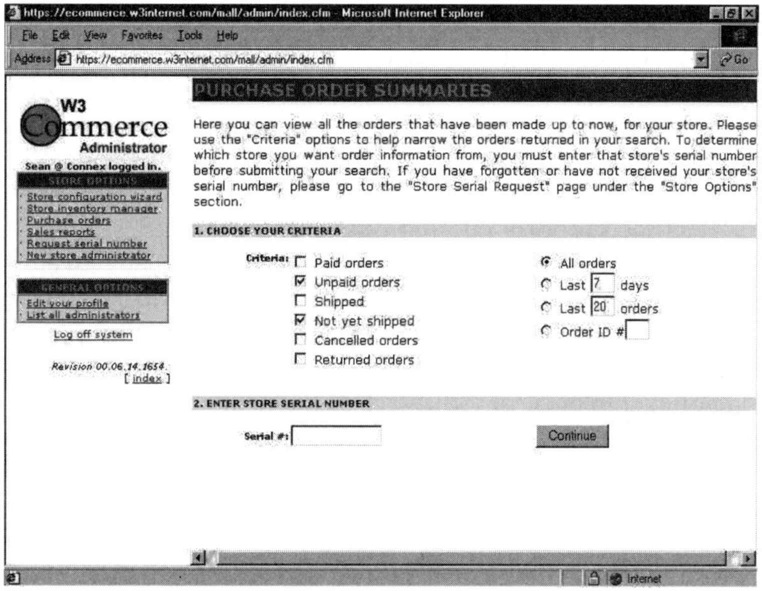

Figure 7.19. Check out your purchase history and recent orders.

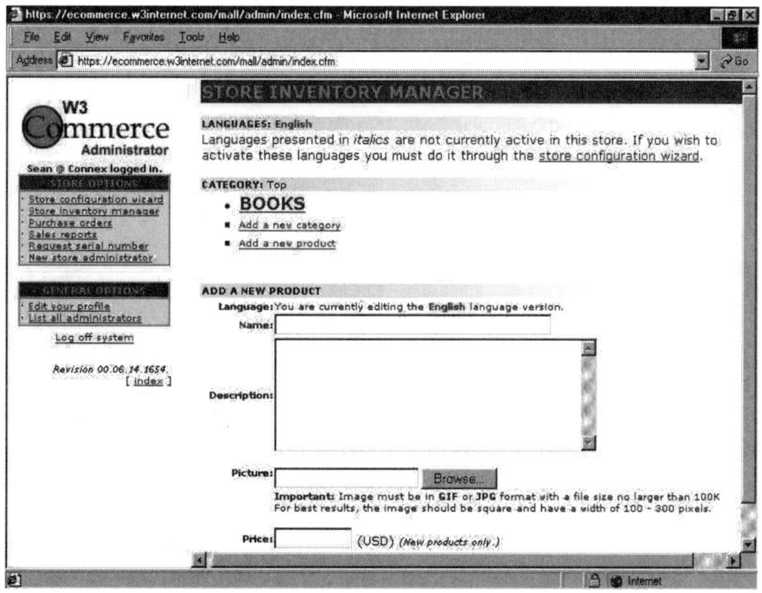

Figure 7.20. Adding new products is easy.

request on CD so that you can experiment with the software. This software package is much like an online template service, but you must install the software on your computer. All changes are made locally, on your desktop, and when you are ready to have them go live, you simply click a button and it updates your site. Actinic is very affordable and comes complete with many customizable features. Actinic supports international currency, taxes, and a number of different payment formats, and it has an excellent inventory management system. If you're looking for the ability to conduct international business but want the ease of setting up a site like a template service, then this solution may be for you. Figures 7.21 to 7.23 show a couple of examples of the software package in action.

What if you already have a site and want to add e-commerce capabilities to it, and you need the ability to seamlessly integrate the storefront with your existing site? This will require some programming and HTML knowledge and perhaps the services of a professional Web developer. However, there are many, many storefront software packages available. For example, you could use Cat@log

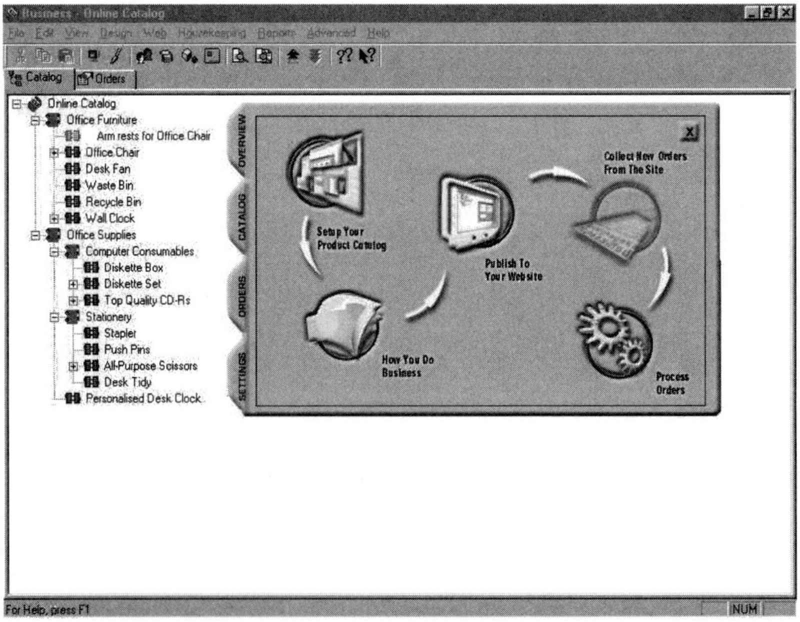

Figure 7.21. Actinic Business software.

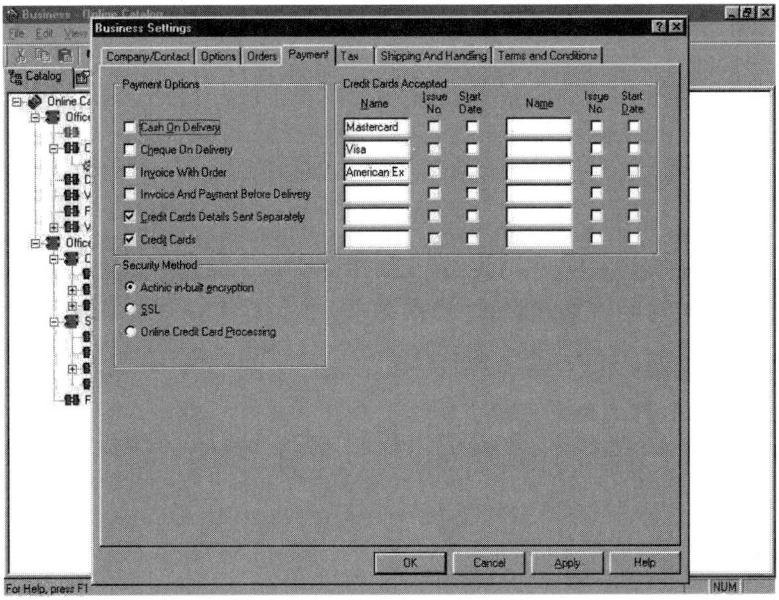

Figure 7.22. There are many options the merchant can configure.

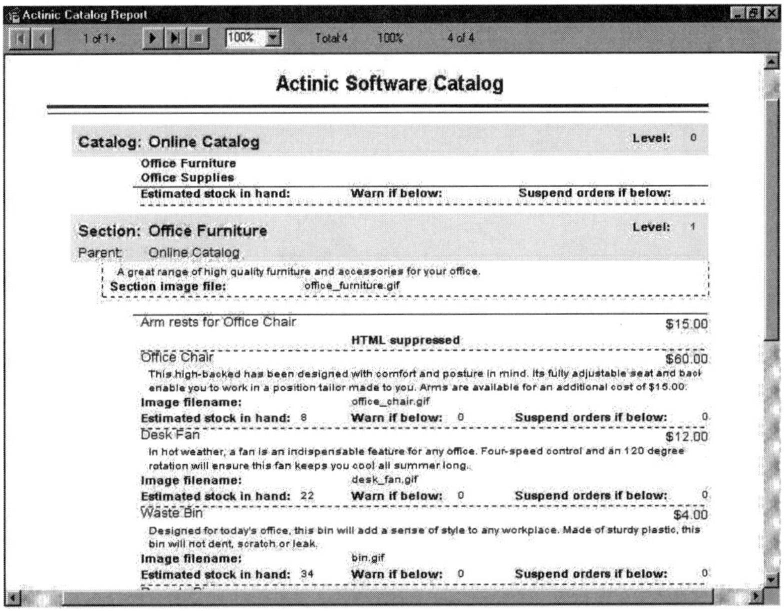

Figure 7.23. Business software generates a number of pertinent reports.

(*http://www.catalogint.com/*), which is aimed at large enterprises with costs starting at a price of $7995 US at the time this book was published, depending on the platform and solution you're interested in. It is marketed toward Web developers and system integrators, not the general public. Cat@log is a very powerful option that supports different levels of integration and personalization as well real-time ordering activity, database connectivity, and complex payment capabilities. This is more likely an option to be selected by a company that plans to implement e-Business Model 4, which is covered in the next chapter. TheShoppingChannel.com (*http://www.theshoppingchannel.com/*), pictured in Figure 7.24, uses a Cat@log solution.

Remember, you need to select a solution that is right for you. There is no point in paying for the capability to do a certain task if you do not need it. Why pay for a software package that supports

Figure 7.24. TheShoppingChannel.com uses a Cat@log solution.

10,000 or unlimited SKUs when you never plan to sell more than 100 items? It is important to note that when you are looking at software products, they are typically going to offer more capabilities than the aforementioned template service and ASP solutions, and as such you can expect to pay more. Software solutions often are employed by medium to large businesses that need the flexibility offered by the product. Some other solutions for you to consider include InterShop's Effinity (*http://www.intershop.com/*), Visual Trends' Online StoreBuilder (*http://www.visualtrends/*), and Mercantec's SoftCart (*http://www.mercantec.com*). Like many e-commerce solution providers, Mercantec has a number of different versions of its SoftCart product (pictured in Figure 7.25), tailored to the needs of businesses requiring different levels of e-commerce. If you're selling under 100 items, then Mercantec's SoftCart Lite might be an ideal solution for your business.

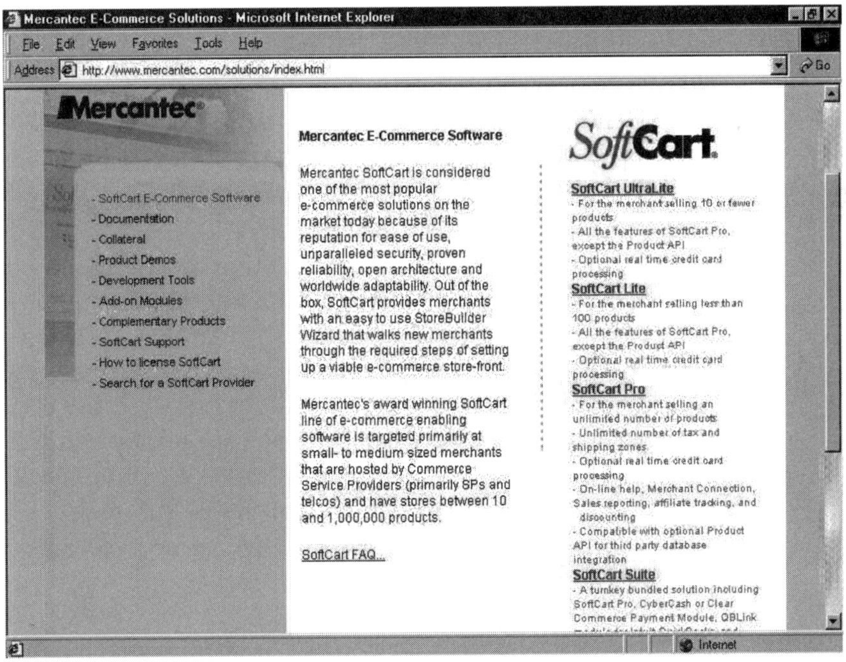

Figure 7.25. Mercantec's SoftCart comes in many different flavors.

Developing Your Own Storefront and Hybrid Solutions

If you have the right knowledge, you can program and develop your own customized storefront solution. Alternatively, you can have an e-commerce Web development team build one for you, but it is only on the rare occasion where another solution cannot fit your needs that a company will do this. Chapter 4 discusses this option in greater detail. Usually a storefront software solution will meet the needs of most businesses.

A hybrid storefront solution is simply the combination of two or more storefront solutions to complete a comprehensive whole. A single solution may not provide you with everything you need, or you may require the services of a Web developer to integrate the storefront solution with your Web site.

MTT's (*http://www.mtt.ca/*) eStore solutions are very cost efficient. One of their more popular options is the "Quick Shop Solution" or "Buy Me Button" which is designed for businesses that already have an existing online presence. If you have products and services displayed on your site and wish to make them available for purchase online you simply attach MTT's "Buy Me Button" to each product or service you wish to sell. In essence, you design the look and feel and MTT manages the e-commerce aspect. When the user clicks on the "Buy Me Button" MTT takes over and the customer is transported seamlessly to their transaction processing engine to complete the sale.

One benefit of the MTT solution is that customer information is stored securely behind a firewall in MTT's electronic commerce database. All customers are stored in the same database. This means that customers who have never purchased from your site before, but that have purchased from another MTT/Aliant powered site do not need to develop a new user account for your site—they can login using their existing account. This creates a sense of community and provides the user with the convenience they look for.

Other Considerations

It is essential that you constantly review and maintain your electronic storefront. Since this level of e-Business does not include backend integration with inventory, it is imperative that you monitor inventory levels. If you sell your products offline as well as online, then you need to monitor inventory levels to ensure that you're not claiming a particular product is available on your Web site when your physical store location actually sold the last one two days ago. You do not want a sale to go through on your Web site for a product you do not have.

If you change the prices for your products, or if you add new products to your inventory, you should immediately update your electronic storefront with this information. This will ensure that you are providing appropriate information to your visitors (i.e., prices, inventory levels, product lines) while optimizing the effectiveness of your electronic storefront.

Providing excellent customer service plays a key role in the success of many online businesses. If a customer feels that the level of customer service that she received was unacceptable when she purchased an item from your online business, you will ruin the chances that she will be a repeat customer. To ensure that this doesn't happen, you should have a customer service department (or one customer service representative if you are a small business) that is dedicated to providing excellent customer service and fulfilling customer requests at all times. All customer requests should be fulfilled within a 24-hour period, if not immediately when the request is received. This is especially important since your online business is open 24 hours a day, 7 days a week, and is accessible from all over the world.

Many consumers are still wary about making purchases online; therefore, it is important that you ensure that your visitors know that your online payment process is 100 percent safe. You can develop an "Is It Safe to Make Online Purchases?" FAQ section on your site, or you can partner with companies such as Trust-e (*http://www.truste.org*) or VeriSign (*http://www.verisign.com*) that offer Web seals of assurance. Web seals of assurance certify that a Web site practices safe and secure electronic order taking. By placing a Web seal of assurance on your site, you will help build credibility for your site in the minds of your target market. For more information on online payment processing, please refer to Chapter 4.

Take your time. Evaluate all of the e-Business models and select the right one for your business. If integration of some or all backend systems with your online storefront is not required, but an online storefront with payment processing capability is, then Model 3 is the right option for you. Your goals, objectives, products and services, budget, target market, and competitive environment will all impact which storefront solution is appropriate for you. Decide which storefront features you need. Do you want to offer gift wrapping? Do you need support for international currencies and taxation? Once you decide on the storefront features to be used, evaluate the storefront solutions available to you. Will a storefront template service provide you with the capabilities and flexibility you need, or do you need the advanced features offered by some of the leading software packages? Once your decisions have been made, you're ready to begin developing your online storefront.

8

e-Business Model 4—The Fully Integrated e-Business Solution

The final model discussed in this book is e-Business Model 4. This model encompasses all of the details incorporated into Model 3 but goes one significant step further. Sometimes the ability to operate a sophisticated online storefront and take online payments is not enough. Depending on the business in consideration, it may be necessary to have different aspects of supporting backend systems (accounting, inventory, etc.) integrated with the online storefront to ensure operational efficiency. It is not the intention of this book to discuss in detail enterprise integration, data integration, and the like, but to bring it to the table and emphasize how it is used in an e-Business environment. Imagine an online business such as Amazon.com trying to run efficiently without integration of supportive back office systems—it wouldn't be possible.

Exploring e-Business Model 4

Model 4, total integration, is the most complex level of e-Business. Integration is exactly what it sounds like—the integration of your online business with all or some of your backend systems. Supporting backend systems that are commonly integrated with online storefronts include:

- Inventory
- Accounts receivable
- Accounting—general ledger
- CRM (customer relationship management)

It is not necessary to integrate all systems with one another; the level of integration used corresponds to the business in consideration. Consider Circuit City as an example. Circuit City is a major retailer of brand-name electronics-related merchandise with over 600 outlets. The company also sells merchandise to via its Web site at *http://www.circuitcity.com/*. (See Figure 8.1.) The Circuit City retail outlets

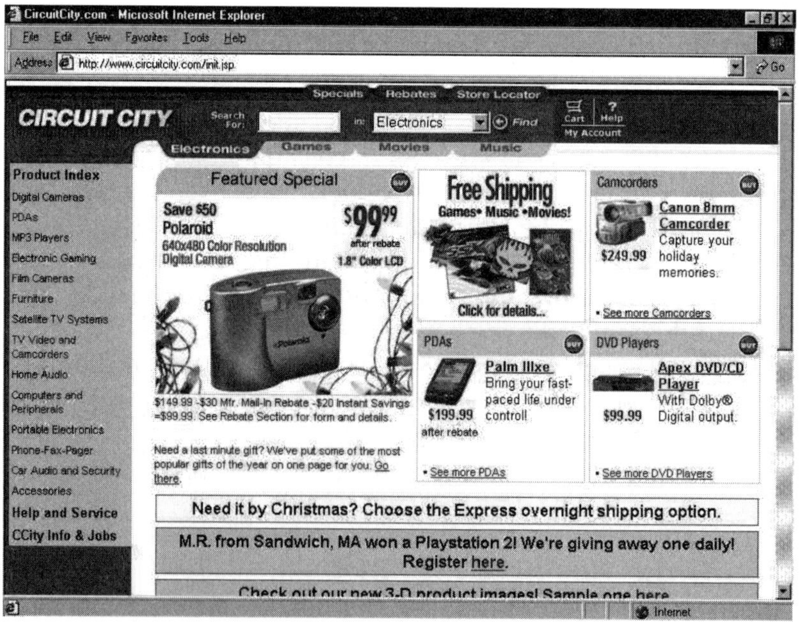

Figure 8.1. Circuit City's homepage.

and its Web site sell the same SKUs, and the merchandise comes from the same central inventory system. If one of the retail stores requests a particular computer for sale in its location, then the central inventory system needs to be able to account for it to manage the inventory properly. Likewise, if the Web site sells a particular computer, the inventory system needs to be able to account for that sale. Circuit City is a large business that pushes large volumes of merchandise. If its systems were not integrated, serious problems could arise in that customers would be sold inventory that is not available. Circuit City also integrates its promotional campaigns. Figure 8.2 illustrates Circuit City's weekly promotions page.

Like Amazon.com, Circuit City could not operate efficiently without the appropriate integration of its Web site and its backend systems. Just imagine what it would be like to manage the inventory of a business the size of Circuit City without having its Web site and inventory systems fully integrated.

Who uses e-Business Model 4? Business-to-consumer (B2C) and business-to-business (B2B) operations both use Model 4. Companies

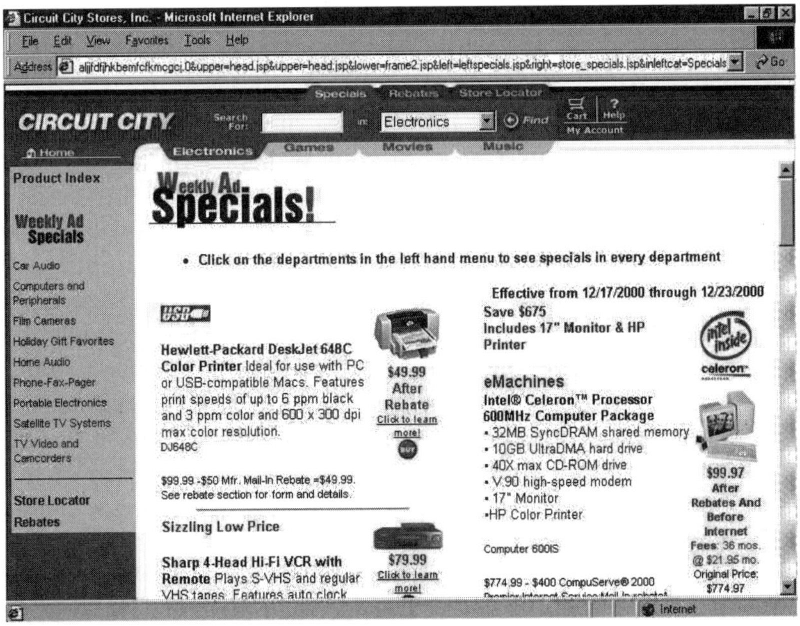

Figure 8.2. Circuit City's Weekly Ad specials are available online.

that are committed to selling online are common users of this level of e-Business, and you will usually find that the investment required is fully supported by management. The costs associated with operating a fully integrated Web site can be significant. Integration costs may be higher than some small businesses can afford or are willing to invest, and as such, it is more common to see medium- to large-sized businesses implementing this level of e-Business. Some small businesses do use this model, however, in part by integrating select components of their business to their Web site. Inventory and accounting are two commonly integrated systems.

Companies that have both an online and an offline presence, share the same inventory, and sell large volumes find this model essential. It is very difficult to manage product flow and cash flow without integration. In many cases, competition will force the implementation of this model. If your competitor is streamlining operations and is providing value-add customer service through the integration of various business components, then it will likely be necessary for you as a competing business to do the same in order to retain market share or to improve your competitive position. In a similar fashion, businesses that operate in both the "bricks and clicks" environments commonly use this level of e-Business as it allows the different components of their operation to work together as a cohesive whole. The Internet is a customer-driven environment, and as such it may be necessary, depending on the area of business you're involved in, to integrate various aspects of your Web site with your enterprise.

A B2B operation may use e-Business Model 4 to assist in streamlining its value chain or a particular aspect of its value chain, such as the supply chain. This enables the company, its suppliers, and its distributors to work together via an integrated Web site or Extranet to minimize delivery delays, costs, and so on. For example, if a supplier has direct access to the manufacturer's inventory system, then the two companies can work together to minimize overhead and to minimize delays because the supplier will always know what the manufacturer requires. As a result, less money will be tied up in inventory. Additionally, the supplier probably has a number of clients, and one client may have certain credit terms or benefits that another does not. The integration of the client database with the Web site or Extranet facilitates daily business transactions enabling the supplier to look up client information and verify credit terms automatically without human intervention. Integration of backend systems can improve the time to market and operational efficiency.

The most prominent example one can give of an online business that currently uses this e-Business Model 4 is Amazon.com (*http://www.amazon.com/*). (See Figure 8.3.) Amazon.com's fully integrated e-Business approach enables the company to provide customers with past purchase history, customer discounts, and purchase tracking, and also the ability to manage their accounts, make changes to orders before they are shipped, manage their ship-to and bill-to addresses, and change or verify credit card information. Amazon.com also allows a customer to set up a user account so that upon return the customer simply has to login using her username and password; this makes using the site more efficient and convenient for the consumer. Each time the customer visits the Amazon.com's Web site, she is presented with "recommendations" based on past history and information Amazon.com has acquired through her preferences and

Figure 8.3. Amazon.com's homepage.

cookies. Amazon.com's inventory management system is tied in with its storefront software, which automatically updates product listings whenever inventory is out of stock. Amazon.com also gives users the option of ordering an out-of-stock item and having it shipped automatically once stock has been replenished. This high level of integration and organization enables Amazon.com to provide its customers with the ultimate online shopping experience.

A section dedicated to the PlayStation 2 on Amazon.com's site, tied into relevant backend systems, offers customers the ability to monitor the availability of PlayStation 2–related merchandise. (See Figure 8.4.)

Other operations outside of the traditional business-to-consumer retail operation use integration as well. Many organizations implement different integration components to facilitate their customers. A number of postsecondary institutions such as Dalhousie University (*http://www.dal.ca/*) (see Figures 8.5 and 8.6) empower students with

Figure 8.4. Check the availability of PlayStation 2 merchandise at Amazon.com

Figure 8.5. Dalhousie University's homepage.

the capability to register for classes, drop classes, make payments, and check their grades online. The Web site is integrated with appropriate systems such as the registrar's database and student accounts. Implementing this strategy impacts operational procedures of the university as well. Employees no longer need to handle extensive line-ups of students wishing to change courses, as students can now do this themselves. Employees can spend more of their time doing other tasks and assisting students who need assistance.

The integration of supportive backend systems with the online storefront presents a number of benefits. Behind the scenes it helps to streamline operations. Staff are able to focus on other tasks as opposed to maintenance procedures that could otherwise be implemented automatically. Integration reduces human error, confusion, and delays with respect to inventory. It facilitates the use of data mining to further the use of one-to-one marketing and assists in building relationships with customers. Integration assists businesses in meeting consumer needs and expectations by enabling a business to imple-

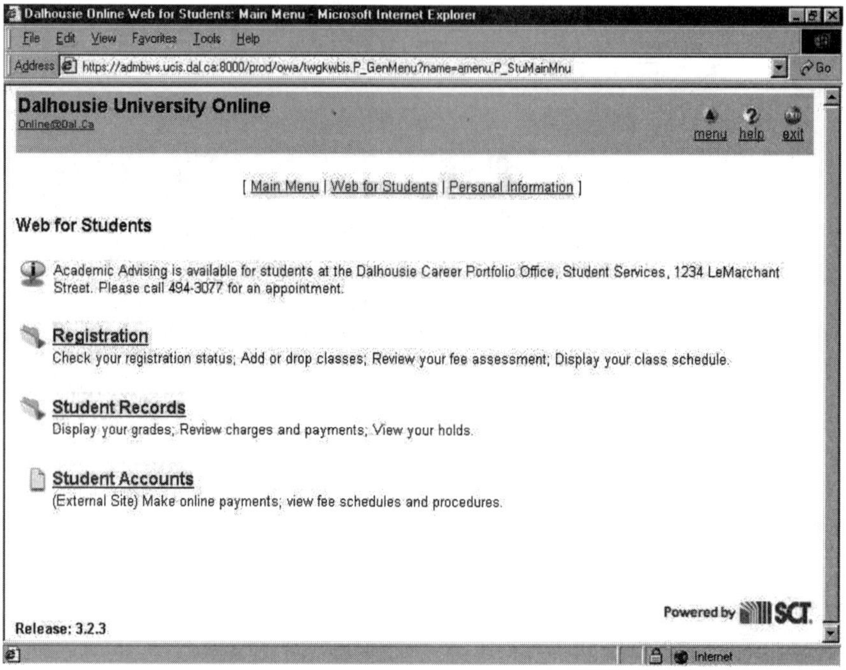

Figure 8.6. Students can add/drop classes, review their grades, and make payments online.

ment personalization features and by providing greater levels of customer service.

A major consideration when deciding on elements to integrate with your Web site is whether or not existing backend systems can be integrated. For example, your customer database may not be able to be integrated with your e-Business solution. This is something you need to consider in advance, but if you do find yourself in this situation, you can rebuild or import your database to the correct format.

There are many companies that offer e-Business integration solutions to businesses. Taviz Technology (*http://www.taviz.com/*) is an example of a company that offers integration solutions. Taviz's e-Integration Suite 2.0 integrates enterprise, Internet, as well as mobile, information to facilitate CRM activities, value chain activities, and e-commerce.

ACCPACC (*http://www.accpacc.com/*) is a commonly used accounting system for small and medium-sized business and has been around forever. A new version of this software offering full integration has recently been developed, making it very easy for existing users to make a smooth transition to selling online. ACCPAC provides affordable solutions that make it easy for companies to buy and sell on the Web with complete integration into their back office applications. All ACCPAC online solutions are delivered on Computer Associates' ASP and e-Business infrastructure.

The following section takes a closer look at some of the different aspects of integration. Remember, the level of integration appropriate for your business depends on the nature of your business, your objectives, your target market, competition, and your budget, as well as other influential environmental factors.

A Closer Look at Integration

Integration can take place on many levels. Integrating your customer relationship management system with your online business provides a number of significant advantages. For one, it facilitates the consumer. The first time a user visits your site he will be required to fill out a personal profile when buying his first item. Once the information is submitted, the user is assigned a username and password so that when he returns to your site he simply logs in using his username and password; he does not need to fill out his personal and credit card information each time he returns. Your customers will certainly appreciate this. Integrating your consumer database facilitates easy referencing of customer information for:

- Selective ship-to addresses
- Credit card details
- User preferences and personalization features
- New product notification
- Order history
- Order tracking and status

Knowing a consumer's personal information and product preferences can be very important when you are announcing new products that you are offering from your site. If you know that certain customers enjoy a particular product brand, you can use this information to notify them when you carry a new product from that brand. This retention strategy is a great way to encourage repeat traffic and repeat sales.

Integrating your inventory management system with the rest of your online business is terrific for providing optimal customer service. If you're out of stock on a particular item, a customer ordering that particular item is immediately notified that the item is "temporarily out of stock." If you can provide an estimated availability message, that's even better. You might provide the user with the option of being notified via e-mail when the item does become available. Integrating your inventory management system and your online storefront allows you to automatically update your virtual storefront and keep your customers informed. This frees up your time and is of great assistance to the consumer.

Integrating your accounting systems with your online business can also be quite beneficial. This enables you to easily track your accounts receivable, manage your bank accounts, and always have current information in your general ledger to facilitate current financial statements. Having a fully integrated and automated accounting system can also cut down on the amount of time and effort your staff will have to allocate to accounting details since the system will run self-sufficiently.

I expect that before too long most businesses will operate on this fully integrated Web site to backend systems model. The cost of the software will come down significantly as more and more competitors enter the market, and the ease of use will also improve significantly.

9

Start with your Objectives

Before you begin to determine your online marketing strategy and certainly before you begin to build your Web site, you must ascertain what your online objectives are and how you are going to achieve them. When deciding what your online objectives are going to be, you must first ask yourself what you want your Web site to accomplish. By determining what you want your online presence to accomplish, you have already developed your primary objectives. You must also consider how to create traffic and keep visitors coming back to your Web site so you can achieve those primary objectives. These are your secondary objectives and are just as important to establish if your online business is going to succeed.

Setting Primary Objectives

Once you have decided to start an e-Business or simply expand your current business to the Internet, you must decide what the purpose of your online business is. Without clearly defining your primary and secondary objectives, it is impossible to design and develop a Web site to achieve those objectives. This is especially true when you are having a third party, such as a Web development company, develop the site for you. Following are some common Web site objectives.

Objective—Advertise Your Products or Services Online

The objective of some sites is simply to advertise but not directly sell an event, product, or service. A prime example of this is a movie studio that develops a Web site to promote a "soon-to-be-released" movie. Their objective is to create awareness or a "buzz" about the movie, generate interest in the film, and, ultimately, have a large number of people attend the movie when it is released. This type of site might include multimedia clips of the movie, pictures and stories of the actors in the movie, viral marketing "Tell a friend about this movie" elements to encourage word-of-mouth marketing, an intriguing story about the film, press releases for entertainment writers, and other elements to help them achieve their objective with their target market in mind.

Objective—Sell your Products or Services Online

Selling products or services online is a common objective. The Internet provides a broad geographic reach and a huge demographic reach. Often businesses combine the objectives of advertising their products or services with trying to sell them through their Web site. This works well because not only are visitors given information about your products and services, but they are given the option of easily ordering and purchasing online. The easier you make it for people to make a purchase from your company, the more likely they will be to buy. You will also have to provide detailed information on your products and services, your return policies, guarantees and warranties, and shipping options.

If you are planning to sell directly from the site, you will need to address security issues.

Objective—Provide Online Customer Service or Support

You may decide that the main reason for your business to have an online presence is to provide more comprehensive customer service and support. A great benefit of a Web site is that you can provide customer assistance 24 hours a day, 7 days a week, 365 days a year. If your company develops software, it would be a good idea to include downloadable upgrades as well as an FAQ section where you can provide solutions to common problems. By providing an easy way for your customers to solve their problems, you will increase customer loyalty. You will also increase the likelihood they will return to your company when they need to improve their system. You should also include the appropriate contact information if customers have more complicated problems to be solved and need to talk to a human.

Objective—Provide Product Information

By using your Web site to provide product information, you are essentially creating an online brochure. If your online objective is to provide customers and potential customers with product information, you will want to set this objective in conjunction with another objective. For example, you might decide that your Web site should provide customers with product information as well as offering a way for them to buy directly through your Web site. Make it easy for your potential customer to make that purchase decision and communicate it to you. Provide him with multiple ways to order—by telephone, fax, snail mail, or e-mail, or through your online order form.

Objective—Reinforce Corporate or Brand Image Online

If you choose to use your Web site to reinforce your corporate image and brand names, you must be sure that your Web site is designed with consistency in mind. This means that all your Web pages should have your company logo prominently displayed and that you use a consistent color scheme throughout the Web site. Of course, reinforcing your brand image is not an objective you would try to achieve on its own, but one you would incorporate with your other online objectives.

Setting Secondary Objectives

Although setting your primary objectives is vital, it is just as important to identify your secondary objectives. By setting appropriate secondary objectives, you will be more prepared to achieve all your online goals. Many companies identify only primary objectives for their Web site and completely neglect secondary objectives that will help them to succeed online. Following are some common secondary objectives for online business to consider.

Objective—Design Your Site to Be Search Engine Friendly

Creating a search engine friendly site should be an objective of every company that wants to do business on the Internet. Search engines are the most common way for Internet surfers to search for something on the Net. In fact, 85 percent of all people who use the Internet use search engines as their primary way to look for information. By using keywords relating to your company in appropriate places on your site, you can improve how search engines rank you. You want these chosen keywords in the "keyword meta tags" as well as in each page's "description meta tag." Some of the other places where you want to have these keywords are your domain name if possible, your page titles and page text, your alt tags for graphics, and your page headers. Recently, many search engines have begun to put emphasis on the number of links to your site to determine your ranking. This means that the more Web sites you can get to link to your site, the higher your Web site will be shown in search engine results. (See Chapter 14 for more information on designing your site for the search engines.)

Objective—Include Repeat Traffic Generators on Your Site

Every Web site should be designed to entice their site visitors to return again and again. No matter if the primary objective of your Web site is to sell your products and services or create brand awareness, generating repeat traffic to your Web site will help you achieve these goals. Generating repeat traffic to your site is a key element of your online success and can be accomplished in numerous different ways. Using contests and competitions, as well as games, advice columns, and many more techniques, will increase your Web traffic. Chapter 15 describes many of these repeat traffic generators in much more detail.

Objective—Getting Visitors to Recommend Your Site

The best exposure your Web site can get is to be recommended by a friend or "unbiased" third party. It is critical that you try to have your Web site recommended as often as possible; therefore, you should have a way for people to easily tell someone about your site. The best way to encourage people to recommend your site is to have a "Tell a Friend" button on your site. You may want to include some variations on this as well. Under articles or press releases you can have an "E-mail this article to a friend" to try to have people refer their friends and associates to your site. Virtual postcards are also a good way to get people to send more people to your Web site. Using virtual postcards on your Web site are discussed in detail in Chapter 15.

Objective—Leveraging Your Sales Force

If your objectives include trying to sell your products, you may want to leverage your sales force by making use of an affiliate or associate program. Affiliate programs once again use the advantage of having your site recommended to create traffic to your site. The difference is that an affiliate program is more formal than just having your site recommended by site visitors and usually involves a contractual agreement. Most affiliate programs involve having an affiliate program agreement, having specific links placed on the affiliate's site to yours, and having software to track where your traffic is coming from so that you can compute and send referral fees to your affiliates as they are earned. The contract will usually state the compensation you will pay to your affiliates for the sales they produce. This is one more way to have other people working to build traffic to your Web site. (See Chapter 16 for details on affiliate or associate programs.)

Objective—Use Permission Marketing

You always want your company to be seen as upholding the highest ethical standards, so it is important not to send out unsolicited e-mail, or "spam," promoting your company or its products. This is why it's important to develop a mailing list of people who have given you permission to send them messages including company news and promotions. When you're developing your Web site, an objective should be to get as many visitors to your site as possible to give you their e-mail address and ask to be included in your mailings. You can do this by having numerous things for your visitors to sign up to receive such as newsletters, notices of changes to your Web site, or new giveaways. Chapter 15 has many examples of what visitors can sign for to receive information or updates about your Web site.

Objective—Create Loyalty with Visitors

The way to create loyalty with visitors is to provide them with some incentives for joining your online community and provide them with proof that you really appreciate their business. You can do this by having a "Members-only" section of your Web site that has special offers for them as well as discounts or freebies. When people sign up to join your "Members-only" section, you can ask for their permission and their e-mail address to send them e-mails regarding company or product promotions and news.

Objective—Include "Stickiness" Elements

To get your visitors to visit your site often and have them visit a number of pages every time they visit, you need to provide interesting and relevant content. You want to have your site visitors feel as if they are part of your online community and to make your site one of the sites they visit every day. You create "stickiness" by including many elements of your site that keep your visitors' attention. Your site could have an advice column for people to read that changes daily, descriptions of your many products, a discussion forum with constantly changing interesting conversations relative to your products, a news section that gets updated daily, as well as a weekly contest they can enter. The combination of these elements would create stickiness for your visitors on your site.

A Final Word on Objectives

Setting your Web sites objectives before you begin building your Web site is essential so that you can convey to your Webmaster what you want your Web site to achieve. You will obviously want to create a number of different objectives for your Web site, but many of the objectives you set work together to make your Web site complete.

Part 3

The Right Web Site

10

Designing a Dynamite Site from the Start

Before you think about promoting your site, you must consider your sites design, appearance, functionality, and features. Once your site is designed to achieve your marketing objectives, looks good, and the layout is easy to follow and understand, you are ready to open your doors.

Building Traffic to Your Site

The phrase "If you build it, they will come" does not work with your Web site as it did in the movies. Unfortunately, building a Web site is only the first step. Generating traffic to your site requires knowledge, planning, time, and effort.

Objectives of Your Web Site

It is imperative that you determine your online objective before you plan your online strategy, and certainly before you begin construction of your site. You must know what you want your Web site to accomplish. Are you planning to sell directly to your customers? Will your site provide information on your products or services? Do you want to provide customer support and service?

Once you have determined the objectives of your Web site, you can begin to build it. If you know your objectives and build your site around them, you will ensure satisfaction at the end of the process.

Clearly Present Your Web Site Message

From the very first page of your Web site, visitors need to be able to instantly understand your message. If your message is not clear, visitors will leave your site just as quickly as they could change the channel on their TV. To capture the surfer's attention, your site needs to load promptly and immediately present your message. Do you want them to buy? Browse? Provide feedback? Order? As with traditional advertisements, you also need to attract the attention of your online audience immediately. However, the benefit of the Internet is that you can deliver more information than you could in a 30-second commercial or a half-page print ad. You must, however, avoid overloading visitors with information. Your site will appear cluttered if you present too much information on the opening page. Try to keep your message clear and to the point.

Take Advantage of Your Competitor's Sites

It is important for you to keep up with the *CyberJoneses*. For ideas to use on your site, visit your competitors' sites or visit sites that are listed on "hot sites" pages. Look at the design of these sites to get a better idea of what you should include in yours. Examine the colors and backgrounds used, see how the information is organized, and look at the features provided.

Some good sites to go to for ideas are:

- Cool Site of the Day—*http://cool.infi.net*
- Your WebScout—*http://www.webscout.com*

- Lycos Top 250—*http://www.lycos.com*
- Web Crawler Top 25—*http://www.webcrawler.com*

The Importance of Your Domain Name

Although it is often overlooked, from an online marketing perspective your domain name is one of the most important parts of your Web site. Your Internet domain name is your exclusive Web address that you can purchase through a domain name registration company such as Network Solutions (*www.networksolutions.com*), an online organization in charge of domain name registration. Some of the benefits of having your own domain name are:

- It builds credibility for your organization.
- The name itself can increase traffic to your site.
- Your presence is mobile when you own your domain name.
- Internet marketing efforts travel with the domain name.

When choosing a domain name, you should always try to use your company name. Keep your domain name simple, easy to remember, and related to the subject of your site.

People will generally try "*www.yourcompanyname.com*" first when searching for your Web site. If your domain name is your company name, customers or potential customers will be able to find your Web site quickly and easily. A catchy descriptive phrase or the subject of your Web site may be a better choice for your domain name if your company is not well known. For example, if someone was searching for information on buying a timeshare and the search results found a site with a URL named *www.howtobuyatimeshare.com,* they would likely click through to that site.

You can also register multiple domain names for your site. You might want to do this if there are several business-related keywords you believe potential customers would search for. An example would be to register a domain name for your company's name, and a separate domain name for each of the products you are selling. You can also have several domain names directing traffic to the same Web site. One of the reasons for doing this is that some of the search engines will give your site a higher ranking if the keyword being searched is found in your domain name.

One of the great benefits of the Internet is that small and medium-sized companies can compete on a level playing field. You create an image of professionalism for your company by having your own domain name. It also projects the image of an established business even if you are just starting operations

Another option for businesses that want an online presence but don't register their own domain name is to use the domain name of the ISP that is hosting their site. Your site address would then have the following address: *http://www.yourISP.com/yoursitename.*

The problem with this type of address is that you can't take it with you should you ever want to move your Web site to another host. If you own your domain name, it is yours as long as you keep your registration fees current. This gives you the option of changing to another ISP without affecting your Web address. So that you don't run into problems moving your site, ensure that you are registered as the actual owner, especially if you allow your ISP or any other party to take care of your domain name registration. You also want to be listed as both the administrative and technical contact so that you receive all information and invoices for your Web site.

Another benefit of owning your domain name is that if you do have to switch to a new ISP, all of your marketing efforts will not be wasted. There is a huge effort needed to promote your site online, such as getting listed in the search engines and directories, developing links to your site, and getting listed in meta-indexes. If you had to change your ISP, all your hard work would be erased and you would lose most, if not all, of the momentum gained by your previous online marketing activities. Having your own domain name allows you to move your site without having a negative impact on any of your previous marketing efforts.

Since on the Internet you are conducting business in an international environment, you need to use the most common top-level domain name, ending in *.com*. Canadian sites often use *.ca;* United Kingdom sites often use *.uk;* Australian sites often use *.au*; and New Zealand sites often use *.nz*—but to be globally recognized, you should use the *.com* designation. Most people associate domain names with

.com and, as mentioned earlier, when a person wants to visit your Web site, the first inclination is to check *www.yourcompanyname.com*.

When registering your domain name, you use a domain registration service such as Network Solutions. Network Solutions has a tool on their site where you can do a search to determine whether your preferred domain name is available. Network Solutions lets you choose among top-level domains: *.com*, *.net*, *.org*, and *.edu*. You can register a domain name with Network Solutions through your ISP or you can do it yourself through the Network Solutions Web site at *www.networksolutions.com*. To register a domain name through Network Solutions, the fee is US $70 for the first two years and US $35 for every year thereafter.

Web Site Design Essentials

Here are Web site design tips that are relevant to all Web sites:

- Your site should be easy to read.
- Your Web pages should have a consistent layout.
- Your online and offline corporate image should be consistent.
- Your site should be easy to navigate (include a site map or a search engine tool, or both).
- Your Web pages should be no larger than 50K.
- Have a "What's New" section to let visitors know what has changed on the site.
- Do not overuse image maps.
- Do not use "Under Construction" pages on your site. When you have information, post it; but don't mention it otherwise.
- Your Web site should steer clear of scrolling marquee text. Scrolling marquees are difficult to read and are not compatible

with all browsers. Simply post text directly on your pages if you have something important to say.

- Design for various screen widths so you can accommodate visitors regardless of the screen resolution they use. Twenty percent of Web users still run their systems at 640 pixels wide by 480 pixels high. Make sure your image sizes are small enough to be fully viewable at this resolution, and use percentage widths in your tables so that your pages are flexible to any screen resolution.

- Use thumbnail graphics where applicable. When you have a page with a lot of large images (i.e., an online photo collection), create small "thumbnail" versions of each image and give visitors the option of clicking through to the larger version of each image. This is a much better option than waiting for a series of large images to load.

- Include contact information on every page. This includes your address, phone and fax numbers, and especially your e-mail address or a contact form. Make it easy for people to get in touch with you.

- Security information: Explain to your customers when transactions or exchanges of information on your Web site are secure. This is important if your site will be accepting credit card orders.

- Privacy policy: Tell people how their personal information (i.e., their name, e-mail address, etc.) will and will not be used. This will make visitors more comfortable submitting inquiries to your site and providing you with their e-mail address to receive your mail list or newsletters.

- Minimize use of background sounds and autoplay sounds. Some people surf the Web from their office at work and wish to discretely go from one site to the next. Background sounds and sounds that load automatically can compromise their discreteness. Allow your visitors the option to listen a sound, but do not force it upon them.

The use of your text and the design of your graphics will set the tone of your Web site. You will want to keep things simple if your target audience is business-minded by minimizing unnecessary graphics and using just enough text to grab the attention and heighten the interest of your audience. On the other hand, a more graphic-oriented site with some multimedia effects like Macromedia Flash would be appropriate for a graphic designer. When designing a Web site, remember to keep your online image consistent with your offline image through the use of logos, corporate colors, and anything else associated with your company.

Be sure that the text content of your site does not leave out any crucial information. Often you may leave out information that is second nature to you but is important data for your visitors. Review all text before you put it on your site and double-check that you have not omitted anything of importance.

It is important to make your key points quickly and succinctly. The reason for keeping your text brief is that almost 80 percent of Web users scan text online as opposed to actually reading it. By using lots of bulleted lists, headers, and horizontal rules, you create visual "breaks" in the content and make it easy to skim and still get all the pertinent information. If visitors are faced with large blocks of text, they will be overwhelmed and too intimidated to read the message.

Choosing your background and font colors is very important because you want your message to be easy to read. By using backgrounds that are too "busy," you obscure the text and do not provide an easily read message. Dark text on a light background is easiest on the eyes. Nothing is more annoying than a hard-to-read Web site.

You should be aware that it may be difficult to read text in your graphics when the page is printed. Also be aware that graphic-intensive sites load slowly; it is sensible to incorporate text content into your graphics.

Don't set your text size too small as this is too hard to read. Don't set it too large as this looks like you are shouting!! Also, avoid using ALL CAPS, WHICH ALSO COMES ACROSS AS SHOUTING.

It is best to use the default colors for links whenever possible. Blue text usually indicates an unvisited link. Purple, maroon, or darker blue usually represents an expired link, and red is the color of an active link. This makes it easy for your visitors to identify your links.

If you decide not to use the default colors, your links should be consistently formatted through font size or style.

It is very important that your site is easy to navigate. Each page should have a navigation bar, placed in a consistent location, with links to all of the pertinent pages on your site. Search engines are able to index any page on your site, so your home page may not be the first page visitors see. It is also important never to have dead ends, where viewers scroll down a page or two but must scroll back up to the top to move to another page (because you have no links at the bottom of the page). A good navigation bar that is consistently placed and has functioning links is the key to easy site navigation.

Avoid dead links or links that don't go anywhere. The viewer usually receives a "404 – File Not Found" error message from the Web server after selecting a dead link. According to a Jupiter Communications study, 46 percent of users have on at least one occasion been driven to alternate sites because their preferred site failed. "Each site should allocate 20 percent to 40 percent of development time to Web application testing to reduce service outages," the study declares. Make a point to verify that all your links still work.

When designing your site, try to use consistency with your font types, headers, footers, navigational bars, buttons, bullets, and colors to project a polished professional look.

The size of your home page should be no more than 50K and be displayed on a maximum of two screens. Studies have shown that most visitors will not wait more than 15 seconds for a site to download. To make sure your site downloads in a reasonable time, use a slow modem to test the speed of your site.

Proper Use of Web Site Graphics

Although graphics are visually stimulating, they may be too time consuming to download, and many visitors to your site may leave before they get a chance to view it. So, remember to be discriminating when adding graphics, because some Internet users are still using 14.4 or 28.8 modems.

Because some people turn graphics off in their browsers, all your information should be in text as well as graphics. By using descriptive ALT attributes in your image tags, the visitors who browse without graphics turned on will still be able to easily navigate your site, since ALT tags give a description of the missing graphic. Also, ALT text is spidered and indexed by many major search engines, so by using keywords in your ALT tags you will improve your ranking in search engines

You should try to avoid using image maps (see Figure 10.1) as well. Image maps are large graphics with clickable "hot spots." They are typically used for navigation and are useful if your Web site contains five or more major sections. If you do decide to use an image map, make it obvious what sections of the image are clickable and where the links will lead. Also try to break the image map into smaller images so that visitors do not have to wait for one large graphic to load. Finally, make sure you provide an alternate text link navigation system for people who surf without using their graphics.

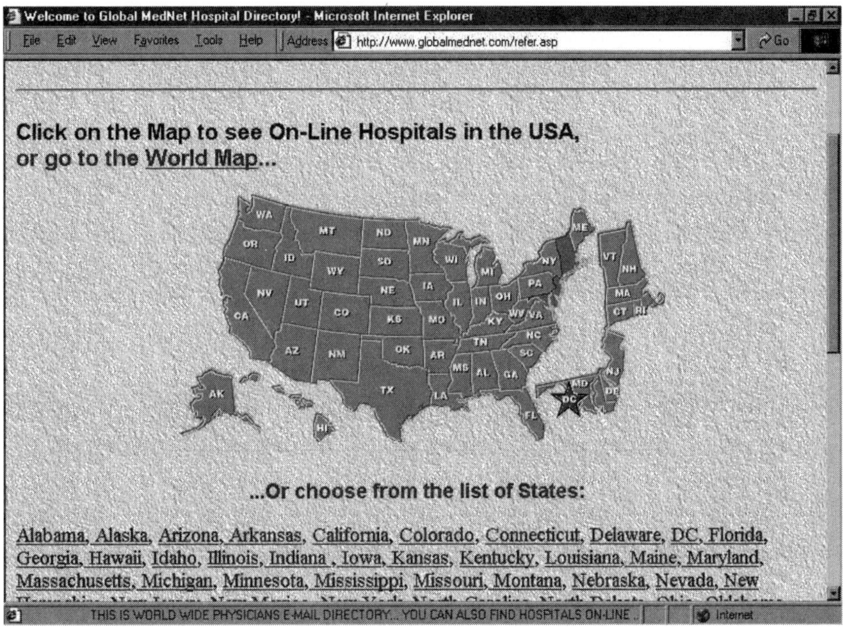

Figure 10.1. This is a example of an image map that has broken the United States into distinct sections and clearly shows where each section leads.

Use Site Maps to Make Navigation Simple

For large Web sites (i.e., those sites consisting of eight to ten major sections) you may want to include a site map that visitors can access from any page in your site. Site maps are usually text-based lists that name all of the site's pages and their contents. This allows users to easily access the information they are looking for. A link on your navigation bar to the site map makes it very easy to access the site map.

Use Page Titles to Identify Your Site

Each of the individual pages in your Web site should be given an appropriate title. The title will be put between the title tags in the header of an HTML document. The title tag information will identify and describe each page. Netscape's Web browser displays a document's title in the top line of the screen. When someone bookmarks your site, it is important the title appears as the description in their bookmark file. This is part of the reason that having each page in your Web site titled appropriately is important.

If you go through your site and bookmark each page, you will see if each title clearly represents the page contents. Also, keep your title short, as longer page titles can dilute the relevancy of your keywords. Keeping your page titles to five to ten words will increase the potency of your keywords and will cause the search engines to rank your site higher. Each page title should also always identify your company.

For some search engines to place your site high in its search results, it must find a relevancy between the keywords you use in your meta-tags with the words you use in your page titles and page content. To increase your keyword relevancy, position your keywords near the beginning of your page titles.

How the Browsers See Your Site

What the viewer sees when your site is downloaded depends on what browser she is using, so use a number of different browsers to make sure your site is displayed properly. You will want to check your site with the most popular browsers:

- Netscape Navigator 4.7
- Netscape Navigator 3.0
- Microsoft Internet Explorer 5.0
- Microsoft Internet Explorer 4.0
- Microsoft Internet Explorer 3.0
- America Online 5.0

Obviously, there are many browsers to consider when developing your Web site, but you should consider your target audience and the browsers they will likely use. If your intended target audience is everyone and anyone, design for the lowest common denominator. Design for Netscape 3.0 and Internet Explorer 3.0 and up, since very few people still use really old browsers.

America Online bases its browser on either Netscape or Internet Explorer; therefore, if your Web site displays properly in these browsers, AOL users will have no trouble viewing your Web site.

If your Web site appeals to a technically inclined audience, you can safely design for the latest browser editions. Using HTML 4.0, Java applets, Active X, or Flash Media may also make your Web site more attractive to these visitors.

In general, design your pages using HTML 3.2 and minimize the number of slow-loading multimedia elements. This lets everyone to enjoy your site without waiting a long time for each page to load.

Meeting Marketing Objectives with Different Web Site Features

It is possible to incorporate many features into your Web site, but it is important to look at each feature from both a marketing and an administrative view before you add it to your site. Although a chat room might seem like a great feature to have, you have to ask yourself: What is the marketing value to our company in having this on our Web site? Will it increase targeted traffic to our site? Will it encourage repeat visits from our customers and potential customers? Will it result in increased sales?

If you can justify a chat room on your site from a marketing perspective, you must decide if it is logical from a financial perspective. What will this feature cost to develop? What is your budget? Can these resources provide a better return on investment if spent elsewhere? Would you achieve your objectives more effectively if you put these financial resources into other online marketing activities?

Using Meta-Information to Guide the Search Engines

One common problem Internet marketers face is how to influence search engines to index their site appropriately and how to make their site appear when people use relevant search criteria. Many great sites on the Internet are impossible to find because they are not indexed with the major search engines. When searching for Web sites, 85 percent of Internet users employ search engines or directories by typing in a keyword or phrase that represents what they are looking for.

Many Web sites do not use the techniques available to them to influence how the search engine list them. Search engines usually evaluate the "meta-HTML" tags in conjunction with other variables to decide where to index Web pages based on particular keywords used.

Meta information can be used in identifying, indexing, and cataloging your Web site. This gives you the opportunity to use these tags to guide the search engines in displaying your site as the result of a query.

Meta and Header Elements

A header without meta-information will look like this:

```
<html>

<head>
```

<title>Game Nation: Gaming Software Specialists</title>

</head>

You should create a header as follows, if you want your site to be displayed properly in search engines.

<HTML>

<HEAD>

<TITLE>Document Title Here</TITLE>

<META NAME="keywords" CONTENT="keyword1, keyword2, keyword3">

<META NAME="description" CONTENT="200-character site description goes here">

<META NAME="robots" CONTENT="index, follow">

<!—Comments Tag, repeat description here?>

<HEAD>indicates the beginning of the header, and the ending of the header is marked by </HEAD>

<TITLE>indicates the title of the page. The end of the title is marked by </TITLE>which is called the closing tag.

<META NAME="keywords" CONTENT="…"> tells search engines under which keywords to index your site. When a user types one of the words you listed here, your site should be displayed as a result. You must use a space to separate the words. Do not repeat any of the words more than five times as a lot of the bots will not recognize repeat words. You should also list the most important words first because some bots read only the first 200 characters. Finally, create a keywords tag for each separate page of your site listing appropriate keywords for each page.

<META NAME="description" CONTENT="…"> should be added to every page of your site since it provides an accurate description of the page to which it is attached. As just noted, keep the de-

scription under 200 characters, or it may not be completely displayed by the search engines.

<META NAME="robots" CONTENT=" "> tells certain bots to follow or not follow hypertext links. The W3 Consortium white paper on spidering (spiders are defined below) offers the following definition and discussion:

> *<url1><META NAME="ROBOTS" CONTENT="ALL | NONE | NOINDEX | NOFOLLOW">*
>
> *<url1>default = empty = "ALL" "NONE"= "NOINDEX, NOFOLLOW"*
> The filler is a comma-separated list of terms:
>
> *<url1>ALL, NONE, INDEX, NOINDEX FOLLOW, NOFOLLOW.*

Note that this tag is meant to provide users who cannot control the robots.txt file at their sites. It provides a last chance to keep their content out of search services. It was decided not to add syntax to allow robot-specific permissions within the META-tag. "INDEX" means that robots are welcome to include this page in search services.

"FOLLOW" means that robots are welcome to follow links from this page to find other pages. A value of "NOFOLLOW" means the page can be indexed, but no links from the page are explored. (This may be useful, for example, if the page is a free entry point into pay-per-view content.) A value of "NONE" tells the robot to ignore the page.

The values of "INDEX" and "FOLLOW" should be added to every page unless there is a specific reason that you do not want your page to be indexed—for example, you might not want a page to be indexed if the page is only temporary.

<!—Comments Tag, repeat description here?—!> is a tag that is read by the Excite and Magellan spiders. A spider is an artificial intelligence agent that reads all of the information on a page and develops a "page description." The comments tag can be used to trick a spider into displaying an accurate description of your pages. The description that a spider usually creates without this tag is not very accurate and usually doesn't convey what your pages entail.

Internet Resources for This Chapter

Web Site Garage
http://websitegarage.netscape.com
This is a one-stop shop for servicing your Web site. Here, you can run critical performance diagnostics on your entire Web site and ensure browser compatibility by seeing your site in eighteen different browsers, platforms, and screen sizes. This speeds up your site by optimizing your images and drives traffic to your Web site. Provided is a comprehensive registration with up to 400 search engines, directories, and award sites. With this tool you can announce news through a Business Wire press release. You can target your industry—an Internet population—and analyze your Web site traffic with a customizable tracking tool. This site will allow you to run a number of diagnostics on your site for free, including: spellcheck, browser compatibility, load time, link popularity, and HTML design.

NetMechanic
http://www.netmechanic.com
This site will check your Web site to find broken links, perform HTML validation to make sure the format is compatible with the most common browsers, optimize your images for quicker loading, and monitor your server's performance for speed checking with different modem speeds. NetMechanic is a free online service.

Northern Webs
http://www.northernwebs.com
Northern Webs' Engine Tutorial is one of the most recognized leaders in exposing the nuances of the various search engines and explaining what makes them tick. See if your site can stand the test of their exclusive Meta Medic!

Meta-Tags and Search Engines
http://www.webdigger.com/meta_tags.htm
Need to improve your search engine standings? Here you can find a few ideas to get you started using meta-tags as well as search engine and Web site design tips.

Meta-tag Analyzer
http://www.scrubtheweb.com/abs/meta-check.html
This will check your meta-tags and your HTML code to help you achieve better placement in search engine results. Let their free Meta-tag Analyzer Program check your meta-tags and help analyze your HTML syntax online.

Using Meta-tags Tutorial
http://searchenginewatch.com/webmasters/meta.html

World of Design
http://www.globalserve.net/~iwb/search_engine/killer.html
This is a tutorial for writing meta-tags for higher search engine placement and good descriptions.

Web Developers Virtual Library
http://www.stars.com
A comprehensive illustrated encyclopedia of Web technology, the WDVL is for Web masters and Internet developers. It's a well-organized goldmine of tutorials, demos, and links to great resources.

Argus Clearinghouse
http://www.clearinghouse.net
This is the premier Internet research library or meta-index to locate everything you need to find on the Web.

11

Going Beyond the Basics

A dynamite site that satisfies your primary and secondary objectives, is appealing to your target audience, and effectively promotes your products and services is an essential component to having a successful online business. Many businesses fulfill this requirement and feel that a properly designed site that is user friendly, has attractive images, and fulfills their objectives is all they need to be competitive in the online world. In some cases this is true, but today we are seeing many Web sites that are going beyond the basics and are implementing Web site features that help create a whole new experience for their visitors while leveraging the marketing power of their Web site. The following elements are just a few of the techniques that could be implemented on your Web site to "go beyond the basics" of online business

Spread the Word with Viral Marketing

Viral marketing, which is often referred to as "word of modem" marketing, enables you to capitalize on referrals from an unbiased third party—the consumer! The power that peers and reference groups have over the purchasing decision is phenomenal. Similar to how a positive testimonial from a reliable source can add credibility to a product or service, the opinions of friends, business associates, and family can also help influence a consumer's purchasing decision. By implementing various viral marketing techniques on your Web site, you are provided with a dynamite opportunity to leverage the opinions of the consumer's reference groups.

You can use viral marketing techniques in a number of different ways throughout your Web site. By placing a "Tell a Friend about This Product" or "Share This Page with a Friend" button on your site, you enable users to quickly and easily spread the word about your site and your products. Visitors can click on the button, provide appropriate information in the "To" and "From" fields (including name and e-mail address of both the recipient and the sender), and a brief message. The important fact to remember is that the message is being sent through the business's site and not the sender's personal account. Although the message is personalized, your business can include additional information about the product, including features, benefits, the price, and a link directly to the page where the recipient can purchase the item. Since the message is personalized from a friend, the recipient will be more apt to visit the site to find out more about the product than he would if the e-mail came from a traditional corporate e-mail campaign.

Amazon.com (see Figure 11.1) is a prime example of a company that has implemented viral marketing features throughout the site. When visitors browse through Amazon.com's 3 million-plus product listings, they are always presented with the opportunity to "Tell a Friend about This Product." Providing this feature leverages the effectiveness of the Amazon.com Web site and ultimately results in increased sales for the company.

In addition to the aforementioned techniques, there are many different ways that you can implement viral marketing techniques on your Web site. If you have a newsletter on your site, you can add a "Tell a Friend about This Newsletter" button on the site. You can also incorporate a message in the body of your e-mail newsletter encouraging readers to forward a copy to friends they think would benefit from the information included in the newsletter. You should also include information in the message on how to subscribe to the newsletter. The recipients will then be able to send a copy of the newsletter to their friends, who will in turn be presented with the opportunity to

Figure 11.1. Amazon.com implements viral marketing techniques for every product listed on its Web site.

subscribe and regularly receive the newsletter. The opportunities for viral marketing are endless.

Leverage Your Site with Permission Marketing

Permission marketing is revolutionizing the way that many companies are doing business online. Permission marketing is basically asking visitors if they would like to be notified via e-mail about a particular subject. Through permission marketing you can promote and sell goods and services to current and potential clients who explicitly agree to receive marketing information through a specified communication channel. The most common example of permission marketing is the development of an opt-in e-mail list. An opt-in e-mail list is used for promotional purposes and contains a list of e-mail addresses that were provided by individuals who are interested in receiving information about a specified subject. Since recipients request the information, they are more apt to read the e-mail message. There are many different ways that you can implement permission marketing opportunities on your Web site. Many of these techniques will be covered more in depth in Chapter 15, "Generating Repeat Traffic and Building Customer Loyalty."

Permission marketing provides you with a dynamite opportunity to increase the exposure for your products and services while generating a large number of repeat visitors to your Web site. The development of a strategic permission marketing strategy is resulting in serious profits for many businesses. Over the years, many offline businesses have asked themselves, "How do we keep our customers coming back to our stores?" The proposed answer to this question has resulted in million-dollar advertising campaigns that offer little in the way of a return on investment. Permission marketing enables online businesses to communicate with thousands of current and potential customers at little cost. This helps businesses keep profitability high for their products and services.

There are a number of different ways that you can implement permission marketing techniques to help leverage individual elements of your site. Developing an opt-in e-mail reminder service for various elements of your site can help to generate significant repeat traffic. For example, if you have a "What's New?" page on your site that is updated frequently, you could ask visitors if they would like to be notified via e-mail whenever you make updates to the page. The e-mail notification would encourage recipients to return to your Web site; thus re-exposing them to your products and services.

If you carry an extensive line of products that is updated frequently, you can ask visitors if they would like to be notified via e-mail whenever you add new products to your storefront. This provides you with a great way to leverage the exposure for the new products. In the e-mail message you can provide information about the new product including features and benefits and the price, and include a link directly to the page where the visitor can purchase the product. This is a dynamite way to increase the sales of your products while generating brand awareness for your company.

If you regularly hold contests on your Web site, you can leverage the effectiveness of the contest by asking visitors if they would like to be notified of the contest winner via e-mail. The e-mail will not only inform recipient of the winners, but will also encourage them to reenter the next contest. This generates repeat traffic to your Web site, which re-exposes visitors to your products and services.

You can include many permission marketing opportunities on your Web site. The more opportunities you have to communicate with your target market at their request, the more traffic your Web site will receive. Once your visitors begin receiving updates about your products, services, company, Web site, and so forth, you will develop an online community of regular visitors. Your current customers and potential clients will appreciate the fact that you have included them in your online community. By maintaining communication with your target audience, you will build customer loyalty for your business's products and services, which will ultimately result in increased sales for your business. For more information on repeat traffic–generating techniques that you can include on your Web site, refer to Chapter 15.

Personalize the Experience for Your Visitors

Do you have a favorite Web site that you have bookmarked in your browser and return to on a regular basis? If so, the owners of that Web site most likely know that you are visiting that site on a regular basis too! Imagine if the next time you visited that site there was new text at the top of the page that read "Hello (Your Name Here), Thanks for returning to our Web site." This is happening quite often these days, as many businesses are now going one step beyond basic Web site technology to help personalize each visitor's Web site experience. By doing so, the business makes visitors feel more important and therefore more apt to return to the Web site, as they feel a part of your online community. But how does the Web site know who is visiting the site?

There are various ways to gain information about your Web site visitors in order to personalize their experience on your site. The most common type of personalization is simply name recognition. Typically Web sites that personalize their site for each visitor have some sort of "Members Only" section on their site. When a visitor registers to become a member of the site, the Web site places a cookie in the visitor's browser that tells the browser to display a specific page when the visitor returns to that site. The cookie is what tells the Web site the visitor's name and any other personal information that the site may be capable of showing. Unless the visitor manually removes the cookie from her browser's directory or has the "enable cookies" option disabled in her browser, her Web site experiences will continue to be personalized. This makes the Web site stand out from the rest.

A more complex example of a Web site that offers personalization is the Excite homepage (*http://www.excite.com*—see Figure 11.2). When you visit Excite's homepage, you are presented with the opportunity to become a member of Excite's online community. When you register to become a member, you are required to fill out a form that asks a series of questions including your name, birth date, sex, geographic location, and a desired username and ID. Once your membership has been accepted and you return to the Excite homepage, the content on the page will change dramatically. In comparing Figure 11.3 to the original homepage image in Figure 11.2, there are noticeable differences. The top of the homepage greets the visitor (in this case his name is John) and also provides information that is pertinent to him. John's local weather is displayed on one portion of the homepage, and his horoscope is present on another. Overall this creates a dynamite visitor experience, which will encourage John to return to the Excite homepage on a regular basis and may be the reason John will choose to use this search engine over others.

Although Web sites typically gather information for personalization by developing a "Members Only" section on their site, there are several other different ways that you can gather information that will provide the same end result. Holding online surveys, encouraging visitors to fill out an online form, or simply getting someone to register for your mailing list can all be ways to gather information to be integrated with a visitor's browser for personalization.

Privacy issues are something that you should watch out for if you decide to implement personalization on your Web site. To avoid any negative perception that your site might receive as a result of personalization, you should reinforce the fact that the users' personal infor-

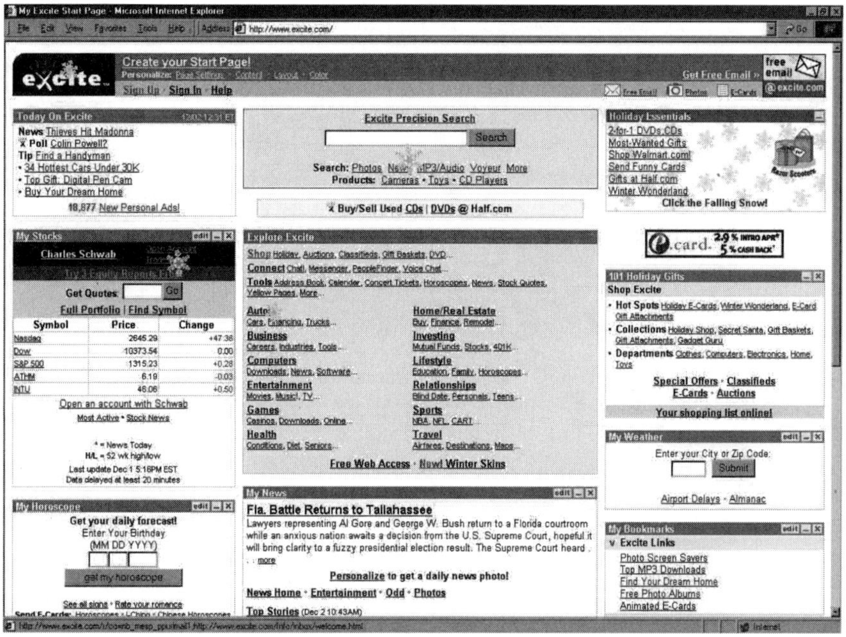

Figure 11.2. The Excite *http://www.excite.com* homepage before Web site personalization.

mation will not be used inappropriately or sold to another business. This will comfort them and will provide a positive Web site experience for future visits to your Web site.

In order to captivate your online audience and draw a lot of repeat traffic to your Web site, you have to stay up-to-date with the latest technology and provide your visitors with something unique. Whether you offer Web site personalization, update reminders, or viral marketing opportunities, it is essential that you go beyond the basics to meet and beat your competition. You should ensure that you constantly include new elements on your Web site that will encourage your visitors to return. At the same time, you should continuously look for permission marketing opportunities that will enable you to leverage the various elements of your Web site, communicate with your target audience, and continue to build loyalty among your online community.

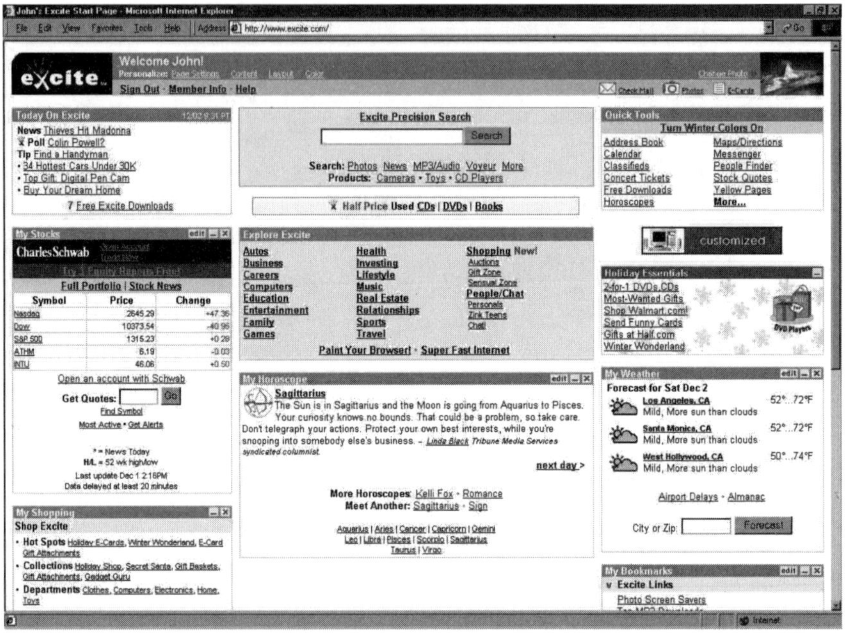

Figure 11.3. The Excite homepage personalized for John's user profile, including local weather, horoscope, and his favorite Excite homepage features.

12

Enhancing the Experience with Rich Media

Webcasting is defined by Netlingo (*http://www.netlingo.com*) as: "Using the Internet, and the World Wide Web in particular, to broadcast information. Unlike typical surfing, which relies on a pull method of transferring Web pages, Webcasting uses push technologies."

In a study conducted by Arbitron New Media and Northstar Interactive, it was found that when listening to or viewing streaming media, 70 percent of the Webcast audience clicks for content information, whereas 60 percent click through for advertising information. It was also found that roughly half of the Webcast audience buy products from online advertising and that 44 percent click on online advertisements.

Streaming and Nonstreaming Media

It is important to explain some of the terms that deal with Webcasting or rich media before we explain the marketing implications. Webcasting comprises primarily video and audio. Whatis.com defines rich media in this way:

> *Rich media is an Internet advertising term for a Web page ad that uses advanced technology such as streaming video, downloaded applets (programs) that interact instantly with the user, and ads that change when the user's mouse passes over it. For example:*
>
> - *A movie ad that includes a streaming video sample of a scene from the movie*
> - *A mouse cursor that is changed to an image on a particular Web site if the user requests it*
> - *A standard-size banner ad that includes an inquiry form about ISDN installation, capturing the user's filled-in personal information and telling the user he will be contacted by a company representative—all simply by interacting with an ad on an online publisher's Web page."*

This chapter discusses both streaming and nonstreaming content, focusing on streaming since it has the highest promotional potential. The difference between streaming and nonstreaming is that streaming is presented as it arrives. On the other hand, you must download the entire clip or file before you can listen to or view nonstreaming media.

- *Video*: This category would include both streaming (Real Audio, G2, and Windows Media Player formats) and nonstreaming video formats (such as AVI and MOV files). Streaming video can be sent from pre-prepared files but be distributed as a live broadcast feed. News clips and movie clips are examples of this.
- *Audio*: Audio includes streaming and nonstreaming formats. RealNetworks is by far the current king, with its RealAudio. Macromedia, with its Shockwave, is another leading provider of streaming audio.

Push technologies involve distributing information across the Internet to your target market. Once an Internet user installs the appropriate software on his system, he can receive content from the Webcaster. For example, he might receive the latest sports scores, the current weather forecast, or current headlines. Technically speaking, e-mail is one of the earliest forms of push technology. This is different from "pull" marketing where the client uses a browser to specifically request content from a Web site.

Advertising with Rich Media

A company can use rich media by purchasing a "commercial" that will precede an online presentation or audio event. A rich media "commercial" can also be developed and used on the company's own Web site to provide a more interactive feel resulting in more repeat traffic. Broadcast.com is a great example of this. Figure 12.1 shows Broadcast.com's home page, which provides current streaming audio and video footage of almost any event you could imagine. You can even listen to the commentary of an entire NHL hockey game. However, immediately before the program starts, you will be greeted by a 25-second audio advertisement.

Why is this good advertising?

- Rich media averages higher recall.
- Rich media advertising leaves a deeper impression on customers than does a static banner ad.
- Higher customer recall of rich media makes it easier to brand a company name or product.
- Rich media has higher click-through rates.
- Rich media is more "likable."
- Rich media increases your return on investment since you don't have to invest as much to achieve the same results as with traditional advertising.
- Because the Internet is not regionalized like TV and radio, there is a potential to reach a much larger audience with rich media.

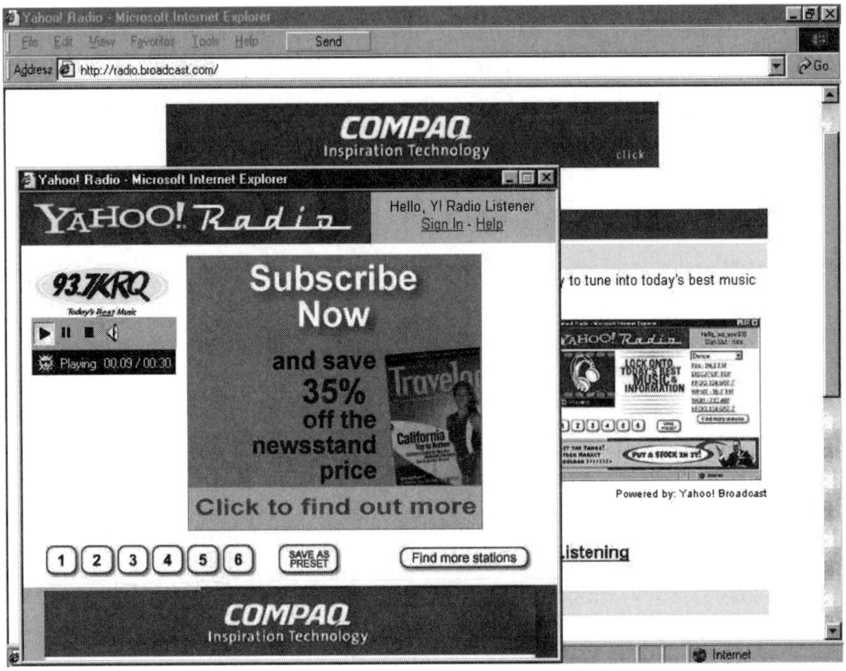

Figure 12.1. Broadcast.com uses rich media on its site to enable visitors to listen to numerous radio stations throughout the United States.

Uses of Webcasting

Although there are a few barriers to using Webcasting as a promotional tool, it is worth investigating if your target market includes early adapters to technology. Some important uses of providing rich media content to the general public include:

- Broadcasts of cable networks and television stations
- Live continuous broadcasts of radio stations and networks
- Coverage of sporting events (both streaming and nonstreaming footage)
- Live music including concerts and club performances (both streaming and nonstreaming footage)

- On-demand shows, corporate events, CDs, audiobooks, video titles, and so on

As bandwidth increases and more people are gaining access to higher-end technology, Webcasting as an advertising medium will soon be a regular part of our lives. The growth of Webcasting is apparent from the large number of prominent players already using this technology.

Internet Resources for This Chapter

Broadcast.com
http://www.broadcast.com
Broadcasting over 36,000 live events, Broadcast.com is a streaming media industry giant. The site was recently purchased by Yahoo!

ChannelSeven.com
http://www.channelseven.com
A large resource for Internet development, marketing, and advertising executives. This site contains information on rich media advertising.

Digital Librarian: Audio, Video, Rich Media
http://www.digital-librarian.com/audio.html
A librarian's choice of the best audio and sound resources on the internet. The site is updated weekly.

International Webcasting Association
http://www.webcasters.org
The IWA serves as the meeting place for companies that are active or interested in the delivery of multimedia (audio and video) services to consumers or business customers via the Net and other networks.

OnTheAir.com
http://www.ontheair.com
A reference site listing the best sites that provide links to live radio and television across the United States and around the world. Over 1,000 stations are available live on your computer.

Streaming Media World
http://www.streamingmediaworld.com
Streaming Media World offers media player reviews, news, tools, tutorials, discussion forums, and cool links devoted to streaming video, audio, MP3, multimedia, and gif animation.

The Media CHANNEL
http://www.mediachannel.com
A guide to video on the Internet.

VideoSeeker
http://www.videoseeker.com
The leading Internet video service, this site offers a wealth of streaming video clips and a complete online video guide. Check out exclusive "Must See" video from NBC, including comedy from SNL, "The Tonight Show," and "Late Night with Conan O'Brien," as well as the latest music videos, celebrity interviews, movie trailers, MSNBC news, live Webcasts, and more.

Yack!
http://www.yack.com
A guide to online events. With co-branding and personalized event services, Yack is the main portal for searching and finding all Internet events. Yack.com lists Webcasts.

13

What the Innovators Are Doing

Technology is changing the way that we do business every day. It seems as though it was just a few years ago when we started using e-mail on a regular basis, and now we are able to monitor, track, and accumulate data on our target market simply from their visiting our Web sites. *Webster's Dictionary* defines an innovator as "someone who begins or introduces something new." In the online business world, everyone is trying to be an innovator. The truth is that only certain businesses will actually take the time to implement a strategy that will enable them to understand their target audience, manage their current customer database, and provide optimal customer service to the end consumer.

CRM in the e-Business World

With an increase in global competition, gaining new customers and retaining current customers is becoming harder every day. So what are the innovators doing about this? They are integrating comprehensive CRM (customer relationship management) programs into their everyday business activities. CRM is changing the ways that companies are doing business. CRM programs are helping businesses learn more about their customers' needs, which in turn helps them satisfy those needs. This results in higher profitability for companies, as businesses are able to focus solely on consumers who will generate revenue for the business.

In the past, businesses would have huge databases of customer sales histories, addresses, contact information, and purchasing behaviors, yet they didn't see the value in this information. Today many businesses are taking the initiative to use this information to the fullest. But what can you truly learn from this information, and is it really worth the investment of time and money to implement a CRM program? The answer is yes.

In such a competitive marketplace, the cost to acquire a new customer is ten times more expensive than the cost to keep one. By analyzing customer data, you can develop an in-depth profile for each client in your database. You can then take these profiles and segment them into appropriate customer groups. For example, if you were an online retailer, you might find a certain portion of your customers only purchase goods from your Web site in November in order to purchase gifts for Christmas, whereas others purchase goods in the spring. To best utilize this data, you would segment those individuals who made purchases in the November time frame and send them an e-mail at the end of September reminding them about your business. Through monitoring past purchase history, you could even mention in the e-mail message that you have a new inventory of a particular item that you know would be of interest to your customer. Once the customer receives your e-mail, she will be reminded of your business, and since you went out of your way to recommend products that the customer would be interested in, she is likely to visit your site and purchase the product. This is just an example of how the innovators are using CRM programs to maximize profitability for their businesses.

CRM programs are also helping businesses to streamline internal operations. If you have an in-depth profile of your target market, the Marketing department will be able to target this market through the appropriate channels. This is helping businesses to receive a greater return on investment for their marketing budget. Accounting and Sales departments can also tighten operations as they can develop more accurate sales forecast, which will play a key role in all other business departments. Overall, implementing CRM programs is helping innovators restructure all aspects of their business. This is helping them gain a competitive advantage over the incumbent firms that choose not to use such a program. In the long term the incumbent firms will not survive, as the innovators will strengthen their relationship with their current customers while accumulating more customers into their database.

When your CRM system is integrated with your Web site and your Web traffic analysis software, you will be able to gather additional information as well. You will be able to track your customers' preferences and purchases and also their visits to your Web site; whether they receive your newsletter, use your coupons, enter your contests; what pages they visit on your site and how long they stay; and so forth. If you integrate this with an internal or external call center for your operation, the contact center rep will have all of this information available on a screen when talking with your customer.

Personalizing the User Experience

Having a dynamite site is a key element to the formula for e-Business success; however, what is the good of your site if the visitor is from another country and doesn't understand the present language on your site, or the visitor's Web browser is not capable of viewing your Web site? These are just a few of the problems that businesses face every day when selling products and services online; however, the latest innovations in technology are enabling businesses to overcome these obstacles.

Java Database Connectivity Driver (JDBC) has been developed to integrate with the server that is hosting your Web site to help solve some of these problems. For example, if your target audience comprises both English- and German-speaking consumers, you may want to have a Web site developed for each customer base—thus an English version and a German version. The problem arises when a visitor from each of the customer groups visits your homepage URL and is presented with the option to select the site that is appropriate for his language preference. The risk that businesses face is that visitors may not select the appropriate option, or will be discouraged from visiting a site that doesn't immediately accommodate their needs and wastes their time. JDBC technology is capable of reading the preferences in a visitor's Web browser to determine his language preferences, screen resolution settings, and whether or not the browser is capable of viewing your site. If a German consumer were to visit your site, this technology would read that the user's language preferences were set for the German language; thus the visitor would be immediately directed to the German version of your site. If you had both a Flash and an HTML version of your site and the visitor was using an older browser that was incapable of viewing Flash, the visitor would be directed to the HTML version of your site. Although these problems seem minute, they do de-stress the visitor, thus creating a more pleasant Web site experience for him.

Some Web sites are using JDBC technology even further by having multiple versions of their Web site readily accessible to attract consumers interested in a particular subject. To illustrate this example, assume that you are a consumer and are researching the costs of a used 1998 Volkswagen Jetta and you are on a Web site dedicated to Volkswagen enthusiasts. On this site you see a banner ad linking to an online used automobile pricing guide. When you click on the banner ad, you enter the site and are surprised that Volkswagen images are used prominently on the homepage of the new site. This is because the used car site is using JDBC technology and knew that you were coming from a Volkswagen-related Web site. If the visitor was directed to the site from a Honda enthusiast Web site, images of Honda automobiles would appear. Innovators are capitalizing on this technology to adapt their Web sites to the interests of their target market. By adapting they will ultimately qualify more leads from their Web site and generate stronger relationships with their current customers.

Providing Optimal Customer Service

Innovators are also differentiating themselves from their competition by providing optimal customer service to current and potential clients. Today customer service is a costly, yet crucial, part of running a day-to-day business, especially for companies doing business online. Advancements in technology are changing the way that businesses fulfill customer service requirements. The following are some of the most common to most advanced techniques being used by industry leaders to provide top-notch customer service to their clients and potential clients:

Call Centers

Although call centers are one of the primary means of providing customer service, they are also the most important. Call centers enable customers to contact representatives who are trained and capable of answering all of their questions. Today many of the leading-edge online businesses have in-house call centers open 24 hours a day, seven days a week. Since online businesses are open on the Internet 24 hours a day, 365 days of the year, it is necessary that there is always a customer service representative (CSR) available to answer any inquiries that consumers may have about the company's products or services. Technology is now enabling CSRs to communicate with customers in real time through various methods. Following are some of the more advanced and most effective ways for CSRs to communicate with consumers.

The Effectiveness of E-Mail

The speed and cost efficiency of e-mail is enabling businesses to lower overhead costs by eliminating unnecessary long distance telephone and postage charges that were incurred when customer service levels were not as advanced. CSRs are required to keep their e-mail program open on their desktop at all times in order to respond to customer requests in a timely fashion. It is recommended that CSRs, or any person who communicates with clients via e-mail, respond to e-mail requests within a 24-hour period. This shows a high level of professionalism and courtesy.

E-mail is also a less time consuming way to communicate with consumers. CSRs can have sample e-mail responses to typical questions that they receive from customers prepared in advance in order to respond to customer requests immediately. The CSRs can easily cut and paste the content from the prepared document into the e-mail message and send the response immediately. This saves time, which will enable CSRs to respond to a larger number of customer requests in a given period of time.

Web Chat

Web chat programs enable CSRs to communicate with clients and potential clients in real time via the Internet. Many online businesses provide a "Chat with a Customer Service Representative" button in a prominent location throughout their site. This enables Web site visitors to communicate with a CSR in real time without having to leave the Web site. Since Web chat happens in real time, a CSR must be available at all times in order to communicate with the visitors. However, real-time communication is superior to e-mail or even telephone because the visitor doesn't have to leave the Web site to converse with the CSR. There is also not a time delay between the response from the CSR, as is present with e-mail communication.

Whiteboarding

Whiteboarding is also becoming a popular Web site feature being implemented by industry leaders. Whiteboarding is similar to Web chat in that it enables CSRs to communicate with visitors in real time; however, it takes Web chat to the next level. A CSR for an online business that has whiteboarding capabilities can actually watch what a specific Web site user is doing while on the business's Web site and can provide assistance. This is particularly useful in situations where a visitor has to complete in-depth forms. To assist the visitor, the CSR is able to have the same form open on his desktop and can actually assist the client fill in the blanks. This innovative Web site feature adds a great deal of value and customer service capability to any business Web site, and will become a more common Web site feature in the near future.

Voice over IP

Although many Web sites don't currently use voice over IP features on their site, this innovative feature will become more common as technology continues to advance. Voice over IP (VOIP) enables people to speak into a microphone or headset that is attached to their computer. The user's voice patterns are then transferred over the Internet; similar to how your voice travels across the telephone cables. This advanced technology is going to revolutionize the customer service industry, and at the same time it will deconstruct the telecommunications industry as the cost to make a telephone call will plummet. At this point in time, it is not feasible for businesses to rely on VOIP technology, as the majority of Internet consumers are not equipped with the technology to be able to communicate using this medium.

Managing Opportunity in Real Time

All of the aforementioned techniques are enabling innovators to leverage the power of their online business to new heights. Through being able to identify, adapt to, and communicate with their target audience, businesses will be able to take advantage of opportunities that would not have been as readily available in the past. For example, when a CSR is communicating with a potential client via Web chat, the CSR is presented with an opportunity to upsell the visitor or cross-promote products on the business's Web site. Since this is happening in real time, the CSR is given the opportunity to participate in such activities on a regular basis. This varies significantly from the traditional sales approach of visiting an offline location or participating in cold calls in order to "close the sale." As technology continues to advance, we can only expect that similar trends will continue to change the regular business models that we have grown accustomed to. In order to remain competitive, businesses will have to adapt to these changes or risk losing their place in the market to the innovators who adapt to technology quickly and respond to the needs of their customers.

e-Tailers are preparing for m-Commerce

Over the past several years, many online e-tailers have been profiting tremendously from the increase in the number of consumers making purchases online. But what if consumers weren't limited to making purchases from a computer? What if they could make purchases while in their automobiles or while climbing the side of a mountain? Well, in selected cities in selected countries, this is already happening as the demand for mobile commerce (or m-commerce) is increasing in popularity. M-commerce is the process of buying goods or services via the Internet through wireless devices such as cellular telephones, palm pilots, wireless laptop computers, and the abundance of personal communication devices coming available every day. Although the wireless infrastructure needed for m-commerce is not yet available in many cities throughout the United States, Datamonitor (*http://www.datamonitor.com*) has predicted that the market for mobile commerce solutions will grow 1,000 percent to $1.2 billion dollars by the year 2005. If this prediction is correct, m-commerce is going to revolutionize e-commerce as we know it, but how does it work?

M-commerce is made possible through wireless application protocol (WAP) technology. This technology enables mobile devices that are equipped with Web-ready mini-browsers to access the Internet from anywhere in the world where this service is available. This means that consumers will be able to purchase goods and services at their discretion. Whether they are stuck in traffic or waiting for an appointment, consumers will be able to access the Web and make online purchases through the use of mobile devices.

Flexibility with regard to when and where you can make online purchases is not the only innovation that will result from the evolution of m-commerce. Consumers will be able to access their e-mail, surf the Internet, read newsgroups, and participate in online chat sessions all through the use of a WAP-equipped mobile devices. Although this technology is still emerging and many cities across North America are not equipped with the wireless infrastructure to handle m-commerce, this will become commonplace in the near future.

Internet Resources for This Chapter

NetworkWorldFusion.com
http://www.nwfusion.com/research/voip.html
This is a dynamite resource filled with lots of great information on VOIP technology.

Customer Relationship Management
http://www.3com.com/technology/tech_net/white_papers/503057.html
This is a terrific report about how networks of communication are enabling business-to-consumer relationships to develop.

ITtoolbox CRM
http://www.crmassist.com/
This is a huge directory containing everything that you will need to know about CRM. You can find out information about anything from starting a call center, to integrating your back office into your Web site.

Java Database Connectivity without Compromise
http://www.openlinksw.com/info/docs/opljdbc.htm
This report, prepared by Kingsley Idehen, the president and CEO of OpenLink Software, takes an in-depth look at JDBC technology. A must-read for anyone interested in adapting to the needs of his target audience.

ThinWeb.com
http://www.thinweb.com
ThinWeb provides next-generation e-Business tools today. They are experts in JBDC.

Part 4

The Right Traffic

14

Preparing Your Site for the Search Engines

When Internet users are looking for a particular product, service, subject, or information pertaining to an area of interest to them, how do they do it? The most common search tool used is the search engine. Because search engines can bring significant volumes of traffic to your site, you must understand how the major search engines work and how the design of your site can influence the indexing of your site by the search engines. This chapter will help you do just that.

Search engines are becoming increasingly complex in their scope of offerings, with the line between search engine, directory, portal, and content site becoming ever more blurred. No longer do search engines just offer their search service. More often than not, you will find a wealth of headline news, rich media entertainment, online shopping, a variety of complimentary directories such as an online version of the Yellow Pages, and the integration of other search engines' and directories' indexed information into their own. Personalization features such as the ability to customize how a page is displayed are also becoming prominent with some of the major search engines. Some search engines, Excite for example, even offer users a free e-mail service! They do this because they have to—people expect it, and it is a part of keeping up with the times as well as the highly competitive environment. Although search engines continue to change, there is one thing that remains constant, and that is that people use them to find what they're looking for. You need to ensure that your site is designed to meet the criteria set forth by the search engines so that your site can be properly indexed and listed.

Understanding Search Engines

Search engines use programs or intelligent agents, called bots, to actually search the Internet for pages, which they index using specific parameters as they read the content. The agent will read the information on every page of your site and then follow the links. For example, AltaVista's spider continually crawls the Web looking for sites to index and, of course, indexes sites upon their submission. Inktomi also uses a spider; however, a user cannot access Inktomi's information directly to search. Instead, the user will submit its site to other search engines and directories that use Inktomi's search engine technology. Inktomi is very important in the search engine community, so be sure your site is easily accessible to its spider. A detailed discussion on submissions to search engines and directories can be found in Chapter 18, "Submitting Your Site to the Search Engines and Directories."

Registering with search engines is fairly simple. In most cases you simply have to submit your URL or Internet address on their submission form. Even if your URL is not registered with search engines, a number of the major search engines will eventually find you since their bots are continually roaming the Internet looking for new sites to index. There are millions of sites out there, so I suggest that you be proactive and register your site to ensure a speedier listing. Once you are registered, some of the bots will periodically visit your site looking for changes and updates.

A common problem faced by Internet marketers is how to influence search engines to index their site appropriately and how to ensure that their site appears when people use relevant search criteria. Many of the interesting and creative sites on the Internet are impossible to find because they are not indexed with the major search engines. The majority (85 percent) of Internet users employ search engines or directories to find what they are looking for on the Web. They do this by typing in a keyword or phrase that represents what they are looking for. The following sections explore how to make your Web site more search engine friendly.

Many search engines and directories either partner with or license the use of another search engine or directory's search technology. MSN Search references LookSmart for results, and Yahoo! uses Google's index for some of its search results. iWON references LookSmart's directory and Inktomi's index. If you submit your site to a search engine that uses Inktomi's index, then the design of your site influences how you're indexed in all search engines that rely on Inktomi for their search results. In a similar fashion, you will find other search engine and directory data intermixed or included in some form with another search engine or directory's data.

When designing your site you must always keep the search engines in mind. Something as simple as a drop-down menu on your site can cause problems with the search engines and the indexing of your site if implemented incorrectly. You want to do everything you can to ensure that your site is designed to meet the needs of your target audience while remaining completely search engine friendly. Search engines can produce a significant amount of traffic to your site if you can manage to be placed in the top search results. The following sections discuss some of the most common issues experienced by individuals and companies with respect to the search engines and Web site design.

To keep up to date with the latest in search engine happenings and trends, I recommend that you join the I-Search Discussion List, published by audette|media (*http://www.audettemedia.com*) and moderated by Detlev Johnson, a leading search engine expert.

Frames

From a marketing perspective you should avoid frames when developing your Web site. Frames may result in some search engines being unable to index pages within your site, or they can result in improper pages being indexed. Also, many people simply prefer sites that do not use frames.

What "improper pages being indexed" means is that content pages will be indexed and when the search engines direct a user to these content pages, he will likely not be able to navigate your site because the navigation frame probably will not be visible. To prevent this, one technique you can use is a Robots meta-tag in the head section of your HTML that does not allow bots to proceed beyond your home page. As a result, though, only your home page will be submitted, which means you have less of a chance of receiving the high rankings you need on the major search engines. Alternatively, you should include textual links to all major sections within your site to accommodate those users who enter your site on a page other than a home page, and to assist the search engines with indexing your site.

Some search engines can only read information between the <NOFRAMES> tags within your master frame. The master frame identifies the other frames. All too often the individuals who apply frames ignore the <NOFRAMES> tags, which is a BIG no-no. If you do not have any text between the <NOFRAMES> tags, then the search engines that reference your site for information will have nothing to look at. This will result in your site's being listed with little or no information in the indexes, or you will be listed so far down in the rankings that no one will ever find you anyway. To remedy this situation, insert textual information that contains your most important descriptive keywords between the <NOFRAMES> tags. This will give the search engines something they can see, and it also helps those users who are browsing with non-frames-compatible browsers.

Now that the search engines have found you, you still have a problem. They can't go anywhere. Create a link within your <NOFRAMES> tags to allow search engines and users with non-frames-compatible browsers to get into your site. Frames are a headache when designing your site to be search engine friendly. To make your life easier and from a marketing perspective, it's better to avoid them altogether.

Image Maps

I recommend that you stay away from image maps when designing your Web site. An image map is a single graphic or image that has multiple links to different pages or resources.

Image maps can prevent some search engines from getting inside your site—you're basically locking the door. This may result in some of the pages on your site not being indexed, or none of your site being indexed at all. If you do use image maps, make sure that your site is easy to navigate with hypertext links. This will ensure that search engines will find all of your pages and index them. Another tip is to create a site map that has text links to all relevant pages within your Web site. This will help the search engines to index all the pages within your site.

Dynamic Pages and Special Characters

Don't bother submitting to the search engines those pages that consist of CGI content or have question marks (?) in the URL. Search engines simply won't index them. In addition, some search engines such as Lycos will not index sites with the ampersand (&) or percent sign (%) characters.

Meta-Refresh

A meta-refresh tag is an HTML document that is designed to automatically replace itself with another, after a certain specified period of time. Search engines generally do not like meta-refresh tags. If you do use a meta-refresh tag to redirect users, then it is suggested that you set a delay of at least seven seconds and provide a link on the new page back to the page they were taken from. Some businesses use meta-refresh tags to redirect users from a page that is obsolete or no longer there. Meta-refresh tags also may be used to give an automated slideshow.

Splash Pages and the Use of Rich Media

A splash page is basically an opening page that leads into a site. Often splash pages consist of a Java or a Macromedia Flash intro.

Some Web sites use splash screens that consist of an eye-pleasing image and an invitation to enter the site. Many splash pages implement techniques that automatically send you to the home page once you've seen the splash page, and others will invite you to "click to enter" in some form or another. Why do people use splash pages on their sites? For one, they usually look beautiful. Another reason is to provide the user with something to look at while images or content for the home page loads in the background. Individuals also use splash pages as a means of advertising. Splash pages are usually very attractive in appearance, but they often lack content relevant to search engines.

If you do use a splash page on your site, be sure you include the proper meta-tags within your HTML header. This is important so that search engines that use meta-tags can access this information. This ultimately affects your ranking and how your site is displayed to users in the search results. If possible, include a paragraph or statement on your splash page that pertains to your site's content. This can help boost your rankings on some of the major search engines that both do and do not use meta-tags. Some search engines will review your opening paragraph and use this information when developing a description for your site that is presented in their search results.

Page Size

The total file size of all of the content, graphics, and media on your site can influence your positioning within some search engines. Some search engines seem to prefer smaller-sized pages, whereas some of the other leading search engines have been observed to place preference on larger-sized pages.

The best way to hedge yourself against this issue is to perform your own research. Do some relevant searches using key search engines and analyze the top pages or sites found. You can use your browser and view the properties of each page to check the total size of the page, or you might use a Web page analysis tool such as Web Site Garage (*http://www.websitegarage.com/*) to get an idea of a particular page's total file size. Sometimes the search engine you're using will list the file size of each page listed. Based on this information, you can gain a good idea of whether or not page size influences the search engine in consideration.

Use of Tables

To a lesser extent, tables can pose indexing issues with some of the search engines. Tables are a common feature found on many Web sites to display information and position content, but if implemented incorrectly they can cause the search engines some confusion. Also, by using tables close to the top of a page, you are potentially forcing the content you want search engines to see farther down on your page. Because some search engines look only so far, you might be hurting your chances of receiving a high ranking. If you are using tables, place any important information pertaining to the page content above the table if possible to help prevent any potential problems.

Here's an interesting problem some search engines suffer from: Assume you have a Web site, the main color of the background is white, and you have a table on the page with a dark background. If you were to use white color text in the table, some of the major search engines would pick this up as using same-color text on the same color background and would ignore your site's submission because it will be considered spam to them. Using tables is okay; many people do it—just be careful with your choice of colors.

Keywords Are Critical

Keywords are an important aspect of every Web page because the search engines use keywords in determining your site's ranking, and these are the words people are most likely to use when they're searching for your site. Selecting the right combination of keywords for each page on your site is critical to your success. When creating your keyword list, don't use just nouns. Think of descriptive words that may be associated with benefits of your products or services. For example, if your site offers information on weight loss, then some of your keywords may be "weight," "weight loss," "diet," "exercise," "nutrition," and so on. You can also add some keywords that describe advantages a person may receive from visiting your site, such as "thin," "slim," "healthy," "in shape," and so forth.

When determining what your keywords will be, always keep the customers or your target visitors in mind. Try to think as they would if they were to do a search for information on your topic. Don't just think about what people would do to find *your* site, but what they would do if they didn't know your company existed and were looking for the types of products and services you provide. If you find this a difficult exercise, then ask around. Talk to both people that know about your business and people that don't. Ask what keywords they would use to find a site like yours. Reviewing any corporate materials, brochures, and so on, can assist you in building your list of appropriate keywords.

Always use the plural when forming your keywords. (Adding an "s" forms the plural.) If you list "game" as your keyword and someone uses "games" to do a search, then your site will not be found. If you include the word "games" in your keywords and someone requests information on the word "game," then your site will be found because "game" is part of the word "games." Don't use both versions because you're then running the risk of spamming the search engines, and you want to be able to use other keywords to increase your chances of achieving high rankings. The only time it is appropriate to use both the singular and the plural is if the plural does not include the singular in its entirety; for example, "dairy" and "dairies"—you should list both the singular and the plural as part of your keyword list. It is also important to note that when most people perform their searches they will use the plural version. You're more likely to search for "computers" than you are to search for "computer."

Your keywords list should always be included in your submissions to directories and in your keywords meta-tags. However, there is much more you can do to be listed in a higher position in search results. You should include your most important keywords in other places, such as the page title; the description; the first 200 to 250 characters of your page; the beginning, middle, and end of your page text; between the <NOFRAMES> tags if frames are used on your site; in "alt" attributes; in the keywords meta-tag, the description meta-tag, and the comments tag; and in any page <H1>headers</H1> used.

Some search engines rank sites by how early the keyword appears on the site. The earlier a keyword is mentioned on your site, the higher your site may be positioned in search results. You want to repeat keywords a number of times on each page of your site. I recommend using important keywords in conjunction with each other.

You can check the effectiveness of your keyword placement and utilization by using Web traffic analysis techniques. You can use Web traffic analysis reports to determine what sites are referring people to you. You can strip down this information further to view only search engine referrals. By looking at this information, you can see exactly what keywords people are using to find you and you can alter the keywords used based on this information. Refining your keywords is one of the key elements to success—you're letting the search engines tell you what you're doing right and what you could be doing better.

Know Your Competition

Check out your competition. I use the term *competition* very loosely. I mean your industry's leaders (whether or not you compete directly)—people who are selling noncompeting products to your target market, as well as your direct competitors. Search their names and see what they are using for descriptions and keywords. Next, search using some of your keywords and see what sites receive top rankings. This research will illustrate why they have received such a high ranking—and you can incorporate what you've learned into your Web site or doorway page for that search engine or directory.

What does this mean? No one knows exactly how each search engines work, but by searching for your most important keywords and observing what the top-ranking sites are using with respect to their page content, title tags, description meta-tags, keywords meta-tags, and so on, you can formulate a good plan of attack. Remember that if you don't appear in the first two or three pages of search results, it is unlikely that prospective visitors will access your site through the search engine.

Check to see what meta-tags your competitors have. Not only can you learn from the sites that catch your eye, you can also learn from your competitors' mistakes. After you have done a thorough job of this market research, you will be in a good position to develop a description that is catchy and adequately describes your site.

To check your competition's meta-tags in Microsoft Internet Explorer, you simply go to their site, then click on "View" from your menu bar and select "Source" from the drop-down menu (Figure 14.1). This will bring up the source code for that respective page in whatever your default text browser is. For most people this will be Notepad, which is what is used in Figure 14.2.

Looking for the same information in Netscape is just as easy. From the menu bar, select "View" and then select "Page Source" from the drop-down menu. The following image is a simplified version of the header portion of the HTML code on a Web site to demonstrate where you should look for keywords.

Keep in Touch with the Trends

Are you interested in knowing what the most popular search terms or subjects on the Web are? Many search engines and directories provide a list of the most popular search terms of the day, week, and so on, for your viewing pleasure; reviewing these lists may give you ideas you can use on your own site! Yahoo!'s Buzz Index (*http://buzz.yahoo.com/*) and AltaVista's A-List (*http://trends.altavista.com/*),

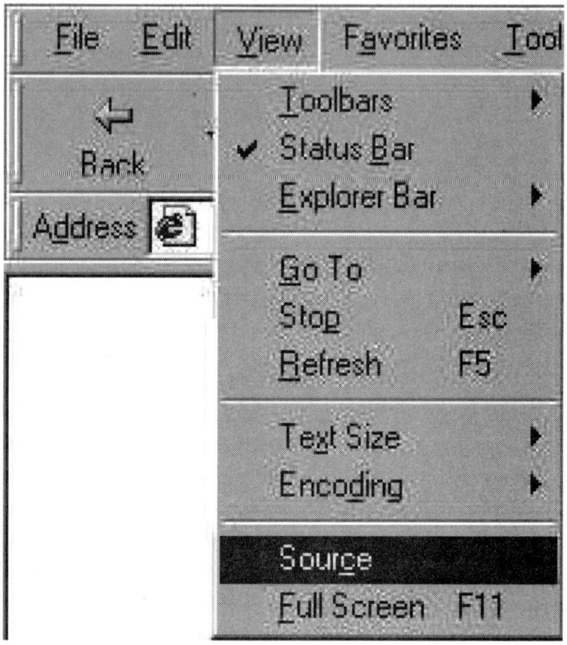

Figure 14.1. Look for the "Source" option under Internet Explorer's "View" menu.

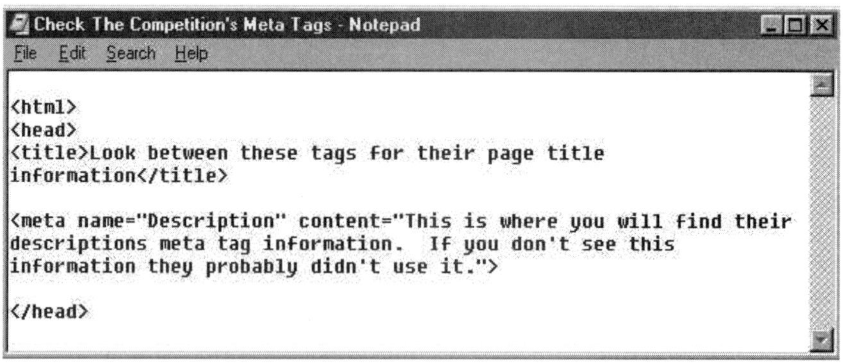

Figure 14.2. This is what you should look for in the source code of the site you're viewing.

pictured in Figures 14.3 and 14.4, show the most popular search information from the related search tool.

There are a number of services available that can help you with selecting the most appropriate keywords for your site. These services base their suggestions on results from actual search queries. WordSpot (*http://www.wordspot.com/*) and Wordtracker (*http://www.wordtracker.com/*) are two such examples. Wordtracker references a number of sources including Infoseek, Google, Lycos, Yahoo!, AltaVista, and Goto for its suggestions and comparisons. Figures 14.5 through 14.9 illustrate Wordtracker's free trial using "Internet Marketing" as the focus.

Use Descriptive Page Titles

Each of the pages in your Web site should be given a title. The title is inserted between the title tags in the header of an HTML document. Title tag information identifies and describes your pages. Titles can

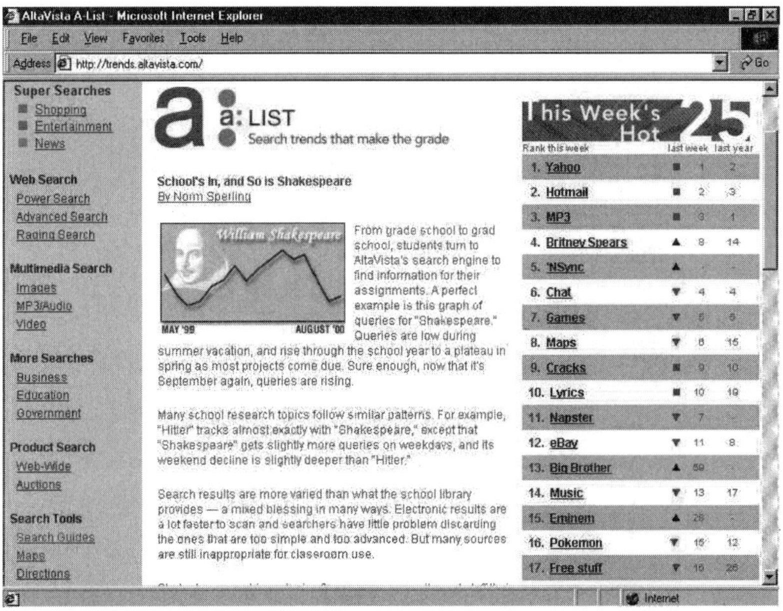

Figure 14.3. Yahoo! posts the subjects most sought by its users every day.

Figure 14.4. AltaVista ranks its most popular search terms on a weekly basis.

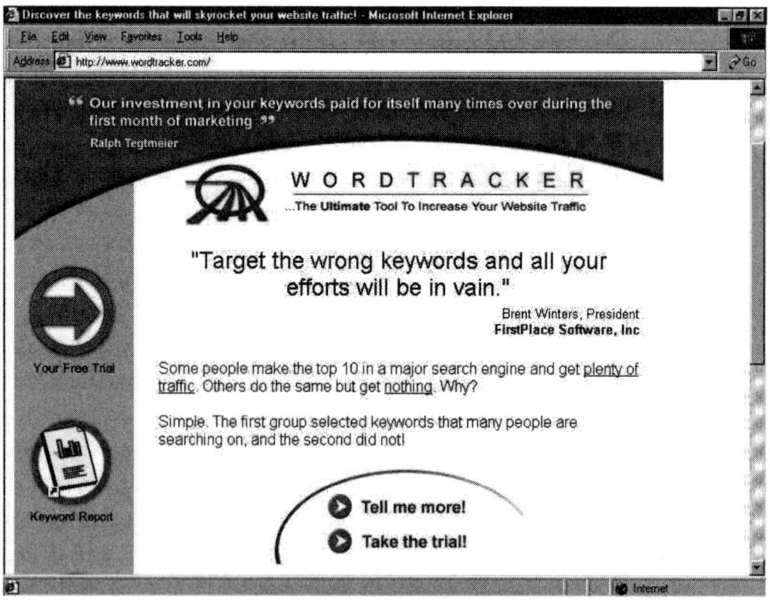

Figure 14.5. Wordtracker helps clients select relevant keywords.

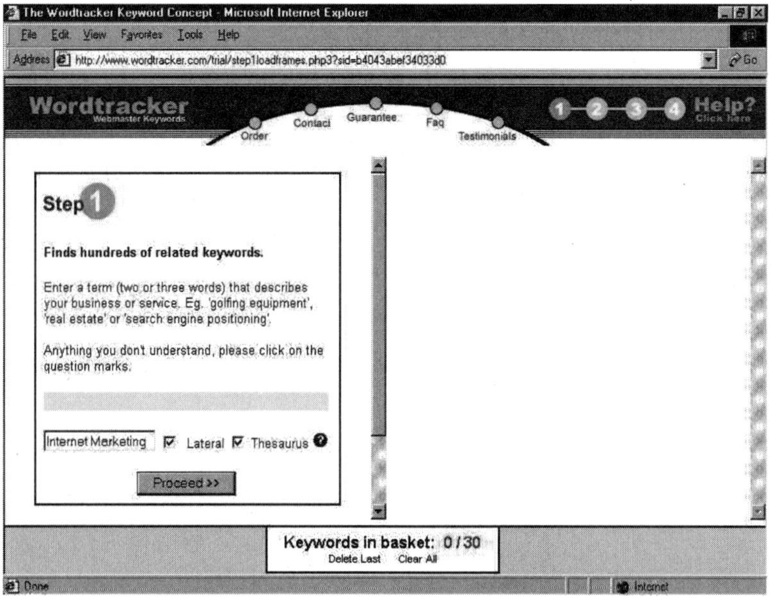

Figure 14.6. Click on "Take the trial" from Wordtracker's homepage and enter a keyword of interest.

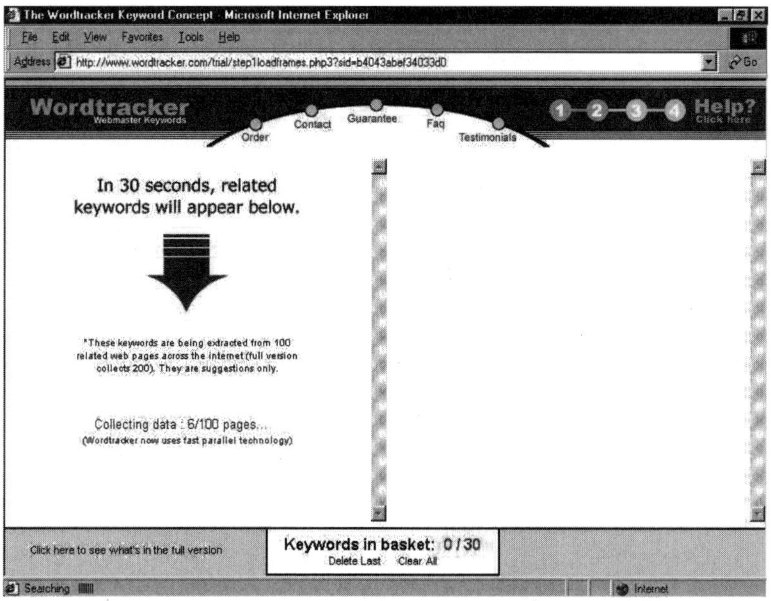

Figure 14.7. Wordtracker extracts related terms.

Figure 14.8. Keywords that relate to your query are displayed.

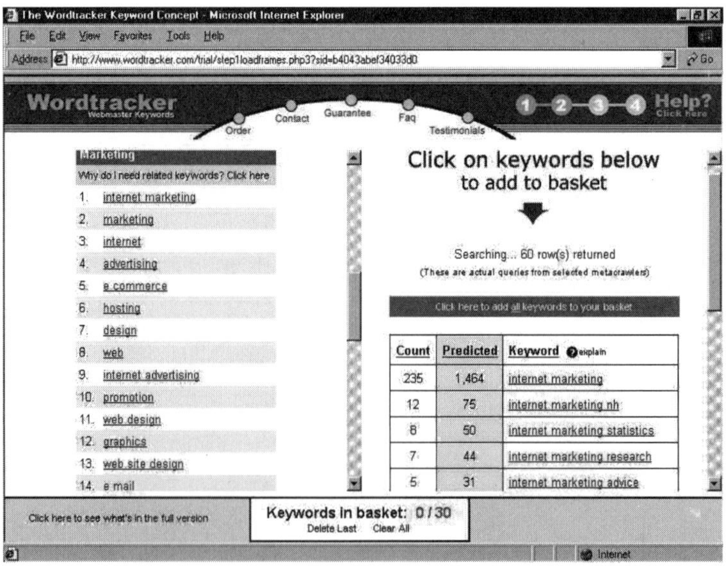

Figure 14.9. You can then view information from actual queries made to various meta-crawlers.

tell readers where the information contained on a page originated. Most Web browsers, such as Netscape, display a document's title in the top line of the screen. When users print a page from your Web site, the title usually appears at the top of the page at the left. When someone bookmarks your site, the title appears as the description in her bookmark file. These are all reasons that it is important that a page's title reflects an accurate description of the page.

Go through every page of your Internet site, bookmark each one, and check that your titles represent each page clearly without being lengthy. Longer page titles can dilute the relevancy of your keywords. Keeping your page titles brief (five to ten words or fewer) will increase the potency of your keywords and earn your pages higher search engine rankings. Also, keep in mind that Internet Explorer will bookmark approximately 50 characters, whereas Netscape bookmarks around 40. Your page titles should always identify your company.

Match the keywords you use in your meta-tags with the words you use in your page titles. Search engines check page titles, meta-tags, and page content for keywords. Your pages will be more relevant, and therefore place higher in the search engines, for certain keywords if these keywords appear in each of these three sections. Position your keywords near the beginning of your page titles to increase your keyword relevancy.

Some of the search engines will retrieve your page, look at your title, and then look at the rest of your page for keywords that match those found in the title. Many search engines use title tags as one of the elements in their algorithm to determine search engine ranking. Among the search engines that use pages titles in their ranking criteria are AltaVista, Excite, Google, HotBot, NorthernLight, WebCrawler, and Yahoo!. Pages that have keywords in the title are seen as more relevant than similar pages on the same subject that don't, and may thus be ranked in a higher position by the search engines. However, don't make your title a string of keywords like "cuisine, French cuisine, imported food..." because this will likely be considered spam by the search engines and you will end up worse off in the rankings or removed altogether. Also keep in mind that people will see that title in the search results, and they're more likely to click on a site that has a title that flows and is descriptive—not a list.

Design Effective Meta-Tags

Retaining a certain measure of control over how search engines deal with your Web site is a major concern. Often Web sites do not take advantage of the techniques available to them to influence search engine listings. Most search engines evaluate the "Meta-HTML" tags in conjunction with other variables to decide where to index Web pages based on particular keyword queries.

The Web Developer's Virtual Library defines a Meta-HTML tag as follows:

> *An HTML tag used in the Head area of a document to specify further information about the document, either for the local server, or for a remote browser. The Meta element is used within the Head element to embed document Meta information not defined by other HTML elements. Such information can be extracted by servers/clients for use in identifying, indexing, and cataloging specialized document Meta information. In addition, HTTP servers can read the contents of the document head to generate response headers corresponding to any elements defining a value for the attribute HTTP-EQUIV. This provides document authors with a mechanism for identifying information that should be included in the response headers of an HTTP request.*

To summarize this lengthy definition, meta-information can be used to identify, index, and catalog. This means you can use these tags to guide the search engines in displaying your site as the result of a query.

Meta-tags are an important part of reaching your goals online. AltaVista, Excite, Inktomi, Lycos, WebCrawler, NorthernLight, and Google are all examples of search engines that use meta-tags in one form or another. Some search engines use your keywords meta-tags and description meta-tag in determining your ranking in their results. Some search engines also use this information as the source of description displayed to the user who is searching for information of interest. For specific information on how and where to place meta-tags in your HTML code, check out one of the many Web development resource sites, such as CNET's Builder.com (*http://www.builder.com*).

Place your most important words first in your description and keywords meta-tags. This will help you achieve higher rankings because most search engines consider the first few keywords the most important in their ranking criteria. Also, what if the search engine you're submitting to looks at only the first 30 or so characters? You're okay because you've placed the most important keywords first.

As a general rule of thumb, keep your description and keywords meta-tags to under 200 characters in length. There are some search engines that allow you to use up to 1,024 characters in the keywords meta-tag. Using this many keywords is not advisable unless you plan to create a doorway page specifically for that search engine. When you use too many keywords, you end up diluting the importance of each keyword, meaning potentially lower rankings in the search engines. Also, do not repeat the same keyword too many times in the keywords meta-tag for a particular page. Stay below five repetitions per page, and mix up the use of your keywords with other words and phrases. Using the same keywords too many times may result in your site's being passed by or penalized for spam.

Another rule of thumb is to use lowercase letters when formulating your keywords meta-tags because most search engines are not case sensitive. Only AltaVista and Infoseek are truly case sensitive, and even then most people perform searches using only lowercase letters anyway.

Page Content Considerations

To achieve optimum online results, I recommend you design your site content carefully. You want to apply the most important keywords near the beginning of your page because many search engines attribute a majority of the weight to the content near the top of a Web page.

Always have a descriptive paragraph at the top of your Web page. Search engines that do not use meta-tags will use this as their source for a site description and keywords on your site. As well, search engines will use the content found within the opening paragraph in determining the ranking of your site among search results. Again, be sure to use the most important keywords first, preferably within the first two or three sentences. This is very important. Infoseek and AltaVista boost pages that use well-placed keywords near the top of the page content. Make sure that the keywords you use flow naturally within the content of the opening paragraph and relate to the content and purpose of your site. You don't want the search engines to think you're trying to cram words in where they don't fit.

Use your HTML <H1>headers</H1> effectively to indicate the subject and content of a particular page. Most people use them only as a method of creating large fonts. Some search engines, including Google, use the keyword content included within the header text in their relevancy scoring.

As you can tell, textual HTML content is extremely important to the search engines, which brings me to my next point. Never create a page that is excessive in graphical content. For example, don't display information that should be displayed in text as a graphic file. I've seen this done numerous times. No matter how great it looks, the search engines can't read the text embedded in your graphics for content.

Before you submit your site, be sure the content on the page you're submitting is completed. Yahoo!, the Web's most popular directory and overall search tool, will ignore your submission if you have an "under construction" or similar sign on your page.

Any time you make significant changes to your site, you should resubmit the site to the search engines. Some search engines revisit on a regular schedule. However, these search engines are growing smarter every day—some monitor how often the site is updated and adjust their "revisit" schedule accordingly.

Additional Design Techniques

Doorway pages, also know as gateway pages and bridge pages, are pages that lead to your site but are not considered part of your site. Doorway pages are focused pages that lead to your Web site but are tuned to the specific requirements of the search engines. By having different doorway pages with different names (e.g., indexa.html for AltaVista or indexg.html for Google) for each search engine, you can look back and see which page is bringing in the most traffic. Those pages that are not bringing in the traffic can then be edited and resubmitted until you get it right.

Due to the need to be ranked high in search engine results and the enormous competition between sites that are trying to get listed high in search engine results, doorway pages have become increasingly more popular. Each search engine is different and has different elements in its ranking criteria. Developing doorway pages allows you to tailor a page specifically for each search engine before submitting to achieve optimal results. Be careful, though; some search engines frown upon the use of doorway pages, so check before creating and submitting one. There are a number of sources online that offer advice for developing dynamite doorway pages. A good place to start is Search Engine Watch, listed in the resources section of this chapter.

Page cloaking is a fairly new tactic companies are using in their quest for top search engine positions. Page cloaking is essentially telling the search engine one thing, but showing the human user something completely different through the use of complex scripting techniques. Sometimes companies do this to prevent competition from mimicking their online promotional activities, and the content that appeals to search engines may not be effective in communicating with the target market. Like doorway pages, cloaking is a controversial subject. Improper cloaking techniques can result in your site's being permanently banned from a search engine. Kloakit (*http://www.kloakit.com/*) and IP Delivery (*http://www.ip-delivery.com/*) are two cloaking products available to you. Fantomas (*http://www.fantomaster.com/*) offers a number of cloaking products.

Consider implementing a "Valuable Resources" or related section on your site. Many search engines attribute a significant weight to link popularity, meaning in general that the more sites that link to yours the better. In your quest to get sites to link to yours, you will encounter those sites that will be willing to do so in return for a reciprocal link. If it would be of great value to you to be linked from that site, then you need a place to put the reciprocal link. Never put links on your home page or in any other extremely prominent location because you do not want people to leave your site and go to another before you get a chance to communicate with them.

Internet Resources for This Chapter

Search Engine Watch
http://www.searchenginewatch.com
Search Engine Watch is a Web site devoted to how search engines work, search engine news, search engine information, tips on using search engines, and more about search engines.

Search Engine World
http://www.searchengineworld.com
A great resource for everything surrounding search engines. Plenty of articles, tips, and information to help you achieve online success. This site also has in-depth information on the various search engine spiders.

PegasoWeb: Web Promotion Portal
http://www.pegasoWeb.com/
Information on promoting your Web site through search engines, e-zines, newsletters, and banner advertising.

Search Engine Showdown
http://www.searchengineshowdown.com/
Detailed analysis of Internet search engines, their features, databases, and strategies.

Search Engine Forums
http://searchengineforums.com/
Information pertaining to search engines and Web site promotion presented in the form of a bulletin board.

Search Engine Guide
http://www.searchengineguide.com/
A comprehensive guide to search engines, portals, directories, and online databases.

LinkPopularity.com: The Free Link Popularity Service
http://www.linkpopularity.com/
A free service that queries AltaVista, Infoseek, and HotBot to check your link popularity.

15

Generating Repeat Traffic and Building Consumer Loyalty

There are many things that you can do to your Web site that will "keep 'em coming back." The following tips, tools, and techniques will get visitors to return to your site again and again.

How to Get Repeat Visits

Just as you would want customers to visit your place of business frequently, the same is true for customers and potential customers visiting your Web site. The more times a person visits your site, the better the chance that they will buy something. When trying to generate repeat traffic, make sure you use techniques that are appropriate for your target market. If your site is targeting children, it would not be wise to have a breadmaker as the prize for a contest you are holding. This would be a fine prize if your target market were families or homemakers but not children. It is important to have a prize that is of interest to your target market. The following elements are worth consideration when selecting repeat traffic generators for your site.

Freebies

Having free items to give away from your site is a great way to increase traffic—everybody likes a freebie. By giving something away each week, you are sure to generate a constant stream of repeat traffic. By having freebies or giveaways on your site, your site can also be linked from the many sites on the Internet that list places people can go to receive free stuff. To find listings of "free stuff," simply use a search engine to do a search on "Free Stuff Index" or "Free Stuff Links."

You don't have to give something away to everyone who visits your site, but you could have a drawing once a week or once a month. Holding a contest gives you an opportunity to e-mail participants and let them know the final results. In this announcement e-mail, you can inform the participants of upcoming contests as well as any other news related to your company. An example of a site that has a monthly draw would be Lobster Direct (*http://www.lobsterdirect.com*). Lobster Direct is a site that ships live Nova Scotia lobster anywhere in North America the next day via FedEx. They also have a drawing for a lobster dinner for four every month. When the drawing is done, Lobster Direct e-mails everyone who was part of the contest to inform them of the winner, and takes the opportunity to remind them of the monthly specials. This certainly can't hurt sales.

If you want to attract only your target market to your site, then try to give away things that only people interested in your industry would be interested in.

If it doesn't matter what traffic you generate to your site—and any traffic is good traffic—then give away generic items such as free downloads and screensavers. It is best to try to have your logo and URL displayed on the items you give away. Good examples of freebies are a neat screen saver that displays your logo and URL or free samples of your product.

You can also use a traditional marketing approach and offer free samples of your product from your Web site. Once you give away the samples, follow up with an e-mail asking the people who received the sample what they thought of it, if they had any problems, and if they have any questions. In your e-mail, direct the samplers back to your Web site for more information and discounts on purchasing the regular version of the product. If you carry a number of different products, you might want to alternate your free samples. Ask if visitors want to be notified by e-mail whenever you change your free sample. Once they have given you permission and their e-mail address, you can write them on a regular basis to let them know about the new free samples. In that same e-mail you can put a little extra information regarding specials or new items on your site. Give them a reason to visit as well as new information regarding your Web site. Make sure you include your signature file in your e-mail message.

Coupons and Discounts

If you offer coupons and discount vouchers that can be printed from your site, people will return to your site again and again because they know they will find good deals. You can also change the coupon on a regular basis to encourage more repeat visits. You may use this strategy in conjunction with a free sample giveaway. People who tried a free sample may be enticed to buy the regular version if they can receive a discount. If they like the regular version, they may buy it again at full price or recommend the product to a friend. This is another chance for you to ask people if they would like to be notified by e-mail when you update the coupons on your Web site.

You can also develop a coupon banner ad that links to your site, and have it placed on sites frequented by your target market.

Another option is to trade coupons with non-competing sites that target the same market that you do. You can arrange to have your coupon on their site link to your site while you have their coupon on your site with a link to their site.

Offering coupons on your Web site can cut down your overhead cost because people are printing the coupons on their own printers, thus not using your supplies. Remember to include terms and conditions on all coupons that are available for printing by having an expiry date on the coupon. The expiration date should be close to the release of the coupon so the visitor will use the coupon quickly and then come back for more coupons.

Recently we have been seeing a number of coupon-related sites appearing on the Internet such as CoolSavings.com (*www.coolsavings.com*), as seen in Figure 15.1. This is an online coupon network where businesses can advertise and place coupons for

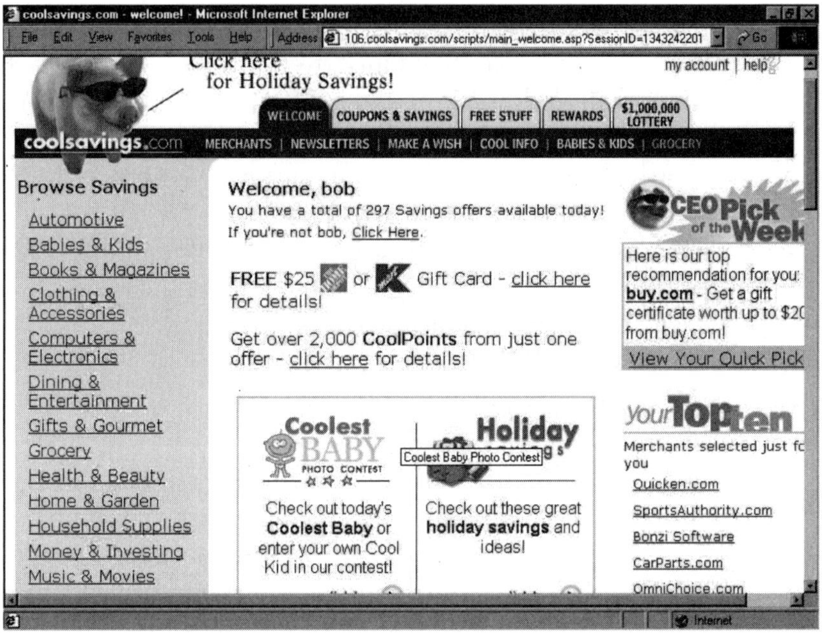

Figure 15.1. Coolsavings.com is an example of a Web site where you can have your company's coupons displayed for its products or services.

their products and services. Sites like this offer another way to promote your business since they receive large volume of traffic. It is a good idea to get listed on these sites if you do offer coupons.

A Calendar of Events

If you keep a comprehensive, up-to-date calendar of events related to your company or your industry on your site, you will encourage repeat visits. A calendar of events for a band might show their scheduled appearances. A calendar of events of what is going on in your business community is very appropriate for a Chamber of Commerce or Board of Trade site. A calendar such as this will encourage lots of repeat traffic so visitors can be kept up-to-date. Calendars of events are also beneficial on community sites because the community accesses these sites to stay posted on what is going on.

Contests and Competitions

Contests and competitions can be a great way for you to build traffic to your site. Many sites hold contests on a weekly or monthly basis in order to generate repeat visitors. By holding a contest, you can find out lots of information about your target audience by requesting certain information on the entry form.

The type of contest you run depends on your Internet marketing objectives. If your objective is simply to increase traffic, it would be best to offer items such as money, trips, cars, or computers. If you are more interested in having only your target market participate, choose prizes that are more related to your product or industry.

You can have people fill out an electronic ballot on your Web site that includes their name, address, phone number, and e-mail address if they want to enter the contest. To find out more information about your participants, ask them to answer a series of question that will give you pertinent information about your target audience.

Another option for a contest would be to find a contest site that would offer one of your products as a prize for a contest they are holding. This would work best if your product is of interest to a wide range of people. You could arrange to set up a picture of your product on their site with a link to your site. This will generate brand awareness for your product and generate traffic to your site. Most contest sites will be more than happy to do this because you are offering to give them something for free that adds value to their site.

A contest could become a competition if you ask entrants to submit their best recipe using your food product or the best photo using your camera equipment, and so on. People will visit your site to see the winning recipes and you may get some ideas for future marketing efforts. Other competitions may include things like best short story about one of your products or the best drawing of one of your products. The closer the contest relates to your product, the better.

You may find that it is best to offer a number of smaller prizes as well as your "grand prize." This makes people feel they have a better chance of winning and they will be more likely to enter.

There are legal issues to consider before you hold any kind of contest. You should check out all of the legal restrictions that may apply, such as needing a permit to hold lotteries.

You should also be sure to ask the entrants for the e-mail address at which they would like to be notified of the winner. This, once again, gives you permission to e-mail them to tell them who the winner was, and also to inform them of the specials that you may have at your site that month.

Resourceful Links

You should provide visitors with links from your site to other sites that are related to your industry. However, it is very important that you do not put any outbound links on your home page as this gives visitors the option of leaving your site before they've had a chance to properly explore what your site has to offer. You should place your links down a level or two so visitors have seen all the information you want them to see before you provide any links away from your site.

A great way to build links to your site is to exchange links with other, related sites so you receive a link from their site to your site. As long as the links on your site are of interest to your visitors, they will come back to see if you have added any new links to sites they should visit.

You might want to ask if visitors would like to be notified when you update your links, or even when you make general updates to your site. By offering this, you have the permission of the people who signed up to send them an e-mail message reminding them about your site as well as offering new information about your site. Remember to attach your signature file with your URL. This allows recipients to link through to your Web site directly from the e-mail.

Providing a Tip of the Day or Week

You may want to have a section on your site that offers cool tips that relate to your business, your products or services, or your target market. These tips can be long or short, but if they provide useful advice, visitors will return repeatedly to find out what other interesting advice you have for that day. Ask your visitors if they would prefer receiving the tip via e-mail or just being notified when the tip has been updated on your site.

Get Bookmarked

Encourage visitors to your site to add you to their bookmark (or favorites) list. It is important to have a call to action such as "Bookmark this site now!" somewhere on your site. Make sure the page title of the page that has the "Bookmark this site now!" call to action clearly identifies your site and its contents. Whenever I see "Bookmark this site now," I always consider it. Sometimes I bookmark the site and sometimes I don't, but I always consider it. Often, when the call to action is not presented, I don't think about it and don't bookmark it. Then, days later when I want to go back there, I wish I had remembered to bookmark the page.

Bulletin Boards

Having a bulletin board can be very interesting as people from all over the world will join just to interact with each other about a topic that relates to your Web site. Be aware that you may have to keep an eye on the messages being posted and may also need to intervene on occasion.

Site of the Day or Week

If you decide to have your own "Site of the Day" or "Site of the Week" listing, it will take a lot of effort searching the Internet for a cool site to add, or looking through the submissions you receive. However, if your audience finds your picks are interesting, you may find that avid Internet users come back every day to see what interesting new site is listed. Keep in mind that this must be updated on schedule; displaying a week-old "Site of the Day" will reflect poorly on your site and your company.

Cartoons, Jokes, and Trivia

You can create a dynamic and fun atmosphere on your site by displaying relevant cartoons, jokes, or trivia. You do not have to create all of the content and features yourself. Glasbergen.com (*http://www.glasbergen.com/y2k.html*), as seen in Figure 15.2, offers cartoons for sale to use on your site if you want. "Laughter is the best medicine" and cartoons or jokes could become a popular feature of your Web page. People also enjoy trivia or a "thought for the day." There are many sources on the Web for you to draw these features from. You will want to update your content regularly so people return. Again, this gives you the opportunity to ask if your visitors would like to be notified when you update your Web site.

Games

It has become more common for sites to feature fun activities and games on their sites. Some games that are held on Web sites range

Figure 15.2. An example of a cartoon you can get from Glasbergen.com to use on your Web site and lighten the mood.

from a Star Wars trivia contest to having guests play an interactive game with other visitors. Games such as these will entice visitors to return to your site to play the games, but in the process they will also be familiarizing themselves more and more with your company and products.

Update Reminders

On your site you can have a reminder service that will allow visitors to sign up if they'd like to be notified when there are updates or content changes to your pages. This works in a similar manner to a mailing list except that you only write to the "list" when changes have been made. This works well when you have a newsletter or a frequently visited calendar of events on your site.

Events Reminders

Event reminders let people sign up to be reminded of something via e-mail on specified dates. A florist originally used this idea to remind people of important dates in their lives. You can use this technique to remind people about any number of things relating to your business. If your business sells fishing and hunting gear, you could offer people to sign up to be reminded when certain fishing or hunting seasons start. You should develop a reminder service that relates to one of your products or services. In the case of the fishing example, your reminder could include suggestions about what fishing fly works best at this time of the year.

E-commerce sites are beginning to use reminder services quite regularly. It is a service that is really appreciated by busy people who are not good with remembering dates. This has saved me on more than one occasion and made it very easy to purchase from the site that provided the reminder. I have five nieces and nephews across the country and I have registered their birthdays with a site that also asked for a few details for the reminder—such as what the date is, the relationship that I have with the person, his age, things he enjoys, and how far ahead of time that I want to be notified. Like clockwork ten days prior to Kyle's birthday I got this e-mail:

> *Susan, your nephew Kyle's birthday is in 10 days. He will be 12 years old. Kyle likes Gameboy video games. We happen to have several that may be appropriate as a gift for Kyle. Click here for more details.*

I am then able to choose the gift that I want to purchase, the paper I want it wrapped with, and the text that I want on the card that will be attached to the gift. Then I simply provide the address I want it sent to, give them my credit card number, and they send it off. Everyone is happy, especially me.

Real-time Chat Sessions

Chat rooms are a very popular way for groups of people to come together to discuss varying topics. If your site has a chat forum, make sure the topic is related to your business and that your target market will participate. By changing the topic in your chat room from day to day or week to week, you will encourage repeat visitors. Chat sessions should be regularly scheduled and upcoming events should be posted on your site so visitors will know what is happening and when. To promote any special events taking place in your chat room, remember to have the information in your signature file as well as making some postings through your appropriate mail lists and newsgroups to inform interested parties.

It is a good idea to post the topics of the discussions at least a week in advance so interested visitors will remember to join the session if they are interested in the topic. It's amazing how many people will schedule time so that they can chat with someone special or knowledgeable in an area that interests them. You will also want to think about asking your visitors if they would like to be notified of the upcoming chat sessions, or special guests that may be visiting your site to chat. This once again gives you permission to send them an e-mail to present them with information that will entice them to visit your site again. You may also want to ask your visitors whom they'd like to see as a guest or topics they would like to see discussed.

Advice Columns

Some Web sites are incorporating advice columns into the site. By having advice related to your industry or product posted on your site, people will return to read the e-mails asking for help and the responses that are given. This is a great way to establish your company image as an expert in your given field.

Virtual Postcards

You may want to have a feature on your site that allows visitors to create original postcards that can be e-mailed to their family and friends. The e-mail you send should have a link back to your site where the postcard can be viewed. This is beneficial for two reasons. First, it causes people to come to your site if they want to see their postcard; and second, it means that you are not sending large attachments to people's inbox. I can't begin to count the number of beautiful cards I have received via e-mail from my thirteen-, twelve-, and ten-year-olds, each with a beautiful verse and complete with audio and video. The cards have come via the Blue Mountain Card site, and I have also noticed that my recent online card purchases happen to be from the same company.

Photo Galleries

If you want your visitors to have a better understanding of what your products look like, you may want to include a photo gallery. It's been said that a picture is worth a thousand words, so why not provide your visitors with a visual image that will give them a clear picture of what you are offering? For example, if you are an online travel agency, you may want to provide pictures of different featured vacations every month. Visitors will be inclined to return so they can see the beautiful pictures of the new "featured vacation." Once again, you have the option of asking visitors if they'd like to be notified when the photos and featured vacation have been updated.

Online Training Sessions

Today we are seeing an increase in the number of organizations providing online training sessions or "virtual seminars" from their Web sites. These training seminars can be used in conjunction with either streaming or non-streaming media. You can also decide if you want to have visitors download the training sessions to watch at a later time, or have the option of watching a real-time stream directly from your Web site. One way to use this online training opportunity would be to have a workshop on how to get the most from a product your company sells. This would work particularly well if your company produced computer software that had some complicated features. This is the kind of seminar that you would want to keep on your site for customers to be able to download and reference if they were having difficulties. You will want to have a calendar of upcoming training sessions and an opportunity for visitors to ask to be notified when you update the calendar.

Loyalty and Reward Programs

One way of generating repeat traffic is to create a loyalty program for your visitors to let them know you appreciate them. You can create loyalty with your visitors by creating a "Members Only" section of your Web site. For entry, you could require visitors to fill out some personal information including name, e-mail, and answers to some key questions that will help gain marketing knowledge in your customers' preferences or profiles. As a reward for becoming a member of your site, they can receive special deals in advance of informing the general public or special coupons. This once again gives you permission to send an e-mail in which you can mention company news and announcements.

Permission Marketing

This form of marketing has been discussed throughout the chapter in the specific applications and is a way for you to get people to give you permission to send them e-mail on a regular basis. By having people sign up to receive information relating to your company, your products, your services, your newsletters, or your promotions, you are being given permission to send them e-mails in which you can also include a little extra company news or company promotions. The more often your name appears in front of your target market, the more they feel a part of your online community and the more often they are likely to visit your site. Review all the elements of your site to see where you can leverage with the use of permission marketing.

Internet Resources for This Chapter

More Hits for Your WWW Site
http://www.adze.com/zine/morehits.html
This site offers tips on "how to get people to keep coming back to your site."

Web Developers Virtual Library
http://www.stars.com
A comprehensive illustrated encyclopedia of Web technology, the WDVL is for Webmasters and Internet developers. It's a well-organized goldmine of tutorials, demos, and links to great resources.

10 Secrets of the Web Masters
http://www.i-strategies.com/10secret.html
This is a guide to Web design and strategy to get visitors and make them return.

Yale Style Manual Table of Contents
http://info.med.yale.edu/caim/manual/contents.html
A good example of a detailed Web design manual to keep visitors coming back.

Web Architect
http://www.argus-inc.com/index.shtml
Archive of Web Review site design features to help you get the perfect layout.

Web Page Design: Introduction
http://www.wpdfd.com
Web design from the perspective of typography and graphics to keep visitors happy; no HTML.

Pulling the Plug-Ins
http://www.cio.com/archive/webbusiness060198_main_content.html
Web plug-ins are finally on the outs with Web designers. So how should you cram all that interactivity in your Web pages without alienating your visitors? Go here to find out.

Conservatism of Web Users
http://www.useit.com/alertbox/980322.html
Statistics show that Web users are adopting new Web technologies at slower rates, affecting how you should design your site.

Features, How to, and Elements of Web Design
http://www.builder.com/Graphics/Design
CNET's elements of good Web design to help in your Web page design.

16

Increase Your Sales Force with Associate and Affiliate Programs

It is a well-known fact that referral business is the easiest and most efficient business to generate. When doing business online, affiliate programs enable you to capitalize on this concept. The concept of setting up a referral business model was first started in 1996 when Amazon.com started paying other Web site owners for referring customers to their Web site. This referral business model caught on, and now many sites are incorporating this model into their everyday business activities. The idea and the corresponding software technology have come a long way since 1996. The software available today makes the process so simple that anyone with basic Web skills can set up an affiliate program or join one within ten to twenty minutes.

Many of the major search engines are now using link popularity as a part of their ranking criteria. An added benefit to having an affiliate program is that each person who signs up for your affiliate program has to develop a link from her Web site pointing toward specific pages of your site. This helps to improve your link popularity, which in turn will help enhance your search engine rankings.

What Are My Affiliate Program Options?

To understand the opportunities available with affiliate programs, you must first understand the different types of affiliate programs. All pay for referral business, but in different ways. Before you decide to participate in an affiliate program, you must first look at your objectives, your products and services, your target market, and more importantly whether or not an affiliate program is appropriate for your online business. Most affiliate programs are designed to automatically track the traffic that you receive from each of the referring Web sites, determine whether or not the referral resulted in a sale, and electronically calculate the commission due to the affiliate. Once you have affirmed that an affiliate program is appropriate for your operation, you then choose the type of program that works for you.

Commission-Based Affiliate Programs

This is the most common type of affiliate program available. A commission-based program offers its affiliates the opportunity to earn a percentage of the sales generated from referrals from the affiliate's site. Typically commissions range from 1 to 15 percent. Some programs offer a two-tier commission structure where you receive a commission for your own sales, plus a commission on the sales of each member that you recruit for the affiliate program. Other programs offer an increased commission for those who have higher traffic sites. ConnexNetwork.com (*http://www.connexnetwork.com*—see Figure 16.1) offers a dynamite commission-based affiliate program (*shameless self-promotion*). Other examples of commission based affiliate programs include:

Beyond.com—*http://www.beyond.com/*

CDNOW—*http://www.cdnow.com/*

Flat-Fee Referral Programs

Flat-fee referral programs pay affiliates a predetermined amount for each new visitor that comes from the referring site to the host's site

Figure 16.1. ConnexNetwork.com offers a dynamite commission-based affiliate program.

and carries out a predefined course of action. This action is most commonly a purchase; however, some flat-fee programs do not depend on purchases. The predetermined course of action could be the download of a free demo, ordering a catalog, requesting information, or any other data-gathering task that the affiliate requests during the onset.

Trevelocity.com—*http://www.travelocity.com/*

JobMatch.com—*http://www.jobmatch.com/*

Click-through Programs

This type of affiliate program pays members per click-through for each unique visitor who reaches the host's site from the affiliate's link. Many banner ad networks operate this type of program. They literally pay you every time a visitor clicks on a banner that is placed on the affiliate's site. Some programs will even pay for click-throughs received from a link that you might place in your mail list. This provides an even greater opportunity for affiliates to earn additional income from their site.

AffiliateClick—*http://www.affiliateclick.com/*

B2Brover—*http://www.b2brover.com/*

Selecting the Right Affiliate Type for You

The first thing that you should do when deciding whether to start an affiliate program is to ask yourself if this fits with your Web site objectives and if the program is something that would be of interest to your target audience. Click-through programs can serve to increase traffic to your Web site as long as your banner ad is designed with your target market in mind and the banner ad is placed on sites that are of interest to your target market. Commission-based and flat-fee affiliate programs can go a bit further in having the referred visitor do what you want her to do when she gets to your site. The referring site knows that it receives a commission only when a certain action has been taken by the visitor, whether that action be a purchase, a quote request, or something else. The referring site has a vested interest in having the referred visitor take that action, and the site is in a position to suggest or recommend the visitor take that action.

How Affiliate Programs Can Boost Traffic and Online Sales

By creating your own affiliate program, you may generate a significant increase in traffic to your Web site. When your affiliates place links on their Web sites linking to your site, you will increase your link popularity. This can generate a significant amount of traffic to your site, but it also helps to increase your search engine rankings. Some of the major search engines use link popularity in their search engine ranking criteria. Once you have successfully launched your affiliate program and have developed a wide sales force on the Internet, you may be surprised by the amount of new traffic you have to your Web site.

The best advantage of an affiliate program is that you can exponentially expand your sales force. If your affiliate program is administered professionally and you communicate with your affiliates effectively all over the world, this will expand your customer base into cultures that were impenetrable before.

To succeed in the affiliate initiative, you must keep in touch and monitor the links of all the affiliates in your program and go the extra mile to get the links from their sites to yours to stand out and appeal to their target market. Concentrate on doing all that you can to exploit and promote your program. Register your site in the Web's affiliate directory sites and ask affiliates to rate your program.

Affiliate Tracking Software

If you want to make the whole process of tracking your affiliates clean, simple, and easy, your best bet is to purchase comprehensive affiliate tracking software. Companies have developed tracking software that can allow you to provide maximum service to your affiliates. Depending on what features you would like to provide to your affiliates, the cost of tracking software can range from $300 to $15,000.

There are many varieties of affiliate tracking software. Some software programs are quite unsophisticated and offer very few features, and others offer them all. There are some features that you should watch for when purchasing your software. Features such as automated signup and tracking, real-time reporting, and automatic payment calculations can all help your affiliate program run more smoothly. They can help you to run a very smooth affiliate program and can save you a lot of time.

My Affiliate Program (*http://www.myaffiliateprogram.com*—see Figure 16.2) is a dynamite affiliate tracking program that enables program operators and affiliates to check their success with the program in real time through a Web interface. This program is extremely easy for operators to use and makes setting up your affiliate program a very fast and efficient process. My Affiliate Program is a very flexible program that allows operators to design their own program, at their own terms, and at their own pace. No matter how advanced your affiliate program needs are, My Affiliate Program likely has the capability to fulfill your affiliate program needs.

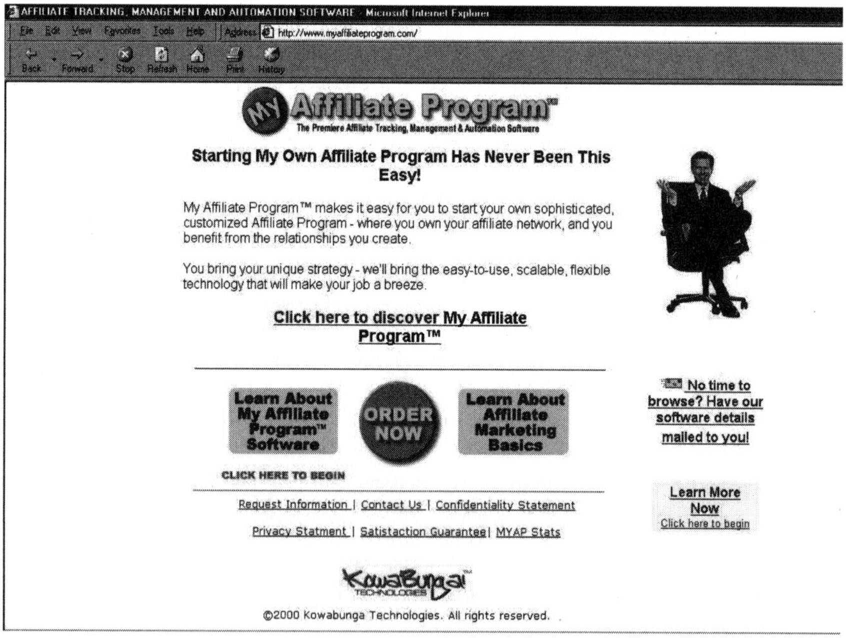

Figure 16.2. My Affiliate Program offers one of the Internet's premiere affiliate tracking software programs.

Internet Resources for This Chapter

My Affiliate Program
http://www.myaffiliateprogram.com
This is the best full-service affiliate software program on the Web yet.

Associate-It
http://www.associate-it.com/
This is the ultimate directory of affiliate programs and associate programs. It is a leading Web portal and community for affiliate, associate, pay-per-click, and revenue-sharing programs. It's categorized and searchable.

Online Business.com
http://www.onlinebusiness.com/revenue/index.shtml
This site features affiliate programs that are recommended because the administrator has positive personal experience with them, or because they provide services and products that can be sold by a wide variety of Web sites, and have a good reputation.

Internet Marketing Center
http://www.marketingtips.com/tipsltr.html
This is an e-zine that offers tips of how to integrate affiliate programs into your online marketing strategy.

17

Setting Up Shop in Cybermalls

Cybermalls are Internet shopping centers that contain "stores" related to a specific topic. Malls that concentrate on a specific type of product or service have become some of the most successful malls. These malls experience success because they bring in interested people searching for a specific type of product or service and not necessarily because they generate a huge amount of traffic. The Hall of Malls is one site that provides a list of cybermalls you can search to determine if any are appropriate for your company.

Cybermall Categories

Cybermalls are often categorized by the type of stores they host or by their target market. Three common ways of organizing a cybermall are by the type of product or service its stores provide, which geographical region they are located in, or the demographic that they are targeting.

Product- or Service-Specific Cybermalls

All of the tenants of a product-specific or service-specific cybermall would be in a related industry and would provide similar types of products. These types of cybermalls are of interest to the same target market. A model-airplane cybermall would consist of a number of merchants all providing products or services related to model airplanes. Other cybermalls that would fit into this category would be computer software cybermalls, electronics cybermalls, environmentally friendly products cybermalls, and vacation cybermalls.

Geographic-Specific Cybermalls

All of the tenants of a geographic-specific cybermall would be located in the same geographic region. Many of these cybermalls are provided by an Internet service provider (ISP) for its clients. Building name recognition with the local customer base, advertising and cross-promotion, and providing easy access through a variety of means for the customer are reasons for participation in these types of malls. (See Figure 17.1)

Demographic-Specific Cybermalls

Often a demographic-specific cybermall will have tenants that provide a variety of unrelated products and services. These tenants should still have a common theme that focuses on the same target market. A children's cybermall that has vendors providing everything from clothing to books to gifts to toys would be a good example of this type of cybermall. A seniors' cybermall could include a wide range of very different products and services of interest to that demographic group.

Selecting the Right Cybermall

You should have an established criteria and evaluation process that you use to determine which cybermall you want to be linked with. It can be tricky to choose a successful mall, but the following guidelines will help you to make the right decision.

The cybermall merchant should have high-speed access with a connection through T1 or ISDN lines. The cybermall's server should be reliable and state-of-the-art and should have lots of capacity to handle the anticipated volume. There should be technicians available to provide technical support and quickly resolve any problems that

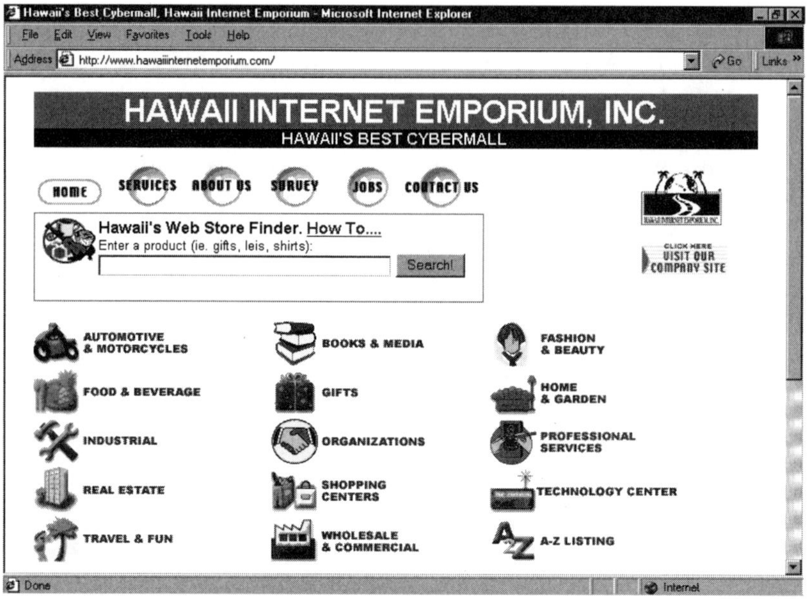

Figure 17.1. A dynamite example of a geographic specific cybermall.

occur. If access is slow, visitors will not wait. A good cybermall should have a high-quality, attractive home page with consistent navigation throughout the site. The mall you choose should also have a logical and easy-to-remember domain name.

There are a number of other things to keep in mind when choosing a cybermall. Before choosing a mall, make sure that your business fits within one of the categories in the mall. Don't join a mall that is targeting a different demographic group from yours. Both online and offline promotion are important, and you should make sure the mall you choose implements its marketing strategy actively. The cybermall owner should be able to provide you with details of their Internet marketing strategy to increase the traffic of their targeted market to their site. Many malls indicate that they promote extensively, but you need to ensure that they are actually targeting shoppers, *not merchants*. You will want to obtain details on mall traffic and the number of unique visitors to the home page of the mall, if possible. Any other count of hits may include hits to the pages of merchants in the mall, which would be misleading. Many progressive malls now provide their tenants with access to their Web traffic analysis reports. Talk with other merchants operating in the mall about their traffic, as well as their experience with the mall itself (fee increases, hidden costs, server downtime, etc.). Many cybermalls will also provide a site search capability to assist shoppers with finding the items they are looking for.

Successful Web sites must be updated on a continual basis. Ensure that the mall provides software tools to make it easy for you to maintain your own site or, if the mall provides the updates, that its fees regarding changes are not too expensive. You will also want to verify that the mall has a secure server that allows you to offer secure credit card sales transactions. Most consumers will not purchase online without it. If you are a small business and cannot accept credit card orders online, you will want to find a mall that provides a credit card merchant account. Some malls will also charge a commission on every sale made on your site. Check the details on all commissions, transaction fees, and other charges. If the mall is responsible for all the traffic to your site, it should be compensated for this activity either through your monthly rental charge or via a commission on sales. If you are making an effort to promote your site yourself and the traffic to your site is the result of your marketing efforts, it is unreasonable for the mall to expect to be compensated for each transaction on your site. Finally, research the mall's history and reputation and find out how long the mall has been in existence. Talk to existing and former tenants about their experiences.

More Than One Cybermall?

If you have a link from the storefront in the mall to your site and are only paying a monthly fee, you might want to consider joining more than one cybermall. If you decide to join a number of malls, you should have some way of tracking the traffic to your site so you can determine which sites are more effective. This can be accomplished quite easily these days with all the Web traffic analysis tools that are available. See Chapter 28 for a full discussion of Web traffic analysis.

What Will It Cost to Participate?

There are a variety of ways that malls can charge their tenants. A mall that hosts one page as a storefront and gives a link from that storefront to your site on a different server from the cybermall generally will charge a flat fee each month. If your Web site is hosted by the cybermall, you may be charged on a flat-fee basis or your charge may be a basic fee with add-ons. You may also be charged on a commission-on-sales basis. The variable charges are generally either on a commission or on a set-fee-per-transaction basis.

Cybermall charges can be anywhere from $25 a month to simply be linked to their storefront to over $1,000 a month, which includes services and a number of features provided by the host.

Where Are Cybermalls Found?

A number of these meta-indexes of cybermalls can be found online. There are cybermall Web rings that can be researched and also cybermalls of cybermalls. There are many locations and sites listed at in this chapter to assist you in finding the appropriate cybermall for your business.

Internet Resources for This Chapter

The Hall of Malls
http://nsns.com/MouseTracks/HallofMalls.html
The most comprehensive listing of all known online malls located on the Net.

The Cybermall.com Directory
http://www.cybermall.com
Evaluation of hundreds of online malls and selection of only what they determine are the very best. Malls cannot purchase a listing on this site (unlike other directories) and are selected exclusively because they provide you with a positive home shopping experience. You get access to the better shopping malls without fighting through hundreds of them. Their categorical listings include brief site reviews to help you find the quality shopping sites you want without all the work.

Malls.com
http://malls.com
Besides providing a range of products and services from their mall, Malls.com provides a huge meta-index of all the malls on the Net at

http://malls.com/metalist.html. This list is a great starting point when doing your cybermall research.

eMall
http://www.emall.com
This is a great location for organic and natural foods. They have a complete health online store, a spice merchant section with the flavors of Asia, fine teas, and sun-roasted Mexican coffees.

ShopNow Market
http://www.internet-mall.com
ShopNow Market's Merchandising Program gives you two key components to successful online marketing: strategic positioning and targeted, focused traffic generation programs. You'll benefit from their partnerships with high-traffic sites such as Yahoo! and PC World as well as from an aggressive advertising and marketing campaign designed to drive hordes of shoppers to this portal—and to your business.

Access Market Square
http://www.icw.com/mall.html
Access Market Square has an "occasion" (birthday, anniversary, etc.) reminder service that also provides personalized gift ideas. They also have a great search engine that allows you to enter names of items, brand names, product types, or store names. The site provides a wide variety of products by category including art, audio-video, automotive, books, clothes, computers, electronics, flowers, food, health, jewelry, music, sports, travel, and others. Access Market Square uses VeriSign for secure ordering capabilities.

iMall
http://www.imall.com
This is an electronic commerce enabler of small and medium-sized businesses that allows them to cost-effectively engage in electronic commerce through the use of iMall's proprietary e-commerce tools and services. iMall offers its electronic commerce services directly to merchants, as well as through partnerships with leading ISPs, Web hosting firms, and financial service companies with an Internet focus. The company professes to operate the largest shopping mall on the Internet, with more than 1,600 hosted storefronts, and millions of visitors monthly.

18

Submitting Your Site to the Search Engines and Directories

A recent study by Forrester Research stated that Internet consumers find Web sites by using search engines 81 percent of the time, making search engines and related search tools a valuable part of achieving success online. There are a variety of search tools (search engines, directories, spiders, etc.) currently used to navigate the World Wide Web; however, you never know exactly what search tool your target market is using. It is for this reason that it is very important for your site to be listed with as many of these search tools as possible. The reality of this information is that not only do you have to be listed in as many search engines and directories as possible, you also have to work hard to achieve rankings within or as close to the top ten results as possible. People rarely venture beyond the first two or three pages of search results. Getting this top ranking is no easy feat, and to do so your search engine submission strategy will have to be timely and well disciplined

Understanding Search Engines and Directories

Search engines are known for their enormous databases of indexed Web sites. A couple of the leading search engines have over 500 million Web pages indexed. Google currently claims that it has the largest index, with over 1 billion indexed pages! Open Directory, Yahoo!, and LookSmart are popular directories, and each has approximately 2 million indexed Web pages.

A search engine will usually have a page on its site where you can add your site to the database by submitting your URL or Internet address. The search engine then goes to the page submitted and grabs the appropriate information it needs to index your site. Another method search engines use to index pages from a site is through the use of "spiders" and "crawlers," which constantly scour the Web in search of pages to add to their index. The number of individual pages on the Web today makes it practically impossible for them to keep up. Be proactive and submit your site or you may never get indexed. Sometimes a search engine will not send its "spider" to your site until a page has been manually submitted to it. The design of a site significantly impacts how a search engine will index it. For in-depth coverage on how the design of a site influences the search engines, refer to Chapter 14.

Directories have a number of unique qualities that differentiate them from their close cousin, the search engine. Directories typically require you to provide more information when submitting your site. When submitting a page or a site, you will have to provide extensive information on your company and the page you're submitting. This is covered in greater depth later in the chapter. Maintaining and indexing sites usually falls upon human administrators who review the submissions, add appropriate sites to their respective categories, and filter out invalid submissions. Some people prefer to use directories for their searches because although their log of sites is smaller they claim that they find the information contained within to be more accurate.

Search Engines and Spiders

Don't know if you're submitting to a directory or a search engine? The submission process and the information requested will usually give a big hint. When you're submitting to a search engine, you commonly will be asked for just your URL and sometimes your email address. It is important to remember that each page of your site has a unique URL. Some search engines will allow you to submit more than one page from your site, whereas others will not. Review the help section of the respective search engine and make sure you understand the submission policies.

Some search engines use spiders to index a site. Some spiders constantly crawl the Web in search of sites to add to their index, whereas others will not visit your site until you tell the spider your site exists through the submission process. When a spider visits your site, it will usually visit each page on your site and index relevant pages, but sometimes it can't for a number of reasons. There may be problems with frames or image maps on a Web site, or the spider may simply miss a page, and so on. Even though a number of spiders constantly crawl the Web looking for sites, I suggest you submit all appropriate pages on your site to the search engines to guarantee that all your important pages are properly listed. Again, you should check the search engine's submission document to ensure that multiple submissions are permitted. All chances that your site may be rejected from a search engine's index should be avoided.

Some of the search engines share or license technology; for example, MSN Search uses Inktomi's technology for some of its results. However, all search engines have different ranking criteria to determine who gets top placement, and you must take this into consideration. Some search engines reference how often a particular keyword appears on a Web page in determining a page's ranking. It is assumed that if a keyword is used more frequently on a page, then that page is more relevant than other pages with a lower usage of that keyword. Some search engines look for the keyword in the title of the Web page and assume that if the keyword is in the title, then that page must be more relevant than those that don't have the keyword in their title. Keywords in page titles are one of the most influential components of many search engine algorithms. Likewise, actual page content can play a large role. Some search engines determine where keywords are used and assume that pages with the keyword in headings and in the first couple of paragraphs are more relevant. Many of the major search engines are now using link popularity as part of their ranking criteria. No two search engines rank sites in exactly the same way, however. For example, you will find that some search engines use information contained in meta-tags, although others don't look at the meta-tags at all.

Getting In-depth with Directories

Directory submissions usually ask for much more information on their submission forms than do search engines. Among the information requested, you will usually need to provide your URL, the category you wish to be added to, the title of your site, a description, and your contact information. Some directories will automatically place your Web site in their index, whereas other directory submissions are moderated by human administrators who will add only those sites that meet their criteria. Since the information that you are submitting may be reviewed by a moderator, it is very important that you prepare an enticing description for your site. This will encourage the moderator to add your site to the directory's index.

When submitting to a directory that is maintained by a human administrator, you can expect to wait a longer period of time before seeing your page appear in the index. In general you can expect to wait between two and eight weeks. It takes longer because the human administrators review every page submitted before adding it to their database. Make sure your page is easy to use, visually appealing, and rich in content because it is the administrators who decide if your page is worthwhile before they include it. Unlike with a search engine, your site's position in directories relies much less on Web site design and more on the initial submission process itself, which is why it is important to review each directory's submission procedure and submission tips.

When you submit to a directory, you will also have to take the time to find the best category for your site. Many directories have top-level categories and subcategories. A top-level category would be something like "Recreation and Sports." Within this top-level category you would have subcategories such as "Travel," "Games," and "Hobbies." Each of these subcategories will likely have additional categories. The deeper you go, the more concentrated the information becomes. Submitting your site to the wrong category could mean a minimal increase in traffic if no one thinks to look for you in the category you submitted to. Also, your site may not be added if you select an inappropriate category.

The Submission Process

When submitting to the search engines and directories, take the time up front to develop the submission material carefully. Organize the information in a logical order in a text file. Then, when you submit, you will be able to copy and paste the content to the appropriate fields on the submission form. Be sure to spell check, check, and recheck everything before you start. The information prepared for each page on the site to be indexed should include:

- URL
- Page title
- Ten-word, 25-word, 50-word, and 100-word descriptions for the page (Different search engines and directories allow different lengths of description.)
- List of keywords for each page
- Description of the ideal audience for the site
- Contact information:
  - Your company's name
  - Contact name
  - E-mail address
  - Your operation's address
  - Telephone and fax numbers

When preparing to submit to different search engines and directories, you should print the submission forms and examine them to determine that you have all the information required for submission. This will not only help you be more prepared for the submission, but it will also help you to become more familiar with that particular directory. Be sure to read the FAQs or instructions first to ensure that you understand exactly what information they are requesting. Figures 18.1 and 18.2 depict AltaVista's and Yahoo!'s submission pages, respectively.

When submitting your Web site to directories, be very careful to fill in every field on the form. Some of the search engines will reject your registration automatically if you have not filled in all the blanks.

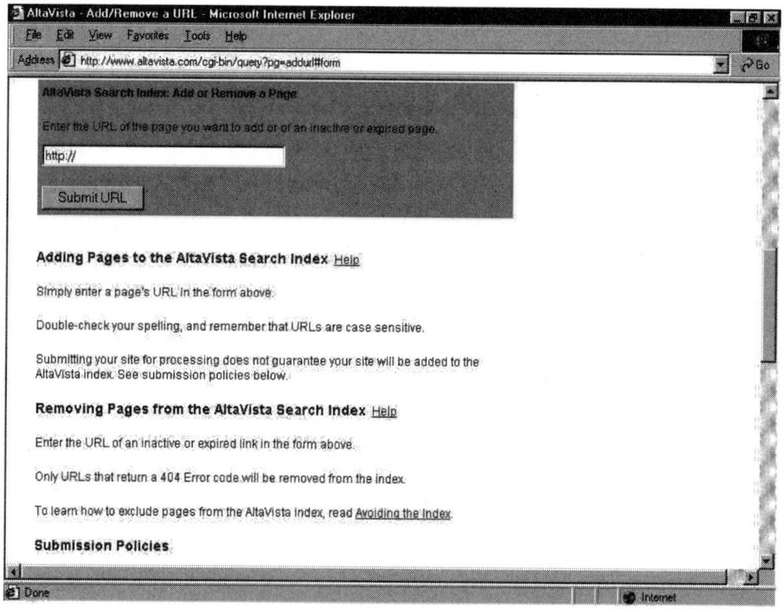

Figure 18.1. Simply enter your Web site's URL to be indexed by AltaVista.

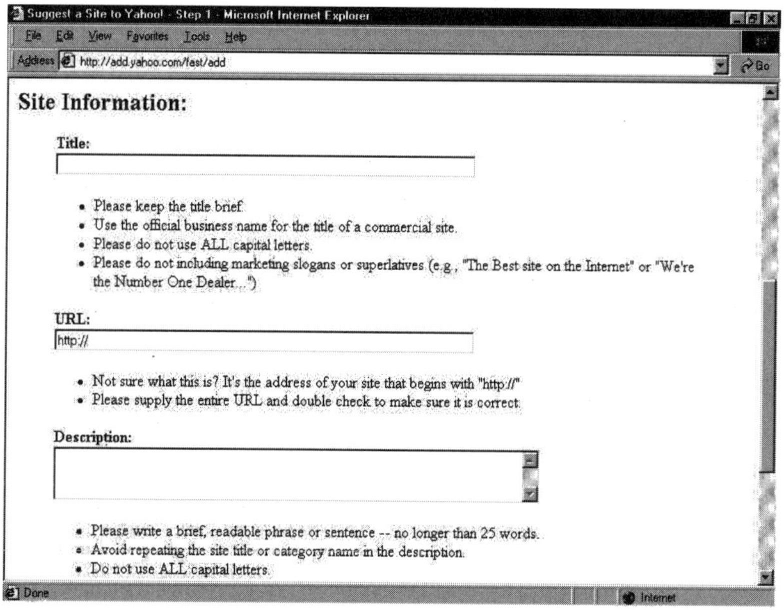

Figure 18.2. Yahoo! requires you to enter detailed information during the submission process.

When selecting the category for your site, do so carefully. It would be a shame to have a great product, at a great price, and a great site, but end up listed in a place where your potential customer would never think about looking for you.

You should always proofread your submission at least twice before you hit the submit button. Since it is hard to control the submission process after you hit "submit," it is vital that your information be effective and accurate. Your listing may be wrong for quite a while before it gets corrected.

When submitting to any search engine or directory, it is important to keep track of where and when you submitted your URL. Many search engines and directories have strict spam policies, which if not followed could hinder your chances of ever being listed in the search engine or directory. It can take anywhere from two days to ten weeks to receive listings in a particular search engine or directory. To avoid spamming the search engines and directories, you should wait a determined length of time before resubmitting. You can also check to see if your site was indexed in the engines. For example, to you want to see if your URL or Web address is indexed by AltaVista or Infoseek/Go, you can enter "*url:yourdomain.com/directory/page.html*" in the search field of each search engine. Check out the help files for each search engine for more information on how to verify that your URL is included in the index.

It Doesn't Always Come for Free

Some search engines and directories are adopting various pay-for inclusion or submission policies. There are a couple general variations you should be aware of:

- Pay-per-click
- Paid inclusion
- Paid submission

The basic concept behind a pay-per-click search engine is that you bid for placement based on a specific keyword or keyword phrase. Every time someone clicks on your link and visits your site, you are charged the amount you have bid. If someone in your industry is paying $1.00 for a certain keyword and has the top ranking site, in theory you could bid $1.01 to overtake the number one position. Of course, if the second most popular site is only paying ten cents for that position, it may be more cost effective for you to target the position depending on your objectives, budget, and the amount of emphasis you want to focus on any given search engine.

Goto.com is the most well known example of a pay-per-click search engine. An important fact to note here is that search engines often reference other search engines for some of their results. Goto.com's listings appear in some form on AltaVista, AskJeeves, NBCi, and Netscape Search, with others on the horizon.

SearchEngineWatch.com has a useful table on its site that provides an overview of information relating to the scope of paid processes used by a number of the leading search tools. I recommend you visit their site at *http://www.searchenginewatch.com/resources/paid-listings.html* for more details.

A paid inclusion search engine or directory does not guarantee you a high-ranking position within a particular search tool; it simply means your site will be indexed assuming that your site conforms to the search tool's submission guidelines and that you will likely have a greater chance of appearing in the search results. Paid inclusion is used by such search tools as AskJeeves, LookSmart, and Inktomi. Details on their specific programs can be found on their respective sites. The "submit a site" section of LookSmart's directory can be seen in Figure 18.3.

Search tools that offer paid submissions as a service make no guarantees other than that your site will be reviewed for inclusion in that particular directory. Yahoo! offers a business express submission service to its users. On the site it clearly states that:

> *Payment* ***does not guarantee inclusion in the directory,*** *site placement, or site commentary. It only guarantees that Yahoo! will respond to your submission within seven business days.*

The key benefit of this type of program is that your site will be reviewed sooner rather than later. It can take months for some search engines and directories to review a site and either index it or reject it.

Purchasing advertising on the most popular search engines and directories will also get you in front of your target audience. Many search tools offer advertising based on targeted keyword buys or sponsorships. Google's new advertising program called AdWords, shown in Figure 18.4, is one such example.

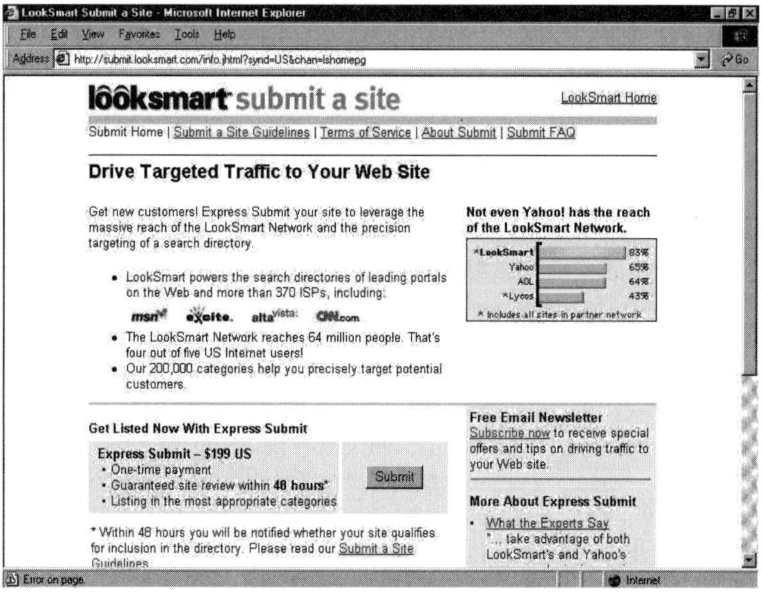

Figure 18.3. LookSmart's "submit a site" section.

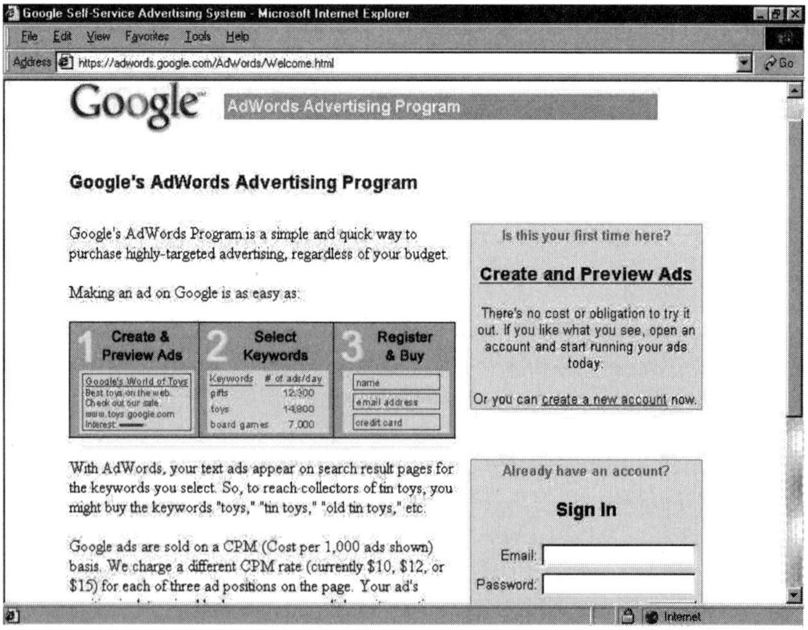

Figure 18.4. Google's AdWords advertising program.

Internet Resources for this Chapter

PayPerClickSearchEngines.com
http://www.payperclicksearchengines.com/
A listing of pay-per-click search engines.

WebReference.com
http://www.Webreference.com/content/search
Search engines and examples, tips, and hints for getting the most out of your search engine—designed for people who work on the Web.

JimTools.com Webmaster's Toolkit Command Center
http://www.jimtools.com/
A number of tools are available on this site that you can use for free. There's information on the search engines, meta-tags, link checker, and a link popularity tool.

Search Engine Matrix
http://searchenginematrix.com/
Learn about search engines and search engine positioning to achieve greater positioning within any given search engine.

Search Engine Chart
http://www.advance-training.co.uk/free/chart.htm

Search Engine Features for Webmasters
http://www.searchenginewatch.com/webmasters/features.html

Comparison of Search Capabilities of Six Major Search Engines
http://www.cyward.com/chart1.htm

AltaVista
http://www.altavista.com/

AOL.COM Search
http://search.aol.com/

Direct Hit
http://www.directhit.com/

Excite
http://www.excite.com/

FAST Search
http://www.alltheweb.com/

Google
http://www.google.com/

Goto
http://www.goto.com/

HotBot
http://www.hotbot.com/

Inktomi
http://www.inktomi.com/

Iwon
http://www.iwon.com/

LookSmart
http://www.looksmart.com/

MSN Search
http://search.msn.com/

NBCi
http://www.nbci.com/

Netscape Search
http://search.netscape.com/

Northern Light
http://www.northernlight.com/

Open Directory
http://www/dmoz/org/

Raging Search
http://www.raging.com/

WebCrawler
http://www.webcrawler.com/

Yahoo!
http://www.yahoo.com/

19

Use Effective E-mail Marketing

E-mail is now a widely accessible and generally accepted form of communication. Because of this, e-mail is rapidly becoming one of the most crucial forms of communication with clients, potential customers, suppliers, and colleagues. CyberAtlas (*http://cyberatlas.internet.com*) reported that there are enough active e-mail addresses for everyone in North America to have his own account. E-mail is an extremely efficient way to build and maintain relationships in the online community. As a marketing tool, e-mail lets you maintain an ongoing dialogue with your audience in a very cost-effective way.

Getting Connected with E-mail

E-mail is a communication medium and, as with all forms of communication, *you do not get a second chance to leave a first impression.* People receive large amounts of e-mail each day, and the following tips will help to ensure that your e-mail is taken seriously.

Maybe the greatest benefit of e-mail is the speed with which you can communicate. E-mail takes seconds rather than weeks to send a message around the world, yet the costs are negligible compared to making a long-distance phone call or sending a fax. The ability to reach millions of people across the globe simultaneously with one e-mail message is also a unique feature of e-mail. This type of mass mailing is done at a fraction of the cost, a fraction of the time, and a fraction of the internal resources it would take with "snail mail." With an autoresponder, information can automatically be sent to customers and potential customers at any time to respond to online requests.

How to Write Effective E-mail Messages

Most people who use e-mail receive lots of messages everyday including their share of junk e-mail. The following tips will increase the likelihood that your message will get prioritized.

The Importance of Your E-mail Subject Line

The subject line is equivalent to a headline in a newspaper in terms of attracting a reader's attention. Only the most interesting headlines get read, so you must make your subject grab the reader's attention. Some people receive more than 100 e-mails a day and cannot possibly read every one. They will choose which ones to read by looking at the subject. People who receive fewer than 20 e-mails a day may have the time to read every message and therefore may not realize the importance of the subject line. You must be aware that just because you can read all of the e-mails you receive, many people do not have the time. The subject line can make the difference between your message's getting read or being deleted.

You should never send an e-mail message without a subject line. The subject line of the e-mails you receive determines which e-mails are read first if at all. Subject lines should be brief, with the keywords appearing first. The longer the subject line, the more likely it will not be completely seen.

Effective subject lines will:

- Be brief but capture interest

- Use action words
- Stress the most important benefits
- Use the keywords first

Effective headlines should grab the reader's attention, making them want to read the rest of your message. Remember to avoid using CAPITALS in your subject since this is the same as SHOUTING AT THE READER! Don't do it!!

To and From Headings in E-mail

By using personal names in the *To* and *From* headings, you create a more personal relationship. Most e-mail programs allow you to attach personal names to e-mail addresses. The help file of your e-mail program will show you how to do this.

Blind Carbon Copy (BCC)

Have you ever received an e-mail message in which the first screen was a string of other people's e-mail addresses to which the message had been sent? Didn't you feel special? This sort of bulk mailing is very impersonalized, and most often recipients will delete the message before looking at it.

You should use the BCC feature when sending bulk or group e-mails so that every person on the list will not see that the message was sent to many recipients. Make sure that you know how to use this function in your e-mail program by doing a test with a number of your colleagues and friends. Make sure you are using the program and features effectively and that all of their addresses do not appear by mistake in each message.

Even more effective than blind carbon copy is using a software application designed to personalize messages to each recipient in your database. E-mail applications like this are far more flexible than the BCC method because there is no limitation on the number of messages you can send, and the field merge capabilities enable you to create a more personalized message.

E-mail Message Formatting

The content of an e-mail message should be focused on one topic. It is better to send a separate message if you need to change the subject in the middle of a message. If you wish to discuss more than one topic, begin your message stating "I have three questions" or "There are four issues I would like to discuss." People read their e-mail quickly and expect you to cover your main points at the beginning of your message.

Similar to writing a business letter, it is important to use correct spelling and grammar in your e-mail. This includes the proper use of upper- and lowercase lettering, which many people seem to ignore when sending e-mail. However, e-mail differs from a business letter in that the tone is very different. The *tone* of e-mail is more relaxed and similar to a polite conversation, which makes it ideal for building relationships.

In general, you should keep your paragraphs short and to the point. Make sure you make your point in the first paragraph and give your readers a call to action. Do not use fancy formatting since many e-mail programs cannot display these features. E-mail is a permanent record, so you will want to double-check for any spelling and grammatical errors as well as improper word use.

Appropriate E-mail Reply Tips

When replying, do not include the entire original message. This is unnecessary and aggravates the original sender because the message takes much longer to download. However, to refresh the recipient's memory, you should include parts of the original message. You will inevitably be asked a number of the same questions repeatedly, so it may be best to create a library of responses to FAQs. This will save you a lot of time since you will be able to copy and paste these answers into e-mail responses. Also remember to double-check the *To* and *CC* lines before you reply. You do not want your response to be sent to an entire mail list.

Signature Files

A signature file is also known as your e-Business card. Your e-Business card should include your company's name, address, and phone and fax numbers, your e-mail address, and your URL. Your signature file is a great marketing tool and should be attached at the end of all your online communication. Also, ensure that the signature files are appropriate for the intended audience.

Proper Use of Attachments

If you need to send a large volume of data, you might decide to send it as an attached file to your e-mail message. However, do not send messages with attachments unless you have the recipient's permission. Also be aware of the file size you are attaching so that you don't send unsolicited attachments that are larger than 50K. The person who is receiving the e-mails may have an old modem that takes two hours to download what took two minutes for you to send.

It is also important to realize when sending an unsolicited attachment that the recipient may have software that is not compatible with the program you used to developed your attachment. A Microsoft Word 2000 document sent as an attachment to someone using a Macintosh with Corel WordPerfect installed will not be able to be read.

As a general rule, avoid sending e-mail attachments unless you have the recipient's permission. When you do send attachments, be aware of how large the file is and whether it is compatible with the recipient's software.

An alternative to sending a large attachment is to post the file on a Web server and direct users via your e-mail to a URL where they can download the file.

Before You Click on Send

Before you send an important message, there are a number of things you should do. You should send a test message to yourself or a colleague so you can confirm the word wrap looks good and that you have properly formatted the text. Also check that there are no typos, errors, or omissions.

Using Automated Mail Responders

Automated mail responders send requested information via e-mail automatically to the person that made the request. Autoresponder services may be available through your Internet service provider (ISP).

Alternatively, you can find a third-party provider by doing a search on "mailbots" or "autoresponders."

Information on your company, your products, your services, and your marketing materials can be easily accessible 24 hours a day, 7 days a week, 365 days a year through mailbots. Through this service you can easily provide information such as:

- Catalogue and price lists
- Brochures
- Reviews and testimonials
- Press releases
- Newsletters
- Annual reports
- Award announcements
- Sample reports

This type of information should also be placed on your Web site. By using an autoresponder to promote these items, you can obtain customer data prior to providing the customers with the information they are requesting from you. Ask them for their e-mail address, mailing address, phone number, and answers to any marketing-related questions you may have. You can use this information for targeting individuals in a future e-mail marketing campaign.

Autoresponders can also be used to personalize, build relationships, and provide outstanding customer service. Even if you are out of the office, you may set an autoresponder to deliver a personal note to let people know that you will get back to them as soon as possible. Clearly, it would be best to respond immediately, but if you are indisposed, an "out of office" message shows outstanding customer service. You are letting your customers know that they are important to you even though you are unavailable.

Autoresponders provide an excellent means of promoting your company. Each time someone sends you a request for information, include a short marketing blurb in the autoresponder that includes the requested information.

E-mail "Netiquette"

When writing e-mails, there are a number of things to keep in mind. Remember to be courteous and remember your pleases and thank-you's. You should reply within 24 hours and be brief. Before you send any e-mail, be sure to check both your grammar and spelling. Finally, do not send unsolicited bulk e-mail and avoid sending attachments.

HTML or Text Messages?

E-mail messages are commonly sent and encoded as regular ASCII text. However, HTML mail is steadily making inroads into the e-mail world. The benefit of sending an HTML-formatted message is that you can send a message that acts and appears like a Web page. It's like a colorful brochure and is much more attractive than a plain ASCII text message. The drawback of using HTML mail is that there are a lot of e-mail clients that cannot properly decode the HTML. Thus, the message is converted to ASCII, loses its formatting, and looks very unattractive. The recipients of these messages will likely delete them.

One example of an HTML message would be a line of hyperlink text such as "Click here to visit our Web site." To ensure that URLs you insert in an e-mail message always display as hyperlink text, simply type the full URLs into your message. For instance, type:

> *"Click on the link below to visit Connex Network:* http://*www.connexnetwork.com"*

If you want to use HTML formatting in your e-mail correspondence, ask your recipients which type of message they prefer. Send HTML formatted messages only to the people who prefer it and ASCII messages to the rest of your recipients.

Some e-mail software packages can send both an HTML and an ASCII text version of an e-mail at once. If your software has this capability, then you can send either type of message without any concern.

Internet Resources for This Chapter

Everything E-mail
http://everythingemail.net/
Information and links to make your e-mail account more productive and fun! Resources, guides, and a glossary make things easier for you to understand. This is an extensive Web site dedicated exclusively to e-mail and e-mail services.

123 Promote
http://www.123promote.com/workbook/plan1.htm
This site is an e-mail guide to e-mail styles, mail merging, auto responders, auto reminders, netiquette, headers, signature files, announcements, press releases, business administration, free designs, mailing list announcements, newsgroup announcements, office automation, mass e-mailing, publicity, form letters, form folders, e-mailed databases, programs, and software.

A Beginner's Guide to Effective E-mail
http://www.webfoot.com/advice/email.top.html
Here's where to get the help in writing the e-mail you need. Formats and why you need e-mail are explained in detail.

Neophyte's Guide to Effective E-mail
http://www.webnovice.com/email.htm
This site goes through, step by step, the important issues you should keep in mind from start to send.

Internet Marketing Newsletter
http://www.arrowweb.com/graphics/news/ap12.html

E-mailAddresses.com
http://www.emailaddresses.com
A directory of numerous free e-mail services including POP accounts, e-mail forwarding, newsletters, and so forth.

CyberAtlas
http://cyberatlas.internet.com
CyberAtlas is your guide to online facts. The site provides readers with valuable statistics and Web marketing information, enabling them

to understand their business environment and make more informed business decisions.

E-mail: The Mining Company
http://email.miningco.com/internet/email/
Updated weekly, this site consists of articles and links to e-mail resources on many topics: beginning e-mail, finding people, free e-mail, greeting cards, privacy, and much more.

20

Reaching Out with Mail Lists

Internet mailing lists have become one of the top online marketing tools. The number of mail lists available on the Internet is growing constantly. Many mail lists are free, whereas others involve a fee. Purchasing or simply downloading previously developed mail lists is a good way to start using e-mail marketing as a part of your online marketing strategy; however, there are some factors to watch out for when using public lists, which this chapter will outline for you.

Connecting with Your Target Audience

The potential of e-mail marketing can only grow in effectiveness. The Internet expands each time a new user goes online, and communication technology continues to simplify the process of mass e-mail marketing pursuits. Mail lists hold the advantages of direct mail marketing campaigns while making the entire process faster, more interactive, and highly targeted.

Avoid the "bulk e-mail" marketing blunder. Publicly accessible bulk e-mail lists have been developed by unsavory means. Most of the addresses on the bulk lists are useless because they are duds or full of people with no desire to receive unsolicited e-mail. Unsolicited bulk e-mail is the single largest form of e-mail abuse.

Administering masses of contact information involves a superior level of professionalism, organization, and responsibility. You want to avoid being accused of spamming at all costs. The definition of "spam" is evolving as mail list marketing matures. It used to mean sending an unnecessary and huge amount of e-mails to an e-mail address. Now a "spam" is any e-mail that a person receives from a mail list that she did not subscribe to or opt in to. In this age of information overload, users need to protect themselves from unsolicited direct advertising. You have several types of publicly accessible lists to pick from. These types are outlined in the next section.

Types of Mail Lists

Discussion Mailing Lists

Discussion mailing lists are quick and easy ways to distribute information to a large number of people interested in a common subject. Everyone on a discussion list receives all messages posted directly to her e-mail inbox.

Discussion mailing lists are publicly available and focus on a particular subject matter. Participating in discussion lists relevant to your line of business can help you attract new customers. People subscribe to receive all of the postings that are sent to the group, generally because they have an interest in the topic. When you post a message to a mailing list, the message is sent out to everyone who has subscribed to the list by e-mail.

Moderated Discussion Lists

This type of list is maintained by a "gatekeeper" who filters out unwanted or inappropriate messages. The gatekeeper's job is to stop users from posting advertisements that are not permitted. Similarly, he screens the list for flames (i.e., publicly chastising another list member). The gatekeeper will also keep the topic of discussion on track when members stray.

Unmoderated Discussion Lists

An unmoderated list is operated without any centralized control or censorship. Most lists are of this type. All messages are automatically forwarded to subscribers. Unmoderated lists tend to have more blatant advertisements and flame wars since there is no gatekeeper to guide the discussion. It is then the responsibility of the list members to police their own actions. Otherwise, the list could end up being a landfill for spammers. Members will simply leave the list if a few individuals spoil the productive aspects of the discussion.

Targeting Appropriate Discussion Mailing Lists

There are many publicly available lists on the net. These sites provide lists of mailing lists. Three of the most popular and comprehensive are:

- The Liszt (*http://www.liszt.com*)
- The List of Publicly Accessible Mailing Lists (*http://paml.net/*)
- Mail Utilities (*http://www.mailutilities.com/*)

There are also companies online that specialize in providing targeted e-mail lists. One such company is Post Master Direct Response at *www.postmasterdirect.com*. This company rents e-mail lists of people who have requested information on a particular topic. However, these are different from the discussion mailing lists that we described earlier in this chapter. E-mail lists are simply that—lists of e-mail addresses. If you subscribe to one of these lists, you are not entering into a discussion. You are placing yourself on a mailing list that will receive e-mail advertisements. However, from a marketing perspective, e-mail lists can be useful tools if they are targeted.

The best way to tackle e-mail marketing is to find a list whose subscribers fit your target market as closely as possible. Be careful to abide by the rules of the list. If advertising isn't allowed, then don't advertise. There is a good chance that sending bulk advertising e-mail will annoy many unknown potential customers. These mistakes have been known to destroy corporate image, and they may potentially damage your professional credibility. In light of this, a targeted list should be used to get a much higher quality response rate. Less is more in this case.

Finding the Right Mailing List

Whether you join a publicly accessible discussion mailing list or choose to purchase or rent an opt-in e-mail list, you want to find a mailing list whose members are your target market. You will have to do your homework here, so be patient and thorough during the setup process.

There are various meta-indexes and directories of publicly available mailing lists where you can search by title or subject. Some of these sites provide detailed information on the mail lists, such as their content and the commands used to subscribe. We have provided information on a number of these resources in the Internet Resources section at the end of this chapter.

Subscribing to Your Target Mailing Lists

The Liszt, *title.net/lists,* and the Internet Publicly Accessible Mailing Lists are great resources and will provide you with not only a huge list of accessible mailing lists but also specific instructions for joining the particular lists you are interested in. Most lists are subscribed to by sending an e-mail to the given address with "subscribe" in the subject or the body of the message. There are variations on this theme, so you must check the instructions for joining each specific mailing list. After you subscribe, you generally will receive an e-mail response with the rules, FAQs, and instructions on how to use the list.

Composing Effective E-mail Messages

If you follow these tips on mailing list behavior and composing e-mail messages, you will be regarded as a responsible member of the online world:

- Your e-mails must be carefully prepared before you post to a mailing list. Remember to make your subject line relevant, keep your messages short and to the point, and include a signature file (sig.file) in all messages.

- Avoid repeating the same or similar messages to the same mailing list.
- Your messages should remain "on the subject." List subscribers don't want to read information unrelated to the specified topic.
- Before making any commercial announcement, you should be a regular contributor to your list. If your mailing list does not allow advertising (most do not), use your sig. file. Sig.files are generally accepted. Ensure that you make effective use of your tag line to get your mini-ad into discussion mailing lists where blatant advertising is not permitted.
- Track your replies when you use a new mailing list. Your messages should have a "call to action" that encourages the reader to visit a specific page on your site or to send e-mail to an e-mail address created specifically to gather the replies from a particular list. By implementing the appropriate mechanism to track responses, you will know which mailing lists are working for you. It's amazing how well calls to action work. For some reason, people tend to do what they're told.
- Set reasonable and achievable goals. As a benchmark, in most e-mail marketing campaigns a 1 to 3 percent response rate is considered good. However, if your mailing list is very targeted, and you are offering something of interest or value to a particular group, your response rates should be significantly higher.

Starting Your Own Private Mail List

Generating your own mailing lists is highly recommended because of the many marketing uses a targeted opt-in list has. The list can be used to maintain an ongoing dialog with existing customers and potential customers regarding updates, support, specials, and so on. It can also be used to communicate with current and prospective customers through distribution of corporate newsletters, price lists, new catalogues, product updates, new product announcements, and upcoming events.

You can use a number of methods for soliciting and collecting e-mail addresses, including an online guestbook or other type of registration form to be filled out on your Web site. However, you must provide people with an incentive to leave their e-mail address with you.

Place a form with a "subscribe here" button on your site where visitors can sign up for the mailing list. Terminology such as "Sign up now to receive our free newsletter" or "Click here to receive our reliable information newsletter" can be useful in convincing people to subscribe. Having people register for your mailing list by offering an informative newsletter is a great way to stay in touch with your target market. If you offer valuable information and deals that your customers and potential customers want, they will gladly give you their e-mail address to obtain your newsletter.

A useful example of this would be Dr. Ralph F. Wilson, director of the popular Internet Marketing resource site for small to medium-sized online businesses located at *www.wilsonweb.com*. The site has a robust e-zine full of focused content; it believes in passing on its knowledge. Since the site began in July 1995, it has consistently offered the Internet community a newsletter called "Web Marketing Today" and also offers a "Web Marketing Info Center." In the past five years of operation, Wilson's site has received awards and excellent reviews as well as the friendship of thousands of subscribers, clients, and contacts all over the world.

The formation of strategic alliances with noncompeting businesses sharing your target market is a great idea. Together you can produce e-mail marketing campaigns that offer potential customers so many deals that it's tough to pass up. When industry partnerships are created, they should be reflected clearly in your e-mail promotion by offering low-cost freebie incentives, discounts, special sales, and timely announcements. Your mail list subscriptions will grow exponentially because people find it hard to keep sweet deals to themselves.

Encourage customers and potential customers to subscribe to your electronic newsletter through traditional marketing techniques including press releases, offline newsletters, advertising, letters, and so on.

If you use hardcopy direct mail, you can design a response system that requests the e-mail addresses through a fax-back, business reply card, or 1-800 number or by asking respondents to go to your Web site or e-mail you directly. You can also ask people to sign up for your mailing list through newsgroup and mailing list postings, signature files, and other advertising.

Boost your response rate by guaranteeing that responders' e-mail addresses will be kept confidential. Internet users are concerned about the privacy of the information they give out. Provide people with your private policy statement. Make them feel comfortable about divulging their e-mail address.

Do not add someone's name to your mailing list without permission. People dislike receiving unsolicited mail even when given the option to unsubscribe. One method of obtaining more e-mail addresses is to suggest to your subscribers that they recommend your mailing list to a friend (or a few friends). Let your subscribers spread the word about your mailing list. Encourage them to pass the newsletter on to a friend. Make sure you have included information on how to subscribe. Some of these people will then subscribe and tell their friends about your mailing list, and so forth. Word of mouth is a powerful force on the Internet.

Starting Your Own Publicly Available Mailing List

When you are creating your own mailing list, the first step is giving it a suitable name that is enticing to your target market. Draw up a schema that describes what your newsletter or e-mail messages to the list will contain. Designate how you want the list members to communicate with you and on what basis.

Mail lists and the sending of many e-mails at a time demand a reliable virtual server for your list. There are many ISPs that host mail lists, or you can use one of the many online mailing list hosting services. For lists and links of hosting service providers, check out Vivian Neou's site at *http://www.catalog.com/vivian/mailing-list-providers.html.*

Create a corresponding Web page for your list that provides information about the list as well as its purpose and guidelines. Your Web site should contain many opportunities for your visitors to opt in to your list. This will add credibility to your mailing list.

Once the list is up and running, you will have to advertise it so that people will actually subscribe. You can promote your list by participating in newsgroups that relate to your mail list topic. Using your sig.file and subtle advertising where permitted while contributing to appropriate discussion lists and newsgroups will enhance your mail list opt-in rate. You can also trade e-mail sponsorships with other mailing lists for promotional purposes.

There are a number of places to appropriately announce your list. One recommendation is the Internet Scout's New List, which you can find at *http://scout.cs.wisc.edu/index.html.*

Get your mail list linked from the many lists of lists on the Internet. We have provided some of these in the Internet Resources section which follows. Keep the standards high for your content. Make the postings worth reading by ensuring that you and others have valuable information on the topic to share.

Internet Resources for This Chapter

Liszt, the Mailing List Directory
http://www.liszt.com
This site offers a very big directory of mailing lists–over 90,000 to date. The Liszt has organized its lists into subject categories. The Liszt provides details on how to subscribe to each of the mail lists in its database and provides information on content as well.

List of Publicly Accessible Mailing Lists
http://paml.net/
The List of Publicly Accessible Mailing Lists is posted on this site and once each month to the Usenet newsgroups news.lists.misc and news.answers. The Usenet version is the definitive copy—this Web version is generated from the database and is uploaded several days after the Usenet version is posted. They continually post to Usenet so that the PAML will be archived at *rtfm.mit.edu.*

The List Exchange
http://www.listex.com/imark.html
This is the Internet's one-stop mailing list resource. It links to a number of list sites and sites with information on building your lists.

Internet Marketing Mailing List
http://www.o-a.com
The Online Advertising Discussion List focuses on professional discussions of online advertising strategies, results, studies, tools, and

media coverage. The list also welcomes discussion on the related topics of online promotion and public relations. The list encourages sharing of practical expertise and experiences among those who buy, sell, research, and develop tools for online advertising, as well as those providing online public relations and publicity services. The list also serves as a resource to members of the press who are writing about the subject of online advertising and promotion.

MailWorkZ.com
http://www.mailworkz.com
MailWorkZ is a dynamite tool that has helped take e-mail marketing to new heights. This software product makes managing mail lists fast and efficient, enabling users to provide their customers with the personal attention they expect and the support they deserve.

Campaign E-mail Marketing Software
http:/www.arialsoftware.com
This is e-mail marketing software used to conduct legitimate e-mail marketing campaigns. Campaign can import your contact database information and send personalized e-mail messages to all of your contacts.

MailKing
http://www.messagemedia.com/solutions/mailking/
MailKing is similar to Campaign in that it can import your contact database information and send personalized e-mail messages to all of your contacts.

Web Crumbs
http://www.thinweb.com
Web Crumbs gathers the e-mail addresses of visitors to your Web site. This intelligent program can also manipulate what the visitor sees based on rules. A downloadable demo is available from this site.

21

The Value of Incoming Links

Developing your link strategy is one of the most crucial but also time-consuming elements involved in Internet marketing. Although it can take a lot of time, developing a large number of incoming links to your Web site can have a great impact on increasing the traffic to your site. There are many different places that you can seek to find appropriate sites to approach for incoming links to your web site. You can find links from targeted Web sites, Web rings, meta-indexes, award sites, and cybermalls and from launching your own affiliate program. The way in which you generate links using the foregoing online mediums are different; however, they all result in the same outcome—incoming traffic and increased link popularity!

It is very important for you to develop as many links to your site as possible for three reasons:

1. If you generate links from Web sites that are frequented by your target market, they can turn into real traffic builders.

2. Many of the major search engines are now using link popularity in their search engine ranking criteria; thus the more links that you have to your site, the higher your site will rank in the search engine.

3. Links have staying power. When you post a message in a newsgroup where you promote your Web site through your brilliant contribution and your signature file, you will receive increased traffic while the message is current and is being read by participants in the newsgroup. As the time passes, your message will move down the list in the newsgroup and eventually disappear. The same goes for other time-sensitive online marketing mediums. Links are different. Links generally remain active for a long period of time, and as long as the site that hosts your link has new traffic, you will continue to receive traffic through it. The beauty of links is that in three months' time that link will still be there and people will still be clicking through!

Finding Web Sites to Link From

There are many different strategies that you can implement to find appropriate Web sites to be linked from. In an ideal world, your Web site should be linked from every high-traffic site that is frequented by your target market. Regardless, it's imperative that you develop a strategy to find all of these sites and attempt to arrange links from them.

When you are developing your extensive list of potential appropriate link sites, you should first start with the popular search engines. The majority of Internet users turn to search engines and directories to find subjects of interest to them on the Net. Statistics reveal that the majority of search engine users don't go beyond the first twenty or thirty results the search engine returns; therefore, these top sites returned by the search engines receive a lot of traffic. By conducting searches, you should collect the top twenty to thirty results using keywords related to your Web site. You should attempt to develop links from as many of these sites as possible. Some of these results will be your direct competition, however, and they likely won't be interested in providing a link to your site. The best opportunity for links is with non-competing Web sites that target the same market as your site. To implement this step, I suggest you take your most important keywords, do a keyword search in the most popular twenty or thirty search engines and directories, and review the top thirty sites in each for potential link sites.

Another effective strategy to find appropriate link sites is to see where the leaders in your industry and your competitors are linked. When I refer to the term *competitors,* I use the word very loosely. The Internet creates a level playing field for businesses by eliminating geographic boundaries found in traditional offline business operations; therefore, when you are competing in the online marketplace, you have many competitors. Your online competitors include your direct competitors, your industry leaders, companies selling non-competing products to your target market, companies selling similar types of products or services to your target market, and companies that compete with you for search engine ranking (i.e., companies using similar keywords). You should see what your online competitors are doing to increase traffic to their sites. Determine where they are linked from, and decide whether these are sites that you should also be linked from. You should be linked from every site that your competition is linked from and then some. The following is an approach to help you do this.

You should first gather an extensive list of competitors. As mentioned previously, a competitor can be any business or site that offers the same products and services as you do, or anyone targeting the same demographic group as your business. Once you have developed your extensive list of competitors and have gathered their URLs, the next step is to find out where these sites are linked.

There are many tools available on the Internet that will assist you in finding who is linking to your site. With many of these tools you simply enter your URL and the tools provide you with a list of sites that are linking to your URL. By analyzing this information, you can measure the effectiveness of your link strategy. However, the tools can also be used to provide you with information about who is linking to your competitors' Web sites by entering their URL instead of your own.

It is important that you stay organized while implementing your link strategy. The following step-by-step guide will help you organize, develop, and deploy an effective link strategy:

1. Gather an extensive list of competitors and their URLs.

2. Choose the tool(s) from the next section that you are going to use for this exercise.

3. Enter the first competitor URL to find the sites linking to it.

4. Copy (CTRL-C) and paste (CTRL-V) the results into a Word, Notepad, or other file that you can access later.

5. Enter the next competitor URL to find the sites linking to it.

6. Copy and paste the results into the same file that you began in step 4.

7. Repeat steps 5 and 6 until you have found all the sites linking to your competition. When it is complete, you have your Potential Link Sites list.

8. Now develop a link request (see the Arranging Links section of this chapter for details) and keep it open on your desktop so that you can copy and paste it into an e-mail when you find a site you'd like to have a link from.

9. Next visit each of the potential link sites to determine whether the site is appropriate for you to be linked from. If the site is appropriate, then send your link request. If the site is not appropriate for whatever reason, delete it from your list.

10. Follow through and follow up. Follow through and provide an appropriate link to those who have agreed to a reciprocal link. Follow up to make sure that they have provided the link as promised to your site, that the link works, and that it is pointing to the correct page on your site.

Tools for Identifying Competitors' Links

The following are some of the tools available that reveal which sites are linking to your site—or your competition's.

Alta Vista

http://www.altavista.com

To find out where your competitors are linked using Alta Vista, simply enter the competitor's URL in the search area like this: *link:yourcompetitorsdomain.com*. This will return all pages in Alta Vista with a link to your competitor's Web site.

Go.com
http://www.go.com
Go to the Go.com home page and click on the Power Search link. Select WEB Advanced Search. Under "search the Web for pages in which the:" choose "hyperlink" in the first drop-down menu. Select "must" in the second-drop down menu and "phrase" in the third drop-down menu. Then key in the URL you want to find in the space provided. Click on Search and the results will show listings, with descriptions, of the sites that provide a link to your selected URL.

LinkPopularity.com
http://www.linkpopularity.com
Just enter your competitors' URLs and see what comes up. This tool (see Figure 21.1) is fantastic as it reads from AltaVista, Infoseek, and HotBot.

Web Site Garage
http://www.websitegarage.com.
This site has a link popularity summary that tells you all of the sites linking to a particular URL. When you visit this site, enter your competition's URL into the URL check query. The results will include a diagnosis of the site, including the link popularity. You then have the option of viewing all sites linking to that Web site.

Hot Bot
http://www.hotbot.com
Enter your competitor's URL in the search box and change the default from "all the words" to "links to this URL." When you type in the URL, remember to include *http://*. The results will contain all Web sites linking to your competitor's Web site.

Arranging Links

Once you have developed an extensive list of potential link sites, you then have to arrange links with these sites. To do this you have to visit each URL that you had collected in the previous step and find the appropriate contact to request the link. Typically the contact e-mail address can be found on the homepage of the site. Titles such as Webmaster@ or any variation on the theme are usually a pretty safe

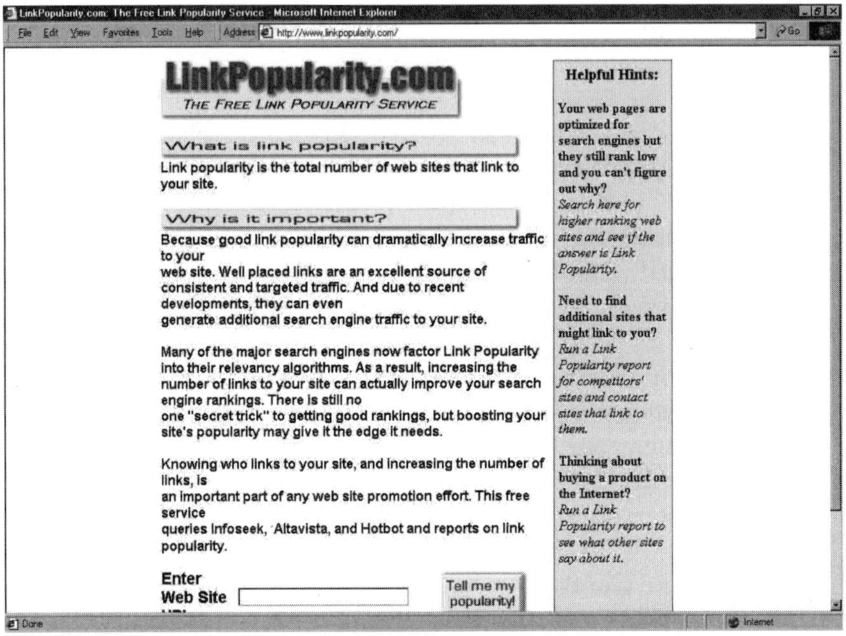

Figure 21.1. LinkPopularity.com is a dynamite tool for checking your web site's link popularity.

bet. If the site does not have an appropriate contact, then try the feedback@ option.

When you request a link, you should send a short note with the appropriate information in the subject line. For example, the subject line for your e-mail might be "Link Request" or some variation of this phrase. Your e-mail should be courteous, briefly describe your site's content, and provide the rationale for why you think reciprocating links would result in a win-win situation for both sites. It doesn't hurt to compliment some aspect of the site that you think is particularly engaging.

It is best to develop a generic "link request" letter that you can have on hand when you are surfing. You should always keep this letter open on your desktop when surfing the Internet so that you can quickly and easily copy and paste the letter into an e-mail. If you don't have a link request ready and open on your desktop and you find a site that you are interested in requesting a link to, you probably will jot the site address down as a reminder to go back to request a link. Quite often it doesn't happen. But if you have the request open on your desktop, when you find a site that is appealing from a link perspective, you can simply copy and paste the link request into an e-mail, do a little editing or customizing, and hit the send button.

The following is an example of a link request e-mail.

Dear Web Site Owner,

I have just finished viewing your site and found it quite enjoyable. I found the content to be very valuable, particularly [customize here]. My site visitors would appreciate your content as I think we appeal to the same demographic group. My site, http://www.mysitename. com, focuses on [my site content] and would likely be of value to your visitors. If you have no objection, I would like to add a link to your site.

Sincerely,

John Doe

Typically when you receive a response from a link request e-mail, it will say that they would appreciate a reciprocal link for their efforts. To facilitate this, you should either have the HTML for the link ready to send or have it available on your site, or both. It is important to remember to follow through and follow up, because you don't want to miss out on a key marketing opportunity. If you tell the respondent that you will provide a reciprocal link, you should do so within a 24-hour period as this shows courtesy and professionalism.

Another great link strategy is to offer your visitors an incentive to link to your site. For example, you could offer your visitors a free sample of your product or the opportunity to have their name entered in a drawing. This also provides you with another dynamite marketing opportunity, as you can have your site listed on sites offering different freebies and contests. There are thousands of freebie sites on the Internet that would love to link to your site to help promote your "free giveaway." Although these sites may not necessarily target your specific target market, they will increase the amount of traffic that your site receives, as well as your link popularity in the major search engine.

What Is a Meta-Index?

A meta-index is a resource site that contains a large listing of links to other sites pertaining to a specific subject category. Typically, meta-index owners will openly add any new links to their meta-index because they want to have the largest resource on the Web, and if your site is relevant for their list you will help them.

There are typically two different ways to submit your site to a meta-index. Some meta-indexes have a "Submit to add your site" area, and for others you have to develop an inclusion request e-mail and send it to the owner of the site. In your inclusion request e-mail, you would let the owner know that you had visited her site and feel that your site would be appropriate to be included, similar to the process described earlier. Review the techniques discussed later in this chapter on how to make your link noticeable with the graphical icon, hypertext link, and the tag line. This will make your link stand out from the rest of the links in the meta-index, which will encourage a visitor to click through to your Web site, as opposed to another link.

How to Find Meta-Indexes

The best way to locate a meta-index is by using a search engine or directory. You simply take your most appropriate keyword and add an extra word such as "directory," "index," "table," "resource," "guide," or "reference." For example, if you were looking for a business resource meta-index, your might use the keyword phrase "business resource directory" or "business resource index." This would return any business resource meta-indexes that might be included in the search engine's database. There are also many meta-indexes of meta-indexes. These sites are great as they provide you with multiple link opportunities.

Enhancing Your Links for Optimal Exposure

Whenever you develop a link from a Web site, you should attempt to differentiate your link from those of your competitors. Once you have an agreement with a site willing to provide a link, you should ask if you could send them an icon and the HTML for the link. The icon (.gif or .jpg format) should be visually pleasing and representative of your company. Perhaps you could use your company logo, or another image that is symbolic of your company. Within the HTML, include a tag line that entices people to click on the link. By including an icon or logo, the tag line, and your company's name, your link will stand out from the rest. The graphical image you include should only be a thumbnail, because you will not be able to take up too much space on the Web site. By having this image and tag line strategically placed on a Web site, the chances that a viewer will click through to visit your Web site are much higher.

You might want to develop a page on your Web site that will include a variety of different types of links to your site that a visitor can easily download. In a prominent location on your site, place a link that says something like, "Would you like to provide a link to this site? Click here." Link this message to a separate page, which hold several options for links. You can provide the viewer with several different sizes of banner ads, which he could place on his Web site. You can also provide him with a thumbnail icon, the HTML, and your tagline, which they could simply right mouse-click and copy and paste into the HTML code on his Web site. Quite often if you offer a viewer the above mentioned opportunities for links, you will have a better chance of receiving these enhanced link features. If you make it easier for him to add the link, he would be more willing to provide the link, for he can do it at his convenience any time of the day or night.

Widening Horizons with Web Rings

Web rings are a free service offered to the Internet community with the sole purpose of linking similar sites into a circle, or a ring. Each link in the ring is directed to a CGI script on the Web ring's server, which sends the viewer on to the next site in the ring. There are literally thousands of rings with subjects such as communications, games, art, real estate, and so forth. The people who visit Web rings are your potential customers who are responsive to the content of your site and are curious about your products and services. They are traveling a ring because they are interested the subject matter. In other words, the traffic that you receive from Web rings is highly targeted.

How Web Rings Can Increase Your Exposure

The major site for identifying potential Web rings for your site is Yahoo! WebRing (*http://www.webring.org*—see Figure 21.2).

There are many benefits to both the users of Web rings and the participating Web sites. Benefits to the users include:

1. Web rings provide a great navigation tool when you are looking for more information on a specific topic.

2. Web rings are easy to use. They provide one of the most efficient ways to find specific content on the Internet.

3. Web rings avoid the duplication found in search engines where a site may appear several times in one search. Each site is linked only once in each Web ring.

4. Web rings speed up search time.

5. Web rings eliminate sifting through mounds of search engine results for appropriate sites.

Benefits to participating Web sites include:

1. Web ring participation increases the number of targeted visitors to your Web site.

2. The organizers of the Web rings make it easy to monitor how successful your ring is. Traffic reports and "top" rings statistics are made available to participants.

3. Web rings drive traffic to your site.

When you have found a Web ring that you are confident attracts your target market, you can participate and enjoy the increase in visitors that you will receive from the ring. Web rings provide an array of other opportunities as well. You can search through the list of participants in a Web ring to arrange reciprocal links, as you share the same target market. You can also search a Web ring for banner advertising purposes. You can either exchange banners or purchase

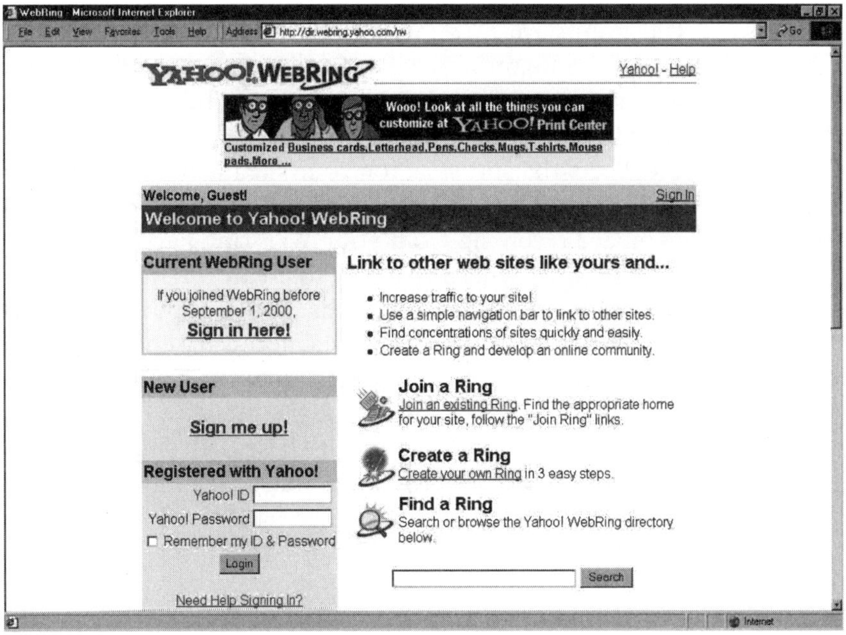

Figure 21.2. Yahoo! Web Ring is the premiere resource for Web rings on the Internet.

advertising on these sites. For more information on banner advertising, see Chapter 22.

How to Participate in Web Rings

The first thing to do is find a Web ring that is for your business and caters to your target market. You can identify potential Web rings at Yahoo! WebRing (*http://www.webring.org*).

Once you have found an appropriate Web ring, you contact the owner to ask permission to join. The owner will review your site to determine whether or not your Web site is appropriate for the Web ring. Once your site has been accepted, the owner will provide you with the required code and accompanying graphics, which you will insert on your page. This code enables you to participate in the Web ring. It is important to remember that the Web ring owner provides all the required material for you to slip into your HTML code. Once the code has been inserted, you're ready to begin. It's that easy!

Once the code is on your site, Yahoo! WebRing monitors the traffic and collects the statistics for your site, as it does for all Web ring sites. This is very beneficial to you because you can see how much traffic you are receiving from your Web ring participation.

Any Web site owner can apply to create a new ring if she feels no already-existing sites suit her needs. If the application is approved, Yahoo! WebRing will provide all the necessary code and instructions to help you establish your Web ring. New Web rings are listed in the directory once they contain at least five sites.

There is no cost to participate in these Web rings—no application fees, no charge for the approval, no charge for the code to be inserted on your pages, no charge for the increased traffic a Web ring brings.

Internet Resources for This Chapter

Virtual Promote
http://www.virtualpromote.com/guest6.html
This tutorial covers how to promote traffic to your Web site with reciprocal links. This is a free service for all Web site developers who want to learn more about announcing their Web site and promoting more traffic to the Internet.

Essential Links: Portal to the Internet
http://www.el.com/
Essential links are provided to the Internet and the World Wide Web. Essential Links is a portal to the Internet portal sites, news headlines, search engines, Web directories, references, and utilities.

Virtual Library
http://vlib.org/Overview.html
The Virtual Library is the oldest catalog of the Web, started by Tim Berners-Lee, the creator of the Web itself. Unlike commercial catalogs, it is run by a loose confederation of volunteers, who compile pages of key links for particular areas in which they are expert. Even though it isn't the biggest index of the Web, the VL pages are widely recognized as being among the highest-quality guides to particular sections of the Web.

Mega Linkage List
http://www.netmegs.com/linkage/
An exhaustive listing of over 1,500 directories, classified ad sites, little-known search engines, FFA pages, and more—all compiled for you alphabetically. Although there are some dead or broken links here, a large majority are active, and you will be hard pressed to visit each one.

Entrepreneurial Trend
http://www.angelfire.com/ct/suremoney/page2.html
This site offers links to hundreds of places to list your site! Free-for-all link pages and search engines. Free classifieds and message boards. Free newsletters and reciprocal links.

Auto Link/Master Link
http://www.career-pro.com/autolink/index.cgi?autolink
AutoLink allows you to type in your site's URL, and with one click automatically list it on over 350 FFA pages, directories, and search engines.

22

A Closer Look at Banner Advertising

The number of businesses now implementing strategic banner advertising campaigns online is increasing every day; however, many businesses are still asking themselves if banner advertising actually works. Some businesses say that banner advertising plays a key role in the success of their online businesses, yet others say that banner advertising is simply a waste of resource allocation. The truth is that banner advertising can be quite effective depending on what your online marketing objectives are and whether or not you implement the right online banner ad campaign strategy for your business. An effective banner advertising campaign comprises multiple elements, including the quality of the banner ads you use, the creative strategy behind the banner ads, your online marketing budget, and ultimately where you place the ads on the Internet. As with any form of marketing strategy, is it vital to keep your advertising objectives, your products and services, and your target market in mind when you develop your banner advertising strategy.

Keeping Your Advertising Objectives in Mind

As with any marketing campaign, when you're developing your online advertising campaign, you first have to determine the objectives of each individual campaign that you run. Typically, the most common objectives for an online advertising campaign include:

- Expanding brand awareness for your business, product, or service
- Increasing traffic to your Web site
- Qualifying leads and generating sales

When developing your online advertising campaigns, you have to do so based upon your objectives. If you were simply trying to increase the brand awareness for your organization, then an effectively designed banner ad on one of the major search engines or directories would be appropriate. The creative approach that you might take with this type of banner might include prominently displaying your corporate ID along with your company tag line. This would increase awareness of your business by providing consumers with information that they can use to identify with your company.

On the other hand, if you want to target a particular market with your advertising campaign, then you should be more selective as to where you place your banner ads. In this case, you would want to place a banner ad on a high-traffic Web site that is frequented by your target audience. Also, if you were launching a targeted marketing campaign, you would want to use a precise creative strategy. For example, if the objective of the banner advertising campaign was to launch a new promotion for one of your new products, the creative strategy used should promote that particular product and encourage visitors to "click through" to learn more about the product.

It is very important for you to keep your advertising budget in mind when you are deciding where to advertise online. Not all businesses can afford to purchase banner ads on the top Web sites visited by their target market. If you take the time to implement a strategic online advertising campaign, you will be surprised how far you can stretch your online advertising budget. However, before you design your online advertising strategy, you should assess your marketing budget and review advertising costs for various sites that appeal to your target market. It makes no sense to design an online advertising strategy if you find out later that you can't afford to implement that same strategy.

If you don't have a significant online advertising budget, there are a variety of ways that you can advertise at no charge. For example, you could participate in a banner exchange program, where you display someone's banner on your site in exchange for your being displayed on another. You can also trade banners with non-competing Web sites that target the same market as you do. The above opportunities, along with others, are discussed in more detail later in this chapter.

The Various Forms of Banner Ads

Before you develop your banner advertising strategy, it is important for you to know what banner advertising options are available for your business. Web sites offering banner advertising opportunities typically have their own banner ad design specifications and advertising guidelines that you must follow when advertising on their sites. Some sites are capable of offering a wide variety of banner ad options, whereas others are less advanced and can provide you with only traditional static banner advertising opportunities. It is important that you review and understand a Web site's banner advertising guidelines before you commit to advertising on that site. For example, you don't want to commit to a site that offers only static banner advertising opportunities if you plan to run a rich media advertising campaign. This could hinder the success of your banner advertising campaign.

Banner advertising technology is changing all the time. Although different Web sites have different banner ad policies and guidelines, following are the most common and most effective banner ad options available.

- Static Banners. Static banners are as the name suggests. They remain static on the same Web page until they are removed. When you purchase a static banner ad on a Web site, your banner ad will be visible on that particular page until your reader moves to another page.

- Rotating Banners. Rotating banners are banner ads that rotate among different Web pages on the same site. Some rotating banners rotate every fifteen or thirty seconds, so a visitor may see several ads while remaining on the page. Other rotating banner ads rotate every time there is a new visitor to the page. Rotating banners are commonly used in high-traffic Web sites.

- Vertical Scrolling Banners. A vertical scrolling banner ad is an advertisement that scrolls vertically down a designated portion of a page, as you scroll down that page. This means that the ad follows you and is present throughout that particular page of the site. This increases the chance that someone will click on the banner.

- Expanding Banner Ads. An expanding banner ad looks like a normal banner ad, but it expands when you click on it, keeping you on the same site rather than transporting you to another site on the Internet. Usually the ad says "Click to Expand," and the viewer can then learn more about whatever the banner is promoting. Some of the more advanced expanding banner ads have e-commerce capabilities, which allow you to actually order products from the banner without actually ever going to the business's Web site. The key purpose of expanding banner ads is to generate interaction between the visitor and the advertiser. If a visitor becomes involved with the banner, she will be more likely to click through to the advertiser's site to learn more about what the ad is promoting.

- Animated Banner Ads. Animated banners are banners that move on a Web site. Animated banners are usually in gif89a format (graphics interchange format) and contain a group of images in one file that are presented in a specific order. When using animated banner ads, you can choose to loop the file so that the banner will continue to move between the images in the files, or you have the option to make it stop after a complete cycle.

- Banners Containing Embedded HTML. Lately we are seeing an increase in banner ads containing embedded HTML. This allows viewers to choose commands from a drop-down menu that relate to the Web site the banner ad is promoting. These banners are great because instead of making a viewer click through and then have to navigate through your site like a conventional banner, these will direct your viewer to the page of interest on your site.

- Interstitial Banner Ads. Interstitial ads are advertisements that appear in a separate browser window while you wait for a Web page to load. Since they are in a separate window, interstitial ads are more likely to contain large graphics, streaming presentations, and more applets than a conventional banner ad. Studies have found that more users click on interstitial ads than on banner ads. Some users, however, have complained that interstitial ads slow access to destination pages. The following are the most common types of interstitial advertisements:

  - Pop-up Interstitials. The most common type of interstitial is a traditional pop-up interstitial. An example of this can be seen in Figure 22.1. A pop-up interstitial is an ad that is launched into a new, smaller browser when a person visits a page and is waiting for the page to load. Since the ad is being launched in a smaller browser window, it can contain standard Web display formatting. This means that you can use HTML, .gif and. jpeg images, and Flash technology.

  - Inline Interstitials. An inline interstitial advertisement is an ad that remains in the main browser window but only appears in between two pages of a site. For example, if a visitor clicks on a link on a site, the inline interstitial advertisement appears for a five-to-ten-second period before the visitor is transported to the desired page. If a visitor is interested in what the advertisement is promoting, he can click through to the advertiser's Web site while the ad is displayed. This provides a unique advertising opportunity, as you capture your visitor's total attention for that short period.

  - Superstitials. Superstitials are similar to pop-up interstitials in that they "pop up" when a user is waiting for a page to load; however, they are unique in the sense that they can incorporate rich media while accommodating a user's download time. When a visitor selects a page that advertises using superstitials, the pop-up window doesn't appear immediately. Typically when a pop-up window appears while a visitor is waiting for a page to down-

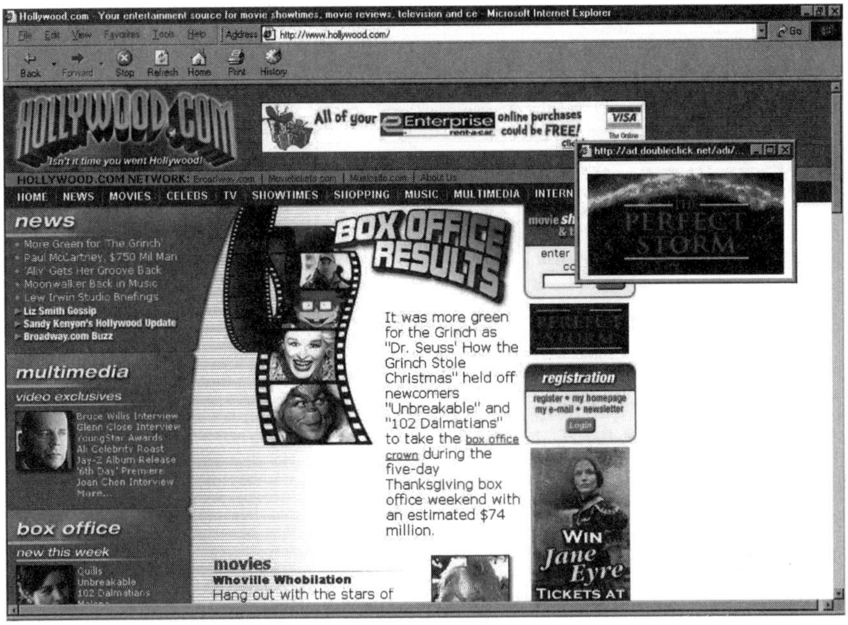

Figure 22.1. A pop-up interstitial is quite effective for promoting the release of the film *The Perfect Storm* on DVD.

load, the visitor closes the window immediately in fear that the pop-up is increasing her load time. To avoid this, superstitials store the advertisement in the browser's cache when the computer is idle (i.e., when the user is simply waiting for the page to download, or has stepped away from the computer). The advertisement then appears when the visitor performs a specific action. For example, if the advertisement is already stored in the browser's cache, the ad might appear when a visitor selects a specific button from the navigation bar. Superstitials are great in the sense that they appear quickly when prompted to "pop up," and for the fact that they are typically larger than a traditional pop-up interstitial. This means that you can combine the latest rich media technology to deliver a clear and powerful image to the visitor that will encourage her to "click through."

- Java and Flash Banners. Java and Flash banner ads allow you to use rich media in your advertisements. By using Java and Macromedia Flash technology, you can incorporate animation and sound into your banner advertisement.

Banner Ad Design Tips

By following the tips outlined below, you can ensure that your banner ads will be optimally designed to meet your online marketing objectives. Resources where you can find further information about banner advertising education can be located at the end of this chapter.

- You should ensure that your banner ad is quick to load. Ideally you want to have a really fast loading banner on a relatively slow loading site. In this situation, your banner ad will appear first before the rest of the site loads. If the Web page loads in its entirety before the banner, then the viewer is presented with the opportunity to click away before ever seeing your banner. You should always try to keep your banner ad size under 10K.

- To see how big files are when using any version of Internet Explorer, you must follow these steps:

  1. Right mouse-click on the banner ad.

  2. Select Properties.

  3. In the Properties window, you will see a Size line that will tell you the banner size.

- To see how large the file for your banner ad is when using any version of Netscape Navigator, you must follow these steps:

  1. Right mouse-click on the banner ad.

  2. Select View Image, and the banner ad will appear on a page of its own.

3. Right-click on the banner and select View Info. Another page will pop up and give you the information on the banner ad size.

- Keep your banner ads simple! Like any ad, if your creative contains too much text or animation, or too many colors and fonts, this will cause viewers to experience information overload. This will not only confuse a visitor, but will encourage them not to click on your banner.

- Make sure your banner ad is clear and legible. Many businesses design extravagant banners that are too busy and difficult to read. Use an easy-to-read font with the appropriate size. Be careful in your choice of color. You don't want to choose a color that would not be appealing to your target market.

- Ensure that you include an ALT tag in your banner for visitors who surf the Internet with their graphics turned off or who cannot see your banner ad for whatever reason.

- Always check to make sure your banner ad links to the appropriate page in your site. It is a common mistake for banners to link either to the wrong page of a businesses site or to nowhere at all simply because someone wasn't careful when they were writing code. This is very annoying to Internet users and counterproductive to your marketing effort.

- Check your banner ads on a regular basis to verify that the link remains active and is pointing to the appropriate page on your Web site.

- If you are using animated banner ads, you should limit your ads to two to four frames.

- Always include a call to action like "Click Here Now" on your banner ads. It is amazing how many people will do what they are told. Your ads still have to be attractive enough to grab a visitor's attention, but the call to action will encourage the visitor to click on your banner once you have captivated him with creative design.

- Test your banners ads with the different browsers, the different versions of these browsers, and at different screen resolutions to make sure that they look the way you want them to.

- If you know absolutely nothing about advertising and graphic design, you should consider outsourcing this activity to a professional. This will ensure that your ads are designed effectively.

Taking Advantage of Ad Networks

A growing trend in the online marketing world is to outsource your banner advertising activities to an ad network. Ad networks are typically used by companies with higher advertising budgets; however, they are being used more and more by small and medium-sized businesses because they offer highly targeted banner advertising solutions.

So what is an ad network? An ad network is an organization that manages the banner advertising responsibilities for a wide range of different Web sites that receive a high number of Web site visitors daily. Ad networks can target a specific industry or they can advertise to the mass public. For example, if you were in the financial services industry, you would want to have your banner ads viewed by users who would be interested in your services. An ad network that managed banner advertising for Web sites related to money and finance would be quite appropriate for your advertising needs; this would enable you to reach your target audience. For a more targeted audience, you will generally have to pay a higher CPM (cost per thousand impressions); however, even though you have to pay a little more initially, it will save you in the long run as the possible return on your investment could be huge. CPM is a standard advertising term. CPM is often used to calculate the cost of banner advertising. If the price of banner advertising on a site was $40 CPM and the number of impressions the ad had was 2,000, then the advertiser would have to pay $80 for displaying the ad.

When you join an ad network, you also receive real-time reports that indicate the success of your banner advertising campaigns. This information can be very useful because it enables you to tweak your marketing strategy if you notice that you are not receiving a good response from your campaign strategy. Perhaps you can take a different approach midway through the campaign. Maybe you could use a different banner design or a different creative strategy. Regardless, the detailed real-time reports give you the opportunity to get the most for your online marketing dollar.

Saving Money with Banner Exchange Programs

Banner exchanges work much as you would expect—your ad is placed on other sites in exchange for someone else's banner ad being placed on your Web site.

Typically when you register with a banner exchange, you have to go through a qualifying process. What this means is that your site has to meet certain minimum standards. Once you have passed the test, the banner exchange will provide you with HTML code to insert into pages of your site where the banner ads will appear. Every time this HTML is accessed, a random banner ad appears for the viewer to see.

This process is monitored and tracked. Each banner that is accessed from the exchange and displayed to a visitor earns you some sort of credit or token. These credits (or tokens) are used within the banner exchange like a bartering system. The credits you earn are exchanged for having your banner displayed on another site.

Sometimes some of the credits you earn go to the banner exchange itself, as a fee for managing the process. The banner exchange will sell the credits to paying advertisers or use them to promote the exchange. Some banner exchanges will allow you to focus your exposure on your target market.

When determining which banner exchanges to belong to, look for restrictions. When banner exchanges have no restrictions, you never know what could be loading to your pages. Don't join banner exchanges without size specifications for the banners. Your site could be displaying huge 150 x 600 pixel banners that make your visitors wait while they load. Ensure that the load time of every banner displayed on your site will be reasonable for your site.

Bartering for Mutual Benefits with Banner Trading

Another technique that you can use when implementing your banner advertising strategy is to barter with other Web sites to trade banners with their site. When you are surfing the Internet and you come across a site that you think appeals to your target market, you should attempt to contact the marketing or site administrator to ask if she would like to trade banner ads. You should send the Webmaster an e-mail outlining your proposition for the trade. In this letter you should include why you think it would be mutually beneficial for the trade, a brief description of your site, where you think you should have your banner on her site, and where you would place her banner on your site.

If you trade banners with a Web site, it is very important that you monitor the results. If the other site receives minimal traffic, more visitors will be leaving your site through their banner then are being attracted to your site. You should also check the other site constantly to ensure that it is displaying your banner correctly for the specified time that you agreed upon. If the site is not following the agreement, you should contact the Webmaster immediately to remedy the situation. If it isn't fixed, you should remove that site's banner ad from your site.

Internet Resources for This Chapter

Link Media
http://www.linkmedia.com/network
LinkMedia Free Exchange is a free service for the Internet community. As a member of the LinkMedia Free Exchange, you will receive free banner advertising on other member sites. In return, you will display banner ads on your site.

123Banners
http://www.123banners.com/
123Banners is a dynamite free banner exchange service designed to help Web sites advertise each other.

Smart Clicks
http://www.smartclicks.com
This site offers free banner exchange with automatic or manual targeting, animation allowed, real-time reporting, and much more!

Ad Resource
http://www.adresource.com
Web advertising, marketing resources, and secrets can be found on this site. Ad Resource offers an extensive price guide about Internet advertising, including what the top 100 sites are charging. This site also has a large number of Web advertising–related links.

Nielsens Net Ratings
http://www.netratings.com
Nielsens Net Ratings provides you with continuously updated statistics on the top advertisers on the Internet, and which banner advertisements are the most commonly viewed on the Internet. The site also offers a wide range of other Internet-related statistics that may prove important to your marketing needs.

TurboAds.com
http://www.turboads.com
TurboAds.com is the ultimate source for "rich media" advertising information. If you are interested in advertising online using Flash, Java, and all other forms of "rich media," you should definitely visit this site to find out what the pros are doing.

Engage Media
http://www.engage.com
Engage Media (see Figure 22.2) is the leading provider of Internet direct-response advertising solutions. The site strives to help companies get the best return on investment for their marketing dollar.

B2B Works
http://www.b2bworks.com
B2B Works has well over 70 different industries in the network and is emerging as an ad network leader. The site can target a specific industry of your choice, or advertise your banner to a mass audience.

Figure 22.2. Engage Media is a very popular ad network.

24/7 Media
http://www.247media.com
24/7 Media is a top-reach network of branded sites in a vast variety of categories. This allows advertisers to zone in on their target market and get the results that they want from their online marketing efforts.

23

Spread the Word through Media Relations

Your online media strategy can be extremely effective in building traffic to your site. Press release distribution can be done easily by building the right list of e-mail addresses and making use of one of the online press distribution services. Most reporters and writers have e-mail addresses that will allow you to directly e-mail them press releases. Most reporters prefer e-mail, but many still receive press releases by fax or mail. When e-mail press releases are sent out, reporters will reply by e-mail and will expect your response within 24 hours. Develop a media kit that you can immediately e-mail out to editors.

Managing Successful Public Relations

Press release distribution can easily be accomplished by developing an established list of reporters and editors or by making using of a press distribution service. You can achieve your best results in media relations when you integrate both online and offline publicity campaigns into your marketing effort.

There are a couple of benefits of maintaining successful public relations. First, press releases can portray your company and products in a positive light. Second, you will reinforce your relationship with current customers and be able to form new customer relationships.

Publicity vs. Advertising

Media coverage, or *publicity*, has a major advantage over advertising. The public view articles written by reporters as unbiased, whereas advertising is paid for. The public will give more credibility to articles published by a media publication than to advertisements.

Another advantage of distributing press releases is that it is much more cost-effective than paying for advertising space in a magazine, newspaper, or Web site, or for a spot on the radio. The costs of writing and distributing press releases are minimal.

One of the disadvantages of a press release is that you don't have control over what is published. The editor may decide to have the article reflect negatively on your company, and there is nothing you can do to stop her. The writer of the piece could also have a personal dislike of your company, for whatever reason, and this may be apparent in the article. Once your press release is distributed, you have no control over what will be written about your company.

You may also lose control over the timing of your release when generating publicity. For example, you may want to have an article released the day before your big sale, but the editor relegates it to a date the following week. There is nothing you can do about this. Never rely exclusively on publicity for important or newsworthy events, because if the release is not reviewed or considered newsworthy, you may be stuck with no promotion at all.

What Is a Press Release?

You should know what press releases are and how to write them before you begin your media campaign. Press releases are designed to inform reporters of events concerning your company that the public may consider newsworthy. Free public attention is the objective of a press release. Companies will not establish a good relationship with the media if they continually send worthless information in a blatant attempt to get their name in the press.

How to Write a Press Release

Your press release should follow a standard format, which is described in the following paragraphs.

Notice of Release
The first thing the reader sees should be:

> *FOR IMMEDIATE RELEASE*

unless you have sent the information in advance of the time you would like it published. In that case, state it as follows:

> *FOR RELEASE: Wednesday, April 14, 2002 (using the date you want it released)*

Remember that no matter what date you put here, the publication can release the information before or after the specified date. If the news is really big, it is not likely that the publication will hold it until the date you have specified.

Header
The header should be in the upper-left corner and contain all of the contact information for one or two key people. These contacts should be able to answer any questions regarding the press release. If the reporter cannot get in touch with someone to answer his questions, then he may print incorrect information or even drop the article altogether. The header should also include the name of your company, the city you are reporting from, and the date you wrote the press release.

> *Connex Network Incorporated*
>
> *75 Brentwood Drive*
>
> *Bedford, Nova Scotia*

Canada B4A 352

Tel 902/468-2578; Fax 902/468-2233

Contact: Susan Sweeney

Headline

The headline of your press release is the most important part and must grab the attention of the reader. Since the headline is so important, you should spend the majority of your time creating a powerful headline.

The Body

Your first couple of sentences within the body of the press release should summarize your headline and immediately inform the reader as to why this is newsworthy. Reporters receive a huge number of press releases, so if you don't grab their attention immediately, they won't read your release. Begin by listing all of the most relevant information first, leaving the details for last.

Ask yourself the 5 W's (who, what, where, when, and why) and answer them immediately. Include quotes from key individuals in your company and any other credible sources. Any statistics that support your main message should also be included. Your final paragraph should be a short company description.

The Close

There are three ways of standard notation to end your release: You should center the symbol "#," the word "end," or the number "-30-" at the end of your message. If your release is two pages long, center the word "-more-" at the bottom of the first page.

Advantages of Interactive Press Releases

Online press releases take the same standard format as offline press releases, but the online press release can be interactive with links to a variety of interesting information that supports your message. This also helps reporters easily find out other facts by following your links.

You may also want to consider additional items to include in your interactive press releases. A link to the e-mail address of the media contact person in your organization is a good idea. You will also want to include a link to the company Web page. It is important to include links to articles both on your corporate Web site and on other sites as well. If your story relates to a product, include a link to a graphic that can be used. The reporter or individual can simply "right mouse-click," "save picture as . . . ," and incorporate the images in her story. Journalists usually include quotes in their stories, so provide links to key corporate players, their biographies, their photos, and possibly some quotes. Finally, you will want to create a link to a FAQ section where you have answered both frequently asked questions and questions you wish were frequently asked.

Sending Press Releases on Your Own vs. Using a Distribution Service

When distributing press releases on your own, you save the money it would cost to have a service do it and will be more targeted than a service would be. A service's list of reporters and editors may not be comprehensive or recently updated.

On the other hand, some services may get your press release taken more seriously. If the reporter recognizes the name of the service, he may be more receptive than if it were to come from an unknown company. Using a service is bound to save you a lot of time.

If you decide to send your press releases on your own, you will have to build a list of journalists. You can do this by reading publications, looking for the names of reporters and finding out their contact information. If you don't know whom to send a press release to, you can always call and ask for the name of the appropriate editor.

By subscribing to a personalized news service to receive articles about your industry, you can find the names of journalists who might be interested in any of your press releases.

There are a number of online resources to assist you in building your press distribution list. Mediafinder (*http://www.mediafinder.com*) provides access to a database of thousands of media outlets including magazines, journals, newspapers, newsletters, and catalogs. Press Access (*http://www.pressaccess.com*) has a large database of journalists and industry analysts. The site's press access editorial database is available online, 24 hours a day, and contains in-depth information on journalists, publications, calendars, and so on. MediaMap (*http://www.mediamap.com*) is another public relations resource that has detailed profiles on more than 20,000 media contacts, including their phone numbers, fax numbers, e-mail addresses, and work preferences. The site also has editorial calendars that tell you who will be writing a scheduled story, what the topic of the story is, and when it will be written.

There are a number of press release distribution services online. You will find some of them in the Internet Resources at the end of this chapter.

Tips for Press Release Distribution

When distributing your press releases, know which editor handles the type of news in your release and address the press release to that person. Don't send the press release to more than one editor in any organization unless there is more than one angle to the information in the press release.

Call ahead, if possible, to discuss and solicit the editor's interest in your press release before sending it. Also, follow up with a phone call a few days later to be sure that it was received and to answer any questions.

You will also want to review editorial calendars of publications in your industry to see if your story may make a contribution to any upcoming articles.

Press Release Timing and Deadlines

One of the most important things to remember when sending a press release or advisory is the deadline. Know how far in advance you should send your information for each of the different media. Following are some time guidelines for your press release distribution.

Monthly Magazines

You should submit your press releases at least two to three months in advance of the issue you want it to appear in. Magazines are planned far in advance because it often takes a number of weeks to have the magazine printed and in subscribers' mailboxes.

Daily Newspapers

It is a good idea to have your press release arrive on the editor's desk at least several weeks in advance. If it concerns a special holiday, you should send it even earlier.

TV and Radio

When submitting press releases to TV and radio, you may be asked to appear on a show as a guest. Be prepared for this before you submit the release. TV and radio move very quickly; a story that has been given to the news director in the morning may appear on that evening's news.

Formatting Your E-mail Press Release

Your press releases can be e-mailed, but some reporters still prefer faxed or mailed releases. Check each reporter's preference before you send your press release. If you send e-mailed press releases, make sure that your e-mails are formatted properly and that your press release is included in the body of the e-mail and not as an attachment. There may also be problems downloading, which may prevent your release from being read, or the reporter may be using software that is not compatible with yours.

Make sure the subject line of your e-mail is compelling. E-mailed releases can easily be deleted or be left unopened by the journalist if the message doesn't catch his attention. Make sure your e-mail is clear and concise and gets to the point with the first sentence. If you don't grab the reader's attention at the beginning of the release, the recipient may not keep reading to find out what your news is. Keep your e-mailed press releases to one or two pages with short paragraphs.

It's very important to be able to send press release information in digital format. The journalist, with a quick copy and paste, will then have the "first draft" of her story. You have made it very easy for the journalist to then edit the draft and complete the story very quickly. Everybody loves to save time, and most journalists are under tight deadlines.

What Is Considered Newsworthy?

Your press release must have newsworthy information for it to be published. Figuring out what is considered newsworthy and what isn't is one of the main concerns for public relations representatives. You have to have a catch and, if possible, it should appeal to some sort of emotion. Some newsworthy items are things such as a merger or partnership between your company and another. A free service or resource offered by your company to the general public or participation in a trade show would also be considered newsworthy. A forum being held by your company with discussions on an already hot news topic or the appearance of a celebrity at a company event would be a reason to send out a press release. Other reasons to send out a press release would be upcoming online promotions, a charity contribution by your company, or an award presented by your company. Finally, you may want to generate publicity for your company if you are developing new strategic alliances, celebrating a milestone anniversary for the company, or introducing a breakthrough in technology.

What Isn't Considered Newsworthy?

Some things that are not news to the general public may be news to targeted trade magazines and journals. Use your own judgment when trying to determine if your press release is news or just an excuse to get your company's name in the press. The following topics are not newsworthy enough to publish.

The launch of a new Web site has not been considered news for a number of years now. Unless the site is based on a breakthrough in Internet technology or serves the public interest in an innovative way, you won't get a mention in the news. Nor is a new feature or change to your Web site newsworthy information. Even if your site has undergone a major overhaul, this is not news to the general public.

Launching a new product also is not newsworthy unless the product is a significant breakthrough in some area. The upgrade of an old product won't grab the public attention.

Preparing Your Press Kits/Media Kits

Your press kit is an essential item at press conferences and interviews. This kit can also be sent to reporters when they request more information about a press release that you have sent them.

Your press kit should start with a folder displaying your company logo and basic contact information. The folder should have pockets inside so different sheets of information can be inserted. Your press kit should include a press release outlining the newsworthy event, a company history, and various articles written about your company. Brochures, pictures, your business card, FAQs, quotes, and background information on key players should also be included.

Develop an Online Media Center for Public Relations

You should consider developing an online media center as part of your site if publicity is a significant part of your public relations strategy. When journalists are seeking information for their story, they want to be able to access information as fast and as easily as possible. An online media center on your site allows journalists this easy access and lets you control the information they receive.

The media center should be easily accessible from your navigation bar. It would include all the components needed by a journalist when doing a story on your company. The journalist should be able to find pictures to include in the story and all the information necessary to do her due diligence. The journalist should be able to send a question to the appropriate media contact within the organization with one click.

The media center should include a chronology of press releases distributed by the company, the company's history, an electronic brochure and links to other articles written about your company. You will also want to create links to pictures of your products. Perhaps you could have a gallery where journalists can choose the pictures they want to include in their article. Finally, you should include background information on key company personnel, with their pictures, bios, and quotes. Figure 23.1 shows an example of an online media center.

When you have a media center on your site, you send a clear message to the journalist saying, "You're very important to me! I want to provide you with everything you need to quickly and easily complete your story on our company." By creating a media center you are providing all the information, in a format the journalist can use, to enable him to do the story no matter when he chooses to do it.

Internet Resources for this Chapter

Press Release Tips for PR People
http://marketing.tenagra.com/releases.html
This site talks about what a public relations person expects to receive and how you should write releases.

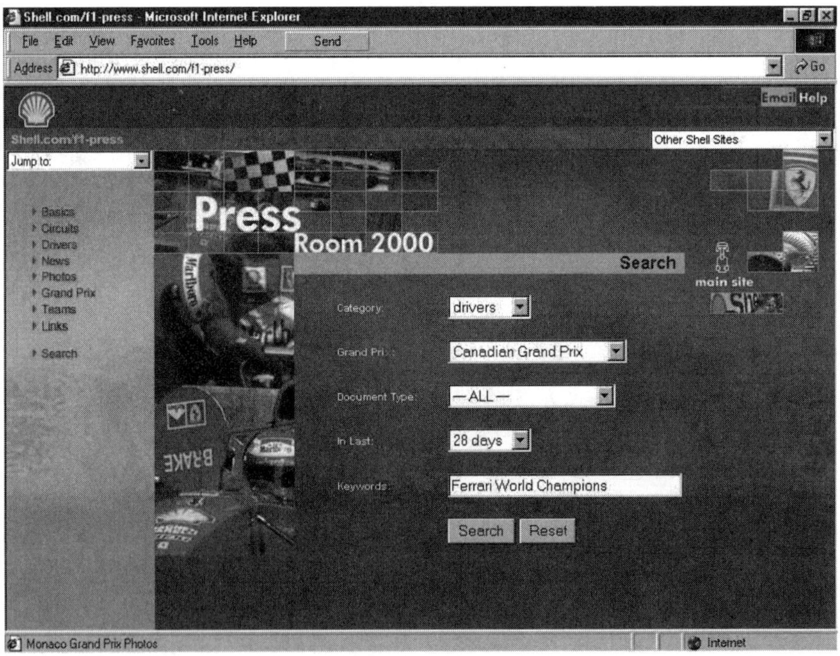

Figure 23.1. The Shell Ferrari Web site makes researching news articles extremely easy with the search function they provide.

Executive Summary: Understanding News
http://www.x-summary.com/tips/980526.phtml
Improve the reception of your press releases by knowing what is news and what isn't.

PR Tips
http://www.profilepr.co.uk/prforum/PRTIPS/PRTIPS6.HTM
A British agency reviews the pros and cons of e-mail press releases.

Xpress Press: E-mail Press Release Information
http://www.xpresspress.com/PRnotes.html
This site offers information on how to write and format a press release to be distributed by e-mail.

A Template for a Killer Press Release
http://www.netrageousresults.com/pr/prtemplate.html
The site offers an example format for a successful press release to get yours noticed.

Partyline
http://www.partylinepublishing.com
This is the standard media placement newsletter for the public relations trade.

PR Newswire Home Page
http://www.prnewswire.com
This site is a leading source for worldwide corporate media, business, the financial community, and the individual investor.

Internet News Bureau Press Release Service
http://www.newsbureau.com
For a fee you, can distribute your press release to thousands of online media outlets here. The site also offers links to a number of good PR resources.

WebWire
http://www.webwire.com/
This is a press release resource for the Internet.

Internet Media Fax
http://www.imediafax.com
This is a custom online news distribution service that creates targeted media lists "on the fly."

Internet Wire
http://www.internetwire.com
The Internet Wire offers online press release distribution via e-mail.

Xpress Press News Release Distribution Service
http://www.xpresspress.com
Press releases are delivered electronically by e-mail to 4,000 journalists and media members in the United States and internationally.

24

E-zines and Other Online Publications

Remember the coined phrase that emerged when the Internet's popularity began? People said: "Content is King." This fact remains true today, and producing original content as fast as it can be distributed (instantly) is the largest challenge for all online publications. Massive media mergers such as that of Time Warner and AOL are a direct indication of the dire need for fresh Internet content. Environmental concerns such as reduced paper usage and costly distribution of printed publications from paper and printing costs to postage are also contributing factors to the growing popularity of online publishing.

Current and useful online content is the commodity that users seek while on the net. Advertising in carefully selected e-zines is an effective way to attract potential customers to your site. When your site is affiliated with or recommended by an online publication that explores issues relating to your business, it establishes credibility, which is difficult to attain at this early stage in online customer relationships.

E-zine editors will tell you that their e-zine is the number one resource for repeat visitors and huge traffic for their site. Advertising in carefully selected e-zines is an effective way to promote your products and services to your target market and also to attract potential customers to your site. Having a story written about you in these e-zines is even better as this appears to be a third-party, unbiased recommendation of your products and services.

This chapter describes various types of e-zines in existence and how to integrate e-zine marketing into your promotional strategy.

E-zines Defined

E-zines, or electronic magazines, are the Web-based version of traditional magazines. They contain focused content that is appealing to a certain interest group in the form of articles and features. Some e-zines are Web site based; others are e-mail based; and some are available in print, html, and e-mail.

Many offline magazines have an Internet version as well. *Glamour, People,* and *National Geographic* are all accessible via the Internet. Some of these provide the full version of their traditional printed issue. Some e-zines are selective about the articles they provide and prefer to publish teaser introductions to featured articles of each issue in order to generate more print subscriptions; others provide a full version of the publication and also archive past editions.

Web-based E-zines

There are Web-based e-zines that have only an online presence. These e-zines are accessed through their Web sites by browsing. They have the look and feel of a traditional magazine. They include lots of detailed pictures and graphical advertisements similar to printed magazines. Usually there is no charge to view the Web-based e-zines; however, some e-zines charge a subscription fee. These e-zines tend to be as graphically pleasing as offline publications and have an edge over traditional magazines because they can be interactive with the visitors and therefore hold a better chance of establishing a loyal online readership.

Web-based e-zines are growing in popularity. Indications are strong that this trend will continue given the overall rising rate of people going online. The free Web-based e-zine is ideal for advertising purposes because the "free" aspect ensures higher traffic levels. The trick here is to find the appropriate e-zine for your marketing effort. You want to participate in those e-zines that are read by your target market.

E-mail E-zines

E-mail e-zines are more content-oriented and therefore tend to be more of a target marketing mechanism than the other types of e-zines. They are not as colorful or attractive as the Web-based e-zines, although rich media e-mail technology could change this reality. E-mail e-zines are usually several screens in length and include several articles and contain classified advertising. Circulation of these e-zines ranges in the thousands and is growing all the time. Most of these e-zines run weekly or bi-weekly editions.

Individuals who are receiving e-mail e-zines subscribe to a list. The chosen e-zine is then delivered straight into their e-mail boxes. Those individuals who are interested in the subject have taken the time to subscribe, and ask to receive the information directly. Once you have found an e-zine that caters to your target market, the e-zine may be a very valuable direct marketing vehicle.

Advertising in an e-mail-based e-zine guarantees certain positive potential customer demographics. Every subscriber to an e-mail-based e-zine has access to the Internet. Your prospective customers are reasonably Web savvy, which means they are probably closer in mindset due to their level of Internet familiarity to purchase online. If you advertise in this type of medium and place your Internet address in the ad, suddenly the user is only one click away from your site.

People subscribe because they are interested. Even if they don't read it immediately when it is received, they usually read it eventually. Otherwise, they would not have subscribed. Therefore, subscribers will generally see your URL and product advertisements or the story on your company sooner or later. For this reason, e-mail e-zines are a great direct marketing tool.

Promoting Your Site through E-zines

Advertising in e-zines is an effective way of reaching the niche group your business serves. Arranging promotional links to your site from high-traffic e-zine pages is a pull marketing strategy rather than a push method.

Chances are high that your potential customers are already on the Net reading e-zine articles that possess information useful to them. The trick is to find the preferred publications of your target market. Once you have defined the e-zines with a readership that matches the demographics of your target market, the next step is developing strategic relationships with them through paid and reciprocal linking arrangements. Most e-zines make their revenue from advertising and have a contact in place to arrange it.

Another useful way of promoting your services through e-zines is by offering suitable professional articles for publications including links to your site. You can write them yourself or hire someone to write them for you. The challenge to produce fresh content is ever present on the Internet. For this reason, online publishers are more accepting of professional article submissions than any other media.

A more permanent way to advertise your services in an e-zine is to create a column where you provide the articles for publication on your own site and in selected online publications that serve a matching target audience. As your own editor, you may strengthen the relationship with your potential customers by exchanging communication with readers in the form of answering questions and providing support. In this circumstance everybody wins. Your site and cooperating e-zines receive timely quality content and enhanced interactivity. You get to establish yourself as an expert and promote your services while learning more about your market. Like other online marketing strategies, e-zine marketing takes organization and persistence, but it has more potential to succeed because you are communicating with volumes!

E-zine Publishing's Three Golden Rules

Depending on your business, publishing your own e-zine could easily be your ticket to prolonged online success. If you do decide to embark on this venture, here are some important factors to remember. There are three golden rules to follow: think of a strategy, plan out the process, and take action.

Strategic thinking at the onset will save tons of time and frustration later on. Before composing the e-zine content, decide what your areas of interest and expertise will be. Determine who your readers are and what type of e-zines they are already reading. Ask yourself what you aim to accomplish by providing the e-zine.

Once your strategy is in place, you'll need to draw up a blueprint of the process that will most likely look like an editor's storyboard with publication dates and distribution details. The blueprint should also include layout and design of the Web site, nature of content, formatting, how you will be archiving past issues, and an outline of how to grow subscriptions.

Taking action is what most e-zines editors want to do first. But haste leads to recurring problems that come from poor preparation. To spare yourself future frustrations, we recommend preparing a set of administrative e-mail responses for anyone who joins your subscriber list. Arrange a relationship with an e-zine distribution service and ascertain which subscribe and unsubscribe processes are most widely used.

There are plenty of tips about e-zine participation and sites available in the resources section that follows.

Internet Resources for This Chapter

Best E-zines
http://www.bestezines.com
This site is an e-zine about e-zines. You can register your e-zine here and subscribe to others.

Free Directory of E-zines
http://www.freezineweb.com/
Based in Australia, this site offers a search engine and static listings of e-zines on the Web.

E-zines Today: Your Newsletters Online
http://www.ezinestoday.com/
This is an e-zine and newsletter site established to provide a location for your newsletters on the internet, including a database for free subscription e-zines.

E-Commerce Management E-zine
http://ecmgt.com
This free e-zine is Web-based and e-mail-based, and it has up-to-date articles about current trends in online marketing. Straight from Silicon Valley.

25

Communication with Your Target Market through Newsgroups

It is estimated that over 10 million people read newsgroups, making newsgroups an ideal marketing vehicle. The number of newsgroups is always increasing, with over 100,000 different topics now estimated. Using proper "netiquette" is important. To do this, read the FAQs and rules, "lurk" first, and stay on topic.

Newsgroups—An Ideal Marketing Vehicle

With over 10 million people reading newsgroups on thousands of topics, it is a perfect place to market you online presence. Usenet newsgroups are hierarchical and are arranged by subject. Each newsgroup is dedicated to a discussion of a particular topic, such as yachting, outdoor adventure, car racing, or The Spice Girls.

Each group's readers are interested in the newsgroup topic; therefore, once you find a newsgroup related to your product or service, you have likely found your target market.

Deciding on the newsgroups you decide to participate in may depend on whether the newsgroup is being read by a small or a large number of people. Large isn't always better. If you join a small newsgroup, it might be read by only your target market, whereas a larger group will provide you with better exposure by sheer volume. Your objectives and also your product or service will determine whether you pick a large or a small group. Posting to a large group will not be of any use if your products or services are not related to the topic of discussion.

The Benefits of Newsgroups

Online marketers can benefit from participating in newsgroups in a number of ways. You are able to immediately reach thousands of your target market with a single message. Newsgroups can help in finding out what people are looking for, the latest trends, customer needs, and what they are talking about. You are also able to provide valuable information to existing customers. Posting messages to newsgroups can direct people to your Web site and increase your traffic. Finally, you are able to build your reputation as an expert in your field by answering questions and solving problems.

Different Newsgroup Categories

Newsgroups are organized into different types of discussions or categories. Each of the major categories has lots of individual newsgroups in which you can participate. Major newsgroup categories include:

- alt—discussions on alternative topics
- biz—discussions on business topics (You may find groups that allow advertising here.)
- comp—discussions on computer-related topics
- K12—education discussions covering such topics as using technology, curriculum, and classroom-to-classroom projects

- misc—discussions of miscellaneous topics that don't have their own category
- news—discussions on Usenet news and administration
- rec—discussions on recreation topics
- sci—discussions on science
- soc—discussions on social issues
- talk—conversations about current issues and more

Each of the major categories has a number of subgroups, and each of the subgroups has a number of sub-subgroups. For example, under the rec major group you will find a subgroup rec.sports. Here the discussion revolves around all kinds of sports. For example:

rec.sports

rec.sports.hockey

rec.sports.hockey.NHL

rec.sports.hockey.NHL.BostonBruins

As you can see, the longer the name the narrower the discussion that is taking place.

Target Appropriate Newsgroups

With such a large numbers of Usenet newsgroups currently existing, it is a huge task to identify appropriate newsgroups for your company's Internet marketing activities. First, you need to determine which newsgroups your prospective customers frequent.

Look for a correlation between a newsgroup and the product or service you are offering. For example, if your company sells software that aids genealogical work, then one appropriate newsgroup for your business might be soc.genealogy.methods. Find and make note of all appropriate newsgroups that might be of interest to your target customers.

There are many ways to find appropriate Usenet newsgroup listings. There are more than 54,000 mailing lists and newsgroups located at the Liszt Web Site (*http://www.liszt.com*) for you to search. You can also do a search using the newsgroup functions of the two leading browsers, Netscape Navigator and Microsoft Internet Explorer.

Most newsreader programs have a search capability and can search the newsgroups for keywords that relate to your target market, your product, or your service. Another place to look for appropriate newsgroups is on Deja.com (*http://www.deja.com*). At Deja.com you can conduct a keyword search of the Usenet newsgroups. The search results are displayed in chronological order, with the results at the top being the most recently used. You should choose keywords appropriate for your target customer or client. A benefit of the Deja.com site is that you can post to the newsgroups directly from the site. You don't have to go through alternative software to do so.

Once you have completed your preliminary research and compiled a long list of the most appropriate newsgroups related to your target market, you can begin to investigate further and qualify your list.

The next step is to go to the Usenet Info Center Launch Pad at *http://sunsite.unc.edu/usenet-i/home.html*. There you can look up the newsgroups on your list. From this site you will be able to find out where the FAQs for each newsgroup are located. The FAQs will usually provide information on the newsgroup's stance on advertising. Info Center Launch Pad will also provide you with details on the number of people participating in the group.

Read the FAQs and Abide by the Rules

Before you post any messages to newsgroups, read the FAQs, charter, and rules about posting and advertising. If the FAQs do not mention the group's stance on advertising and announcements, conduct a search on Deja News based on the group's name and charter. It is very important that you abide by all the rules.

"Lurking" for Potential Customers

Spend time lurking or monitoring the types of messages that are being posted without participating yourself. Determine if the participants are, in fact, your target market. Is there an opportunity for you to contribute? Research the newsgroup to determine if it will appeal to your customers. Take the time to confirm that the discussion in the newsgroup is relevant to your product.

Posting Messages on Newsgroups

Different Types of Newsgroups

Newsgroups can be designed for discussions, news announcements, postings related to particular topics, and even buying and selling goods. Make sure to always stay on the newsgroup topic of discussion. People participate in specific newsgroups because of that subject and don't appreciate off-topic postings.

Follow the Rules

After you have become familiar with the rules of your selected newsgroup, you may begin to post messages. If the rules do not allow advertising, then do not blatantly post an ad. Remember to abide by the rules! To take full advantage of the newsgroup, you have to earn the trust of its members. With one wrong message you could outrage all of the potential customers who participate in the newsgroup.

Run a Test First

Doing a test, by posting to a newsgroup, shows how the posting works and prevents you from making a mistake when it comes to the real thing. For a test mechanism, go to the newsgroup *misc.test*.

Importance of the Subject

Newsgroup participants will decide whether to open or pass your posted message based on the words in the subject area. Make your subject short and catchy so that your message will be read. Try to put the most important words of the subject first. This is a very critical part of posting a message to a newsgroup. Some people adjust the screen to see only the first few words in the subject area. When responding to a message, use the reply option to stay on the same thread. When you reply without changing the subject line, your message will appear immediately below the message you are responding to in the newsgroup. This makes it easy for others to follow the discussion.

Keep your Message Short

Message length should be no longer than 24 lines. Messages should briefly discuss main points and ask if readers would like to have more information. Informed quality responses to people's questions will give you credibility with the group and reflect well upon you and your company. If you post positive and informative information, visitors will return to the newsgroups and look for your posts. Once people show an interest in the information you are offering, your message can be as long as needed.

Public or Private Response

When responding to a message in a newsgroup, determine if it is more appropriate to respond to the individual who posted the message privately or to respond through the newsgroup. If your message will be of value to the entire group or will appropriately promote your company's capabilities, then post the response to the newsgroup for all to see. If you think that you have a solution for the individual only, deliver a private response. Sometimes you may choose to do both. Whichever approach you take, make sure that you respond as quickly as possible.

Signature Files as Your e-Business Card

A signature file, or sig. file as it is commonly referred to, is your e-Business card. It is a short message at the end of an e-mail. Signature files are discussed more in depth in Chapter 19.

Advertising When Advertising Isn't Allowed

Advertising is not welcome in most newsgroups, and many charters specifically disallow the posting of ads. Read the FAQs before posting a message. If the newsgroup does not allow ads, don't post them. By responding to queries or providing information that is of interest to the newsgroup, you have the opportunity to attach your sig. file. A sig. file can be as effective as an ad if it is designed properly. If your information is of value to the newsgroup, the fact that your sig. file is an advertisement will not matter—in fact, it may add credibility to the information you have provided and enhance your company's reputation.

Internet Resources for this Chapter

Newsgroups
News.newusers.questions; News.announce.newusers; News.newusers
These sites provide information to new Usenet users on posting, finding appropriate newsgroups, netiquette, and other frequently asked questions new users are faced with.

Reference.com Search
http://www.reference.com
Reference.com has searchable directories of newsgroups and mailing lists. Newsgroups are archived, but mailing lists are only archived and searchable with the permission of the list owner.

Deja.com: The Source for Internet Newsgroups
http://www.deja.com
The Web site where you can read, search, participate in, and subscribe to more than 50,000 discussion forums, including Usenet newsgroups. Deja.com is a resource for finding people, getting noticed, and getting answers to all sorts of questions. You can find discussion forums on any topic imaginable.

Liszt of Newsgroups
http://www.liszt.com/news
This site offers a complete listing of newsgroups organized by different categories. Over 30,000 newsgroups are listed, making this the largest directory of newsgroups on the Web.

How to Advertise on Newsgroups
http://www.nsmi.com/noflames.html
How to Advertise on Newsgroups shows step-by-step techniques to follow so you won't get blacklisted. It includes everything you need

to know about how to advertise in newsgroups and mailing lists without getting flamed.

Open Newsserver Search
http://www.muenz.com/sdienst/html/sgroup_e.html
This is an English-German search engine that finds open news servers that carry newsgroups matching your search terms.

Free Agent
http://www.forteinc.com/getfa/getfa.htm
Free Agent furnishes newsreader software.

Talkway
http://www.talkway.com
This membership site attempts to provide a friendlier interface to the arcane structure of Usenet newsgroups.

26

Winning Web Site Awards and Being Voted "Cool Site of the Day"

There are literally hundreds of Sites of the Day, Cool Sites, Hot Sites, and Pick-of the-Week Sites. Many of these sites require you to submit, whereas others are selected based on things like awesome graphics, uniqueness, fun features, and dynamite content. Being selected for one of these sites can cause a huge increase in the number of hits to your site. You must be organized so you can cope with the swell of traffic. An increase in traffic will also result in an increased demand for online offerings.

How Do You Get Nominated?

There are sites on the Internet that use established criteria to analyze other sites and acknowledge the best ones by giving them an award. The criteria for what sites are "hot" or "cool" can be very discriminating and are used to determine what sites will receive awards.

Each awards site will use different criteria to select its award winners. To be considered, you may be required to send an announcement or submit a description of your site. Some of the more common criteria are the site's graphics, uniqueness, content, and its "fun" factor. Other awards sites have much more relaxed criteria, and awards may be given out based solely on the personal likes and dislikes of the site owner.

The Webby Awards are taken just as seriously as the Academy Awards and are presented annually to worthy sites in a number of different categories. The nomination procedure for a Webby Award is very comprehensive. Visit their Web site for more information regarding this process.

Choosing Your Awards and Submitting to Win

Some awards are easier to receive than others. Commercial sites often give out awards simply to increase traffic to their own site. Giving an award increases traffic because the award on the winner's site is a graphic link that leads back to the award giver's site. Awards are often used as a way to increase traffic, and some Web masters give awards to everybody who makes a submission.

Having awards posted on your Web site is a valuable asset. The average Web user cannot distinguish between the prestigious awards and ones that are given to anyone who submits. Therefore, submit to any awards you want, but ensure that your site is ready for the surge of traffic.

Once you have received an award, you will be expected to place a promotional graphic and a link on your site. Where you place these awards is important. If you receive a lot of awards, your Web page can become cluttered and will load more slowly as a result. A separate awards page linked from your navigation bar may be the best way to display your many accolades.

Before you submit your site for an award, you must determine whether or not the increase in traffic will be advantageous to your site. If you sell T-shirts emblazoned with WWW cartoons, then any traffic is good traffic, and awards will benefit your site. If, on the other hand, you are a marine biologist specializing in red tides in the Arctic, then the traffic that a "Site of the Day" award would bring may be more of a hindrance than a help in marketing your services. Before using any marketing tools and techniques in your online marketing strategy, you must determine if they will increase hits from your target market.

A quick way to increase traffic to your site is to get mentioned on one of the many high-traffic "Cool Sites" lists. This may be one of the single biggest ways to increase traffic to your site. You must be prepared for the abrupt increase in traffic after you win one of these awards. If your site offers its visitors something free, be sure you have a huge volume of whatever it is so that you can distribute it readily. If your site offers a free download, plan to have alternate FTP sites available to your visitors. An additional telephone system and staff will be needed to handle the huge volume of calls you may get if you have a "call-in" offer. A plan will also be needed to handle the huge volume of e-mails you will get.

When you have determined the type of traffic that winning an award will create and believe that it fits with your marketing strategy, be sure your site has the qualities of a winning site and submit it to as many award sites as possible.

There is a different level of prestige associated with winning an award from various award sites. Some awards, such as a Starting Point Hot Site (*http://www.stpt.com*) award, are an honor to receive and are very competitive due to the number of submissions they receive.

Cool Sites: What's Hot and What's Not?

Most of the awards sites will provide you with their selection criteria. Some awards sites look for and base their selection on valuable content, whereas others look for innovative and unique capabilities. Although sites vary on what they consider "hot" or "cool," they are fairly consistent on what doesn't make the grade, as summarized below.

What's Hot	What's Not
• Awesome graphics	• Single-page sites
• Great, original content	• Single product promotion
• Broad appeal	• Offensive language or graphics
• Fun feature	• Lengthy download time

Posting your awards on your site

Displaying the awards your Web site has won is the next step. All awards you receive for your Web site are expected to be displayed in return for the recognition you have received.

There are a couple of reasons that you should not post the awards you have won on your homepage. First, additional graphics must be downloaded and will slow the load time of your home page. Second, an award is a link that leads visitors out of your site, and links leading out of your site should not be on the first page. This gives people the opportunity to leave your site before they have had a chance to explore it thoroughly.

Where, then, should you post your well-deserved awards? The best solution is to create an awards page. This allows you to post your awards without affecting the load time of your homepage and keeps visitors from making an early exit from your site.

Internet Resources for this Chapter

Webby Awards
http://www.webbyawards.com
The Webby Awards have been embraced by the online community as the leading creative honors for digital media. The awards recognize the most creative and innovative Web sites of the year and the talented editorial, technical, and design teams behind them.

Best of the Planet Awards
http://www.2ask.com
This has been called the "people's choice award," where you can decide who's best.

PC Magazine's Top 100 Web Sites
http://www.zdnet.com/pcmag/special/web100/index.html
This Web site offers a list of top sites listed in five categories—everything from amazing online stores to essential computing resources, with a couple of stops along the way for fun and entertainment.

Jayde.com
http://www.jayde.com/goldlnks.html
The site awards the Gold Diamond Award to sites with great style, design, and content. Jayde.com also has an award for commercial sites.

Cool Site of the Day
http://www.coolsiteoftheday.com
Cool Site of the Day is a wildly popular Internet awards site that features interesting, provocative, and irreverent Web sites from around the world.

Starting Point Hot Site
http://www.starting-point.com
Votes are taken from the site's What's New section for sites worthy of a Hot Site Award.

100 Hot Web sites
http://www.100hot.com/
This site offers a directory of Web sites based on Web traffic and organized by category.

Virtual Reference Meta-Index of Award Sites
http://www.refdesk.com//textcool.html
The site comprises a listing of different sites that host sites of the day, hot sites, and so on.

Web Pages That Suck
http://www.webpagesthatsuck.com
Keep your site from being nominated to Web Pages That Suck, and you are probably doing well. However, you can learn a lot from this site about how to properly design your site from a marketing perspective.

Free Links Award Sites
http://www.freelinks.com/awards.html
This is a free service to aid and simplify your Web site promotion efforts. You can also find information on databases, search engines, and link pages where you can list your site for free.

Links2Go: Site Awards
http://www.links2go.com/topic/Awards
Here you can find links to dozens of award sites.

27

Generating Online Exposure the Offline Way

There are many benefits to promoting your Web site using traditional media and print materials. Your Web site can answer a lot of questions and provide more information than you can print in a magazine or newspaper ad. Your site can be kept up-to-date with the latest information available. People can request additional information or order online.

Offline Promotion Objectives

Offline promotion can direct visitors to request additional information or order online. Because of this, you should promote your URL on every piece of promotional material you produce! The more exposure your URL receives, the more likely people will remember it when they go online.

Be creative with your offline promotion campaign. Brainstorm with innovative thinkers to come up with a number of good places to promote your URL; for example, try displaying your URL in your TV and radio commercials, magazine and newspaper ads, and billboards. The more places your URL appears, the more it will get noticed. Some businesses even incorporate their URL into their building and vehicle signage. Answer your telephone by saying, "YourCompanyName.com, Good Morning." This is effective in providing callers with your URL and letting them know that you want them to visit your Web site. Next time they have a question or want to place an order, they may go directly to the Web site.

By displaying your URL in traditional media, you are encouraging people to visit your site for more information about your company. Another benefit is that people can usually order from your Web site. Naturally, your site should be up-to-date with all of the latest information on products, prices, and sales promotions. If a six-month-old advertisement is seen in a magazine, as long as the URL is displayed in the ad, readers can go to your site and get current information. Even though your Web site is your most effective advertisement, it is an advertisement that people have to know about before they can view it.

URL Exposure through Company Material

It is important that your corporate image be consistent in your online and offline promotional campaigns. Businesses should use the same logo, tag lines, colors, style, and fonts on all of their marketing materials. As a general rule, try to place your URL on everything you put your logo on—which means just about every piece of corporate literature. Make sure to include your URL on the following:

- Letterhead
- Report covers
- Business cards
- Flyers
- Corporate brochures
- Advertisements

- Envelopes
- Direct-mail pieces
- Checks
- Newsletters
- Fax coversheets
- Press releases

URL Exposure through Promotional Items

If your company uses promotional items as giveaways at trade shows and events, it is a good idea to incorporate your Web site marketing with these items. Examples of some promotional items are seen in Figure 27.1. Promotional items that are used in and around computer workstations are ideal because your URL is visible when people are in a position to actually visit your site. Some examples are:

- Mouse pads
- Coffee mugs
- Diskette holders
- Coasters
- Screen cleaning kits
- Letter openers
- Software
- Stress balls
- Screen savers

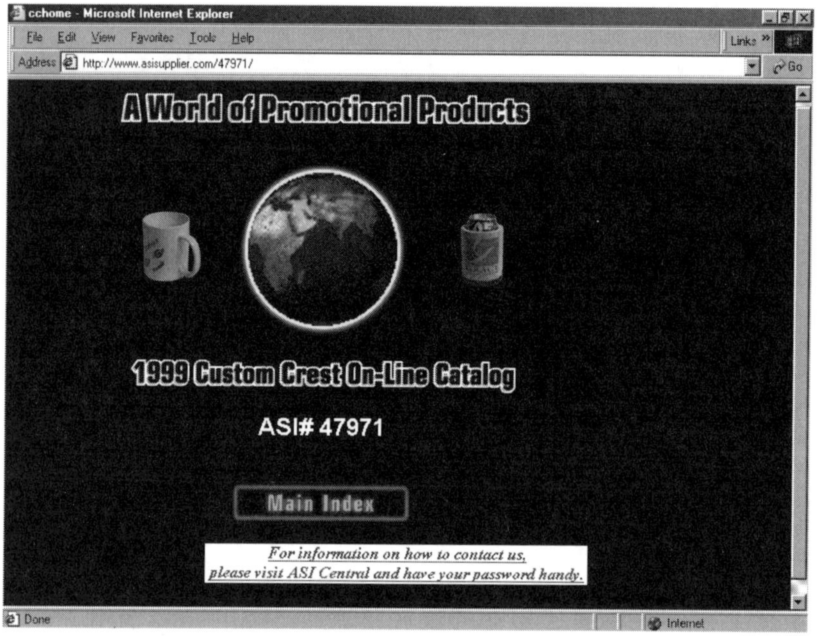

Figure 27.1. A great site for offline promotional products.

- Sticky notes
- Pens and pencils
- Calendars

URL Exposure through Clothing

Articles of clothing are another great promotional item. When someone wears an article of clothing with your URL on it, she becomes a walking billboard for your site. If you have a corporate uniform, your URL could be displayed on the pocket or across the back. Put your URL and a catchy phrase or tag line on items such as:

- Golf shirts

- Hats
- T-shirts
- Aprons
- Sweatshirts
- Jackets

URL Exposure on Novelty Items

Novelty items are another effective place to print your URL. The following items will appeal to a variety of age groups:

- Frisbees
- Key chains
- Balls
- Magnets
- Beach towels
- Chocolate bars
- Sunglasses
- Bumper stickers

URL Exposure on Your Products

If possible, put your URL on your products themselves. Joe Boxer is a great example of a company's using this innovative idea. The company URL is stitched into the waistband of their underwear.

Internet Resources for This Chapter

Bizine
http://www.bizine.com/profit.htm
"Increase your profits by coordinating online and traditional offline marketing" by Bob Leduc.

Free Pint
http://www.freepint.co.uk/issues/040399.htm
"12 Offline Ways of Promoting Your URL" by Nikki Pilkington

WebCMO
http://www.webcmo.com/report/opss1/offline.htm
This site offers a survey report on offline promoting.

PC Mojo
http://pcmojo.com/pcmojo/offline.htm
Information is offered on why you need to promote your site off the Internet.

Promotional Products
http://asisupplier.com/47971/
This is a great site for purchasing promotional material from mouse pads to coffee mugs.

28

Measure Your Success with Web Traffic Analysis

To succeed in the offline marketing world, it is essential that you understand what motivates your target market. Similarly, in the online marketing world you also have to understand your target audience, but how do you do that? Through the latest advancements in Web traffic analysis technology, we can now gather, process, and analyze data that will give us invaluable information about what motivates our target market to perform particular tasks online. Many Web sites are now using comprehensive Web traffic analysis software because the information they can gather from the software can play a key role in the success of their online marketing strategy. Web traffic analysis software can tell us what page of the Web site a visitor came to first, where she came from, how long she was there, what she did while she stayed, and a whole lot more.

Do You Know Who Is Visiting Your Web Site?

Understanding your online audience is a crucial element of the success of your online marketing strategy. Without targeting your online audience in a manner that will motivate them to do what you want them to, you are not only wasting your time, but you are also allowing your online competition to capture a greater market share. Web traffic analysis software is helping companies to focus on their target market like never before. It is helping them to understand the traffic on their Web site, and is enabling them to identify what motivates them to perform specific tasks on their site. But how does Web traffic analysis work?

What Is a Log File, and What Can It Tell You?

All Web servers log a list of all the requests for individual files that people have requested from a Web site. These files will include the HTML files and their imbedded graphic images and any other associated files that are transmitted through the server. By analyzing these files with Web traffic analysis tools, you can generate the following data:

- The number of visitors to your homepage on per hour, per day, per week, per month, or per year
- Where the visitor came from in terms of his unique IP address
- How many times each page on your Web site was requested
- What time, day of the week, and season that people access your site
- Which Web browser your visitors are using
- Which keywords or phrases your visitors are using to find your site using a search engine
- Which advertisements are viewed the most on your Web site
- What motivates your target market to perform specific tasks on your Web site
- Detailed information on visitors and demographics

Some of this information may not sound as though it would play an important role in the success of your marketing strategy; however, there are some very amazing things you can do with the data you can collect from your log files.

Web Traffic Analysis Options

Whether you host your own Web site or not will determine what your options are with regard to Web traffic analysis software. For Web traffic analysis software to work, it has to be installed on the server where you host your Web site. If you host your own site, you are definitely going to have to purchase your own copy of Web traffic analysis software. However, if you are paying an ISP to host your site, the ISP typically has some sort of analysis software available for clients to use. Most people are unaware that this software is available, and most ISPs don't promote this complimentary service. Since you are the ISP's client, and you are paying for services, you should ask the provider to use the Web traffic analysis software of your choice. Typically an ISP will not oppose such a request because it doesn't want to lose your business. In some cases you may be charged an additional fee for this service.

Popular Web Traffic Analysis Software

If you do decide to purchase your own Web traffic analysis software, there are many different brands that do many different things. The following is a list of the more popular brands of Web traffic analysis software:

WebTrends Enterprise Suite
http://www.webtrends.com/
The WebTrends Enterprise Suite is one of the most comprehensive Web site analysis software available. It provides you with reports on everything from the number of views your banner ads receive on another Web page, to which keyword was used when a visitor found your site using a search engine. You can easily target specific hits and user sessions that include file types and names, entry pages, time and

day, user addresses, or any other medium that may have pointed a visitor to your page. WebTrends develops detailed advertising reports, which tells you how often banners on your Web site are viewed and how often people click through. This assists you in selling and billing space to your clients. This is an all-in-one piece of Web traffic analysis software that does more than answer the question of who is actually visiting your site.

NetGenesis 5
http://netgenesis.com/products/netgenesis.cfm
NetGenesis 5 is an extremely comprehensive Web-based analysis platform. This means that statistics on your Web site's activity levels can be accessed from all over the world through your Web browser, which proves to be very convenient for day-to-day global business operations. NetGenesis 5 produces in-depth visitor reports that will enable you to define new target user segments while retaining existing customers.

Learning from Log File Analysis

By analyzing the data from your log files, you can generate results that could significantly increase the popularity and success of your Web site. Knowing what motivates your visitors to perform specific tasks, how they came to your Web site, and what they did while they were on your site will assist you to finetune your online marketing communications strategy to better accommodate the needs of your target market and influence their actions.

Identifying Valuable Information about Your Target Market

Log files can provide you with interesting statistics about your target audience. You can see how the majority of your audience came to your site, and what they like to do while they are there. "What they do" means whether they request information or not, if they download products, or if they are interested in free giveaways. You can use this information to find out if your site needs to be changed to accommodate the needs of your visitors. For example, if you find that many of your visitors are spending a lot of time on your "What's

New" page, maybe it would be in your best interest to start a monthly mail list to inform your audience of the happenings of your Web site.

The log files can tell you when your audience is entering your site. For example, if the log files indicate that your traffic is mostly at night, you could predict that most people visit your site from home. Since most homes do not have high-speed access, you may want to check your graphic sizes to make sure that it is not taking too long for your site to load. If your analysis tells you that not many people visit your site on Saturday, you may want to select this day as your maintenance day. You don't want to make changes to your site on days when you receive high traffic because it is very displeasing if your visitors receive HTTP 404 error messages because your site is temporarily down.

You can also see your visitor's IP address, which the software will translate into the geographical location of your visitor; some software is even capable of narrowing the data down to the city. From a marketing perspective, this can benefit you in planning your marketing efforts in other media. If you are planning a television campaign for your business, for example, you may want to start in a city that frequently visits your site, thus increasing the chance of a successful campaign.

It is very common for Web traffic analysis software to indicate which browser your visitors are using when visiting your Web site. Although you want to have a Web site that is designed to be compatible with both older and newer browsers, this data can be used to your advantage. Older browsers that cannot read Java scripting properly and that do not have the proper plug-ins for a Flash introduction may still be in use by your viewers. However, if a higher number of your viewers are using the latest browsers, you could incorporate more of the latest technology into your site. Remember that you should always offer a "skip flash" option on your site and the latest Java plug-ins for people with older browsers.

Which Pages Are Popular, and Which Pages Are Not?

When you look at the log files and see where your audience is spending most of its time on your site, you can also tell where it is not. You can then take this information to determine what the popular pages on your site incorporate that the less popular ones do not. Perhaps the popular pages are similar to the less popular, but are visited by a specific source (i.e., search engines, newsgroups). Maybe there is a content problem on the less popular pages, or maybe they take longer to load than the other pages and visitors do not want to wait for them to load. Whatever the case may be, you can take this information and attempt to fix the problems that would keep visitors from spending time on all the pages of your site.

Find Out How Each Visitor Found Your Site

By finding out how each visitor came to your site, you can boost your traffic tremendously. You can use this information to help you with the allocation of your online advertising budget. For example, if most of your traffic is coming from the Excite search engine *http://www.excite.com*, you could consider purchasing a banner advertisement on that page. The same theory goes if your traffic is coming from a newsgroup, meta-indexes, and so on.

If you have a number of doorway pages, it would be good to know which ones are drawing the most attention. If the statistics reveal that four out of ten doorway pages are sending traffic to your site, you should analyze the six other doorways to see if you can make them more effective. Maybe the keyword prominence is too low and they are not as effective as you thought when you designed them. If so, you should tweak these pages, then resubmit them to their corresponding search engines.

You can also find out where your visitors go when they leave your Web site. You want your viewers to stay at your site as long as possible. If you notice that the majority of your viewers are not traveling through your entire site and are not viewing important information that you want them to see, you may want to manipulate the layout of your Web site to decrease the "flight effect." If you notice that your top exit page is your homepage, you may want to try a whole new approach because people seem to be turned off from searching through your site right from the beginning.

Single-access pages are pages on your Web site that are accessed through a link or search engine and then are immediately exited. If a high percentage of your Web site traffic is a result of these pages, it is very important that you convey a strong message while you have the visitors' attention. If you have pages like this, you should reevaluate what is on those pages and try to come up with content that will entice your visitor to search through the rest of your site.

Some of the more advanced software can tell you which keywords and phrases your visitors used to find your site using a search engine. This is extremely valuable information because you can use these keywords to increase your popularity in the search engines. By knowing the most popular keywords your visitors are using to visit your site, you can make sure you use them in your meta-tags, alt tags, and page titles and in the text of your page for higher placement in the search engines. Also, by seeing which search engines are being used more by your visitors, you may choose to purchase a banner ad or keywords for that engine to achieve maximum visibility to your visitors.

Another benefit of observing who is watching your site is that you can see when spiders and crawlers from search engines have crawled to your page. This means that your site most likely is indexed on their corresponding search engine. This is good to know, because it not only reassures you that you are going to be indexed, but also because by knowing this you do not resubmit your site to the search engine and risk spamming. As explained previously in Chapter 14, if you are caught spamming some of the search engines, you will banned from their index.

Identifying Your Target Market

After you have collected data from your log files and used the Web traffic analysis software to determine which demographic groups are actually visiting your site, you then must determine whether these are the groups that you want to target. If they are not, you must then determine how you are going to reach your target market. For example, maybe you will find that you should change your online advertising campaign. Or perhaps you should reevaluate your Internet marketing strategy, taking into consideration the new data that you have collected.

Find Out What Forms of Online Promotion Work for Your Site

When you first launch your Web site, you are going to aggressively implement your Internet marketing strategy by experimenting with all of the different forms of online marketing. However, when you analyze who is actually visiting your site, and you find out where the majority of your traffic is coming from, you can then determine where to focus the majority of your marketing efforts. You may find that a link on a particular Web site is resulting in a high amount of traffic to your site; therefore, you may want to consider purchasing a banner advertisement on that site. The same goes for all of the other forms of Internet marketing.

If after a short period of time your analysis software tells you that you are receiving low traffic (if any) from a banner ad that you had purchased, you may want to pull it off that site and designate your investment to another site on the Internet. This is a good way to make sure you get the most for your investments in online marketing.

Managing Your Online Business

If you are involved in selling online advertising on your site, Web traffic analysis software can save you a lot of work. When you place a client's banner advertisement on your site, the analysis software can not only track how many people have viewed that specific banner, but also how many people have clicked through. This makes billing your clients very easy; all you have to do is read the reports generated by your software. If your clients pay per clickthrough, you simply look up the figure and charge them the appropriate fee. The same goes for paying based on CPM.

What Motivates Your Target Audience?

With any type of marketing it is vital that you know what motivates your target audience. Web traffic analysis reports can assist you to gain a clearer understanding of what motivates your target market. You can monitor the activity on your Web site to determine what works and what does not work to motivate your target market. For example, you may be selling products on your Web site and to get a visitor to purchase the item you used a blue button that reads "BUY." After monitoring your Web site activity, you might notice that sales for that item are mediocre and that people are not spending much time viewing the listing for this product. You can run a testing period by replacing the blue button with a red button that reads "BUY

NOW," or some other variation of change. If traffic levels and product levels rise as a result of this change, it can be concluded that your target audience is motivated by the color red, or assertive calls to action. There are numerous ways that you can run tests on your site to ensure that you are optimizing your Web site to motivate your target market.

Internet Resources for This Chapter

Wusage 7
www.wusage.com
Wusage is a dynamic and affordable Web traffic analysis software product that helps measure the popularity of the documents on your Web server. Detailed activity reports provide you with valuable marketing information that can help you enhance your overall marketing strategy.

TheCounter.com
http://www.thecounter.com
TheCounter.com provides free tracking services to its members. By placing a small image on your Web site, they will tell you information such as when your visitors came, from where, and by using what browser. If you are just experimenting with Web traffic analysis, you can't go wrong with TheCounter.com.

The Hitometer
http://www.hitometer.com
The free Hitometer service offers an extensive choice of counters and reporting of URL statistics, such as how many visitors visit your site per day, month, or year. You can receive your reports online or have them sent to your e-mail address.

Web Developer's Journal
webdevelopersjournal.com/articles/site_promotion/site_promotion_logfiles.html
"Traffic-building Ideas from Your Log Files (Part 1)," an article written by Charlie Morris, discusses different traffic-building ideas you can implement from analyzing your server's log files.

CNET Builder.com
http://www.builder.com/Servers/LogFile/index.html
"Demystify Your Log Files," an article written by Olufemi Anthony, explains in detail how your log files produce traffic analysis data. Written in 1998, the article goes over different terminology and gives descriptive examples that can help you to understand what exactly goes on in your Web server's log files.

Web Developer's Virtual Library
http://www.wdvl.com/Internet/Management/index.html
"There's Gold in Them There Log Files," written by Charlie Morris, touches on the different things you can interpret from log files when analyzed by Web traffic analysis software. It touches on different features that are available with different software.

About the Author

Susan Sweeney, C.A.

Renowned industry expert and consultant, Susan Sweeney C.A., tailors lively keynote speeches, full and half day seminars and workshops for companies, industries, and associations interested in improving their Internet presence and increasing their Web site traffic and sales. Susan is the founder and President of **Connex Network Inc.** an international Internet marketing and consulting firm. Susan holds both her Chartered Accountant and Certified General Accountant designations. She is an experienced Internet Marketing professional with a background in computers, marketing, and the Internet. Susan is the author of several books on Internet Marketing as well as numerous articles concerning Marketing on the Internet, Export Marketing, and The Internet and Business. She is a member of the Canadian Association of Professional Speakers, the National Speakers Association, and the International Federation for Professional Speakers. Susan is also the Treasurer and an executive on the Board of Directors of the Information Technology Industry Association of Nova Scotia, as well as a member of the Board of Directors for the Canadian Association of Professional Speakers.

Connex Network is a marketing firm, providing Internet and international marketing consulting and training services to industry and government. Their clients range in size from single person start-up operations to multi-million dollar international firms. Their primary services include Internet Marketing Workshops, Internet Marketing Strategies, Web Site Report Cards, Internet Marketing Consulting, Market Research and Competitive Analysis. During their workshops and training sessions they ensure their clients have a complete understanding of the principles involved with developing a strong online presence. The team of Internet marketing analysts at Connex is highly trained in the area of Internet marketing and all stay up-to-date with the latest technological advancements and industry trends in the online marketing world. Every person on the team has extensive practical hands-on experience and the necessary skills to use proven tips, tools, and techniques to generate high volumes of traffic to your site.

As a result of technological change and global competitiveness the need for a strong Internet presence is essential. Susan instructs individuals with her enthusiastic personality combined with her vast hands-on international marketing experience, which keeps her listeners informed, and captivated. Let Susan help you increase your traffic and make your business prosper!

Susan Sweeney, C.A.
Connex Network Inc.
75 Brentwood Drive
Bedford, Nova Scotia, Canada B4A 352
Phone: 902-468-2578 Fax: 902-468-2233
www.connexnetwork.com
susan@connexnetwork.com

Appendix A

Terminology

ASCII Text File (American Standard Code for Information Interchange) The worldwide standard format for text files in computers and on the Internet. The code represents all the uppercase and lowercase letters, numbers, punctuation, and so forth. There are 128 standard ASCII codes in which a seven-digit binary number, 0000000 through 1111111, represents each character.

ASP (Application Service Provider) An ASP is a company that offers individuals or enterprises access over the Internet to applications and related services that would otherwise have to be located in their own personal or enterprise computers. Sometimes referred to as "apps-on-tap," ASP services are expected to become an important alternative, not only for smaller companies with low budgets for information technology, but also for larger companies as a form of outsourcing.

Autoresponders A computer program that automatically returns a prewritten message to anyone who submits e-mail to a particular Internet address, whether an individual or a Web site. Autoresponders are widely used by Web sites for the purpose of immediately responding to visitor comments and suggestions.

Backbone Large transmission lines that carry data being transferred from smaller lines. These lines or paths connect local or regional networks together for long-distance communication. The connection points are known as network nodes or telecommunication data-switching exchanges (DSEs).

BBS (Bulletin Board System) A computer that can be reached by computer modem dialing (or by Telnet) for the purpose of sharing or exchanging messages or other files. Some BBSs are devoted to specific interests; others offer a more general service. The definitive BBS List says that there are over 40,000 BBSs worldwide.

BCC (Blind Carbon Copy) In most e-mail programs, BCC allows you to send a single e-mail message to numerous recipients and make it appear as if you sent the message to only one person. This makes the message seem more personalized as well as protecting your mail list.

Benchmark A point of reference by which something can be measured or compared. In surveying, a "bench mark" (two words) is a post or other permanent mark used as the basis for measuring the elevation of other topographical points.

Browser The software used to view the various kinds of Internet resources or sites.

Cache A place to store something more or less temporarily. Web pages you request are stored in your browser's cache (pronounced "cash") directory on your hard disk. When you return to a page you've recently looked at, the browser can get most of the information from the cache rather than the original server. A cache saves you time and saves the network the burden of some additional traffic. You can usually vary the size of your cache, depending on your particular browser.

CGI (Common Gateway Interface) Guidelines that define how a Web server communicates with another piece of software on the same machine, and how the other piece of software, the CGI program, talks to the web server. Any piece of software can be a CGI program if it handles input and output according to the CGI standard.

Cgi-bin This is the most common name for the directory on a Web server that holds a CGI program. Most programs located in the cgi-bin directory are text files, scripts that are executed by binaries located elsewhere on the same machine.

Chat Room On the Internet, "chatting" is talking to a group of users from anywhere in the world who are using the Internet at the same time you are. Most chats are focused on a particular topic of interest, and some involve guest experts or famous people who "talk" to anyone joining the chat.

Cookie On the Internet, a cookie refers to a piece of information sent by a Web server to a Web browser. The browser software is expected to save the cookie and send the information back to the server whenever an additional request is made. Cookies may contain information such as user preferences, registration or login information, online shopping cart info, and so forth.

Crawlers Crawlers quietly comb through Web sites and index the information they find.

CRM (Customer Relationship Management) An information industry term for methodologies, software, and usually Internet capabilities that help an enterprise manage customer relationships in an organized way.

CPM (Cost per Thousand Page Views) This is a measure taken from print advertising. Since not all page views result in seeing the ad (for example, if a page scrolls, an ad may initially be out of view), CPM is often interpreted to mean the cost per thousand ad views. (The "M" is the Roman numeral M.)

CPTM (Cost per Thousand Targeted Ad Views) This implies that the audience you have targeted is of a particular demographic group. See also Demographics.

Cybernaut A person who uses the Internet.

Cyberspace Used to describe all areas of information resources available through computer networks and the Internet. William Gibson originated the term in his novel *Neuromancer.*

Demographics Specific data about the size and characteristics of a population or audience that can be used for marketing purposes.

Domain Name The unique name that identifies an Internet site. A domain name always has two or more parts, separated by dots. The part on the left is the most specific, and the part on the right is the most general. A given machine may have more than one domain name, but a given domain name points to only one machine. For example, the domain names *everyopportunity.com* and *support.everyopportunity.com* can both refer to the same machine.

E-mail (Electronic Mail) Mail messages, usually text, sent from one person to another via computer. Messages can also be sent automatically to a large number of addresses on a mailing list.

E-wallet Also known as a virtual wallet; a software mechanism that allows commerce users to store and use credit card and electronic payment information.

Ezine, e-Zine Used to describe an electronic magazine, including those of print magazines such as *National Geographic* and *Newsweek* that have electronic editions. Thus, E-Zine Database includes both electronic-only magazines and electronic-edition magazines.

FAQs (Frequently Asked Questions) Documents that list and answer the most common questions on a particular subject or problem area. There are hundreds of FAQs on subjects as diverse as car repair and franchise advice.

Firewall A set of related programs located at a network gateway server to protect the resources of a private network from users of other networks.

Flame, Flaming Flaming usually involves the use of harsh language directed toward a group or individual for sending unwanted messages (marketing) on a newsgroup or mail list.

Forums Another name for a newsgroup in which people are formed together in a group to chat and discuss.

FTP (File Transfer Protocol) The common method of moving files between two computers through the Internet medium. FTP is a special way to log in to another computer or Internet site for the purposes of retrieving or sending files.

Hit A single request from a Web browser for a single item from a Web server; thus, in order for a Web browser to display a page that contains three graphics, four "hits" would occur at the server: one for the HTML page and one for each of the three graphics. Hits are often used as a rough measure of visits on a server.

Home Page, Homepage The main Web page for a business, organization, or person—or simply the main page of a collection of Web pages.

Host Any computer on a network that can hold files available to other computers on the network. It is quite common to have one host machine provide several services to other machines, such as WWW and Usenet.

HTML (HyperText Markup Language, HTM) The coding language used to create documents for use on the World Wide Web. These documents have a file extension of html or htm. HTML code looks a lot like old-fashioned typesetting code, where you surround a block of text with codes that indicate how it should appear. HTML or HTM files are meant to be viewed using a World Wide Web client program, such as Netscape or Internet Explorer.

HTTP(HyperText Transport Protocol) The most important protocol used in the World Wide Web for moving hypertext files across the

Internet. Requires an HTTP client program on one end and an HTTP server program on the other end.

Hypertext Clickable text that links to another document—that is, words or phrases in one document that can be clicked on by a reader, causing another document to be retrieved and displayed.

Image Map A single graphic that has multiple hot links to different pages or resources.

Intranet A private network inside a company or organization that uses the same kinds of software found on the public Internet, but that is only for internal use and cannot be viewed outside the network.

IP Address A unique number that is assigned to any device connected to the Internet.

ISDN (Integrated Services Digital Network) A quicker way to move more data over existing regular phone lines. Rapidly becoming available around the world, it is priced comparably to standard analog phone circuits. It can provide speeds of roughly 128,000 bits per second over the regular phone lines.

ISP (Internet Service Provider) A provider that allows access to the Internet. Usually there is a cost to the consumer, although there are still some free community networks.

Java Database Connectivity Driver (JDBC) Technology JDBC is an application program interface specification for connecting programs written in Java to the data in popular databases. The application program interface lets you encode access request statements in SQL that are then passed to the program that manages the database. It returns the results through a similar interface.

Java Programming Language Specifically designed for writing programs, it can safely be downloaded to your computer through the Internet and immediately be run without fear of viruses or other harm to your computer. Using small Java programs, called "Applets," Web pages can include functions such as animations, calculators, and other fancy tricks that cannot be done by normal HTML.

LAN (Local Area Network) A network limited to the local area, usually the same building or floor of a company.

Log Files A record of network activities. These activities can include access record errors and financial transactions.

Login The account name used to gain access to a computer system, not a password. Also can mean the act of entering onto a computer system.

Lurking Reading Usenet newsgroups, consumer online service forums, or Internet mailing lists without posting anything—just reading. A lurker is a person who observes what everyone else is doing within that group.

Mailbot A software program that automatically responds to all incoming e-mail. A mailbot, or autoresponder, replies to them by sending the author a file or message.

Mailing List Manager A software program that collects and distributes e-mail messages to a mailing list.

Mail List, Mailing List A system that allows people to send e-mail to one address, whereupon their message is copied and sent to all other subscribers to the list. This method allows people with different kinds of e-mail to participate in discussions together.

M-Commerce The process of buying goods or services via the Internet through wireless devices such as cellular telephones, palm pilots, wireless laptop computers, and the abundance of personal communication devices coming available every day.

Merchant Account A written, commercial bank account established by contractual agreement between a business and a bank or a payment gateway. The agreement contains the respective rights, warranties, and duties with respect to accepting bankcards such as Visa or MasterCard. You must apply for this account directly from your bank or from the payment processor.

Meta-HTML Tags Meta information can be used in identifying, indexing, and cataloging. You can use these tags to guide the search engines in displaying your site as the result of a query.

Meta-Indexes A listing of Internet resources pertaining to a specific subject category, intended as a resource to those who have an interest in specific topic. A meta-index is simply a collection of URLs for related Internet resources, all arranged on a Web page by their titles.

Net The shorthand version of Internet.

Netiquette Internet etiquette.

Netizen From the term "citizen," referring to a citizen of the Internet or someone who uses networked resources.

Netpreneur An online entrepreneur.

Netscape Web browser and the name of a company. The Netscape browser was based on the Mosaic program developed at the National Center for Supercomputing Applications (NCSA).

Newbie A newcomer to the Internet

Newsgroups Name given to discussion groups on Usenet.

Nonstreaming Nonstreaming video is a sequence of "moving images" that are sent in compressed form over the Internet and can be displayed by the viewer once the file is completely downloaded. A Web user must wait to download the file before seeing the video or hearing the sound.

Password A code used to gain access to a locked system known only to one person or a specific group of individuals. Good passwords contain letters and nonletters and are not simple combinations such as *john12.*

Pixels Pixels (a word invented from "picture element") are the basic units of programmable color on a computer display or in a computer image. The physical size of a pixel depends on how you've set the resolution.

Posting A message entered into a network communications system, such as a newsgroup submission.

Rich Media An Internet advertising term for a Web page ad that uses advanced technology such as streaming or non-streaming media.

Search Engine The most popular way to find resources on the Internet. There are numerous search engines, each with its own unique styles and capabilities.

Server A computer or software package that stores information and makes these files available to other users on a network or the Internet.

SET (Secure Electronic Transaction) Implemented to protect the security of electronic financial transactions on the Internet.

Signature A block of information used at the end of every message or online document sent by that user.

Site A unique location on the Internet to post your information and get noticed.

Spam, Spamming An inappropriate attempt to use a mailing list, Usenet, or other networked communications facility as if it was a broadcast medium by sending the same message to a large number of people who didn't ask for it.

Spider An automated program that indexes documents, titles, or a portion of each document acquired by traversing the Web.

Splash Page An initial Web site page used to capture the user's attention for a short time as a promotion or lead-in to the site homepage or to tell the user what kind of browser and other software he needs to view the site.

SQL (Structured Query Language) A specialized programming language for sending queries to databases.

SSL (Secure Socket Layers) Developed by Netscape and supported by all leading Web browsers. SSL is currently the implied standard encryption protocol in the industry for managing the security of file transmissions around the Internet.

Storefront A set location on the Web that stores and displays a collection of information about you and your business.

Streaming Streaming video is a sequence of "moving images" that are sent in compressed form over the Internet and displayed by the viewer as they arrive. A Web user does not have to wait to download a large file before seeing the video or hearing the sound. Instead, the media is sent in a continuous stream and is played as it arrives.

T1 The T1 carrier is the most commonly used digital line in the United States, Canada, and Japan. T1 lines use copper wire and span distances within and between major metropolitan areas.

Tag line A short advertisement or catch phrase at the end of your signature file.

Telnet A program that allows people to log on to other computers or bulletin board systems on the Internet and run software remotely from their location.

Template A form, mold, or pattern used as a guide to making something.

Upload The transfer of a file from your computer to a server online.

URL Uniform Resource Locator The standard way to give an address of any resource on the Internet that is part of the World Wide Web (WWW). The most common way to use a URL is to enter into a WWW browser program, such as Internet Explorer, Netscape, or Lynx, and type it in the location bar.

Usenet A system of discussion groups. Comments are passed among hundreds of thousands of machines, with over 10,000 discussion areas, called newsgroups.

User session A person with a unique address that enters or re-enters a Web site each day (or some other specified period). A user session is sometimes determined by counting only those users who haven't re-entered the site within the past 20 minutes or a similar period. User session figures are sometimes used to indicate the number of visitors per day.

VaporLink A link within a site on the Internet is supposed to lead to more information (hypertext); a vaporlink is one that has become nonexistent and does not lead anywhere—a dead link.

Voice over IP (VOIP) VOIP enables people to speak into a microphone or headset that is attached to their computer. The user's voice patterns are then transferred over the Internet; similar to how your voice travels across the telephone cables.

Web The shorthand version of World Wide Web.

Webcasting Term used to describe the ability to use the Web to deliver live or delayed versions of sound or video broadcasts.

Web rings A way of linking related Web sites so that you can visit each site one after the other, eventually returning to the first Web site. Typically, users can also elect to go backwards through the ring of sites, skip a certain number at a time, visit sites randomly, or see a list of all the sites on the ring.

Web Server A program that, using the World Wide Web's Hypertext Transfer Protocol, serves the files that form Web pages to the end user. Every computer on the Internet that contains a Web site must have a Web server program.

Wireless Application Protocol (WAP) Technology This technology enables mobile devices that are equipped with Web-ready mini-browsers to access the Internet from anywhere in the world where this service is available.

WWW (World Wide Web) The whole constellation of resources that can be accessed using Gopher, FTP, HTTP, Telnet, Usenet, WAIS, and some other tools. Also referred to as the universe of hypertext servers (HTTP servers), which are the servers that allow graphics, text, sound files, and so forth, to be mixed together.

Appendix B

Implementation and Maintenance Schedule

To accomplish the best results from your Internet marketing strategy, you should develop an implementation and maintenance schedule.

Schedule

Every implementation and maintenance schedule will be different since every company's Internet marketing strategy will be different. (See the table that follows for a sample schedule.) The remainder of this appendix provides brief explanations to help further clarify the items included in this sample. (Figure B.1.)

Domain Name

You should ensure your domain name registration is paid on an annual basis.

Check:	Weekly	Biweekly	Monthly	Bimonthly	Quarterly	Yearly
Domain Name						✓
Search engine submissions	✓					
Press releases				✓		
Banner advertising			✓			
Update/rename titles			✓			
Cool sites			✓			
Check competitors					✓	
Cybermalls					✓	
Newsletter			✓			
Newsgroups	✓					
Public Mail list postings		✓				
Guest book	✓					
Signature files			✓			
Private Mail list Maintenance			✓			
Links		✓				
What's new	✓					
Calendar of events	✓					
Employment opportunities	✓					
Affiliate Program	✓					
Viral Marketing	✓					
Permission Marketing	✓					
Marketing Offline					✓	
Tune-ups					✓	
Web browser testing			✓			

Figure B.1. Implementation and Maintenance Schedule.

Search Engine Submissions

You should take your list of directory and search engine submissions and divide it into four groups. Each week, you should take one group, go to each of the directories and search engines in that group, and search for your company by name and also by several keywords. If you appear in the first ten or twenty search rankings and are happy with the description, you don't have to do anything with that search engine or directory.

If, however, you do not appear or are not satisfied with the description, you should resubmit all your pages to that directory or search engine. Search engines and directories purge their databases from time to time to ensure that all entries are current. The following weeks, go through the same process with the next groups. This way you check every directory and search engine at least monthly to ensure that you are still there and are easily accessible.

Press Releases

Press releases should be scheduled at least bi-monthly. If you have a major announcement, the press releases may be more frequent.

Banner Advertising

Check banner advertising locations of your ads at least once a month. Determine the effectiveness of these ads and look for new sites for more exposure. Check prices and traffic flow of these new sites to determine how relevant they may be in increasing the traffic to your site. Adjust your banner advertising strategy accordingly.

Update/Rename Titles

Update and retitle your pages monthly unless you add a new section that requires more frequent updates (for example, Tip of the Week). Retitling your pages and updating your site is useful for two main reasons. First, spiders, crawlers, and bots are continuously visiting sites to see if there have been changes. (They update their information accordingly.) Second, many of your site visitors use software that lets them know when their bookmarked sites have been updated. They will revisit your site only when they know there have been changes.

Cool Sites

Submit to Cool Sites, Site of the Day, or Top 5%. In order to better your chances of becoming one, you should check on how often to apply, usually monthly.

Check Competitors

You should regularly review your competitors' sites.

Cybermalls

Cybermalls continually change, as does everything, so periodically do a quick check to find new malls or changes to the ones that interest you.

Newsletter

A newsletter should be scheduled monthly so you are getting your name and information in front of clients and potential clients on a regular basis.

Newsgroups

Newsgroups that you participate in should be visited every couple of days, and you should try to post messages. The more often you post, particularly providing answers to queries or assistance, the more recognized and valued you are (and is your expertise). Make sure you attach your sig. file for maximum marketing effect.

Public Mail List Postings

New publicly accessible mail lists appear daily. Review (and update if appropriate) those that you participate in on a monthly basis.**AU: the table shows mail list postings to be bi-weekly; mail lists occurs twice on the table.**

Guest Book

Your guest book should be monitored so you can see who is visiting and what they have to say. Every week you should copy the new contact list to the appropriate databases (e-mail lists, newsletter, etc.).

Signature Files

Keep your sig files current. Review and change them on a regular basis with new information or achievements.

Private Mail List Maintenance

Ensure you update and maintain your internal mail lists on a monthly basis. Mail should be sent to those on your private mail list on a regular basis. Remember to change your tag line in your signature file.

Links

The more reciprocal links you can get the better. You should constantly be looking for additional, appropriate sites from which to be linked. As a minimum, you should schedule time bi-weekly to actively seek appropriate link sites.

What's New

Your What's New Page should be updated weekly if possible.

Calendar of Events

If you choose to have a calendar of events on your site, ensure that it is kept current. It should be updated at least weekly.

Employment Opportunities

This section should also be monitored and updated weekly, deleting positions that have been filled and adding new positions as they become available.

Affiliate Program

Afilliate programs require constant monitoring and maintenance, perhaps even daily. Staying on top of paying your affiliates their due and keeping up with new recruits will help to ensure the success of your affiliate program and your online business.

Viral Marketing

Providing refreshing content to encourage positive "word-of-mouth" exposure is important to all businesses. Keeping your viral marketing techniques up to date can encourage significant amounts of referral traffic. "Word-of-mouth" exposure is the best kind of exposure you can garner.

Permission Marketing

Permission marketing can be integrated with a number of your other online marketing tactics, so you should take them time to implement permission marketing whenever possible. For example, if you update your site once a week, then you should provide your users with the opportunity to sign up to receive an e-mail notification of site updates. Take advantage of permission marketing opportunities.

Marketing Offline

Make sure that your offline marketing materials and your online materials are consistent (message, logos, corporate colors, etc.). Also ensure that, where appropriate, you include your URL in your offline promotion materials. This should be checked at least quarterly.

Tune-Ups

Tune-ups should be done quarterly unless changes are made to the site. One location to check is Web Site Garage at *http://www.websitegarage.com*. Here you can check spelling, browser compatibility, HTML design, link popularity, load time, and much more.

Web Browser Testing

Test your site with the major Web browsers. This should be done whenever there is a new release of Netscape or Internet Explorer. You should check monthly to determine if there have been new releases.

Appendix C

Storefront Features Selection Chart

Before you begin searching for a storefront solution, take the time to fill out the following chart. You need to know what storefront features are "necessary" to your business, which ones would be "nice to have," and which ones you can eliminate altogether. Use the forms on the following pages as a guide when reviewing different storefront options and compare them with your requirements that you have identified. It will help you select the storefront solution most appropriate for your business. If you are unsure of what any of the storefront features mean, refer to Chapter 4, where each of the features is explained in depth.

Feature	Necessary	Nice to Have	Not Necessary
Shopping Cart			
Backend Integration			
Thumbnail Image Capability			
Searchable Product Database			
Tax Calculations			
Shipping and Delivery Options			
Automatic Purchase Notification			
Customer E-mail Notification			
Order Tracking			
Customer Information			
Ship-to Addresses			
Technical Support			
Tracking and Report Generation			
Payment Platforms			
Promotions and Discounts			
Third-Party Support			
Domain Name Support and Storefront Hosting			
Maximum Product Limit			
Digital Content Sales			
Template Customization			
International Options			

Flexibility and Value-Add Components (e.g., gift wrapping, "New" product announcements). In the space provided below, you should write down any additional features you're interested in, for easy future reference when inquiring about your storefront solution.

Notes:

1.

2.

3.

4.

5.

6.

7.

8.

9.

10.

Index

Reader Feedback Sheet

Your comments and suggestions are very important in shaping future publications. Please email us at *moreinfo@maxpress.com* or photocopy this page, jot down your thoughts, and fax it to (850) 934-9981 or mail it to:

Maximum Press

Attn: Jim Hoskins

605 Silverthorn Road

Gulf Breeze, FL 32561

101 Internet Businesses You Can Start From Home
by Susan Sweeney, C.A.
520 pages
$29.95
ISBN: 1-885068-28-X

e-Business Formula for Success
by Susan Sweeney, C.A.
360 pages
$34.95
ISBN: 1-885068-60-3

Exploring IBM RS/6000 Computers, Tenth Edition
by Jim Hoskins
and Doug Davies
440 pages
$39.95
ISBN: 1-885068-42-5

Exploring IBM @server iSeries and AS/400 Computers, Tenth Edition
by Jim Hoskins and
Roger Dimmick
560 pages
$39.95
ISBN: 1-885068-43-3

Exploring IBM S/390 Computers, Sixth Edition
by Jim Hoskins
and George Coleman
472 pages
$39.95
ISBN: 1-885068-30-1

Exploring IBM Network Stations
by Eddie Ho,
Dana Lloyd, and
Stephanos Heracleous
223 pages
$39.95
ISBN: 1-885068-32-8

Exploring IBM @server xSeries and PCs, Eleventh Edition
by Jim Hoskins
and Bill Wilson
384 pages
$39.95
ISBN: 1-885068-39-5

Exploring IBM Technology, Products & Services, Fourth Edition
edited by Jim Hoskins
256 pages
$54.95
ISBN: 1-885068-62-X

To purchase a Maximum Press book, visit your local bookstore
or call 1-800-989-6733 (US/Canada) or 1-850-934-4583 (International)
online ordering available at ***www.maxpress.com***